A GAME OF BIRDS AND WOLVES

Also by Simon Parkin

Death by Video Game

A GAME OF BIRDS AND WOLVES

The Ingenious Young Women Whose Secret Board Game Helped Win World War II

SIMON PARKIN

Little, Brown and Company
New York   Boston   London

Little, Brown and Company
Hachette Book Group
1290 Avenue of the Americas, New York, NY 10104
littlebrown.com

First US edition, January 2020
First published in Great Britain in November 2019 by Sceptre

Little, Brown and Company is a division of Hachette Book Group, Inc. The Little, Brown name and logo are trademarks of Hachette Book Group, Inc.

The publisher is not responsible for websites (or their content) that are not owned by the publisher.

The Hachette Speakers Bureau provides a wide range of authors for speaking events. To find out more, go to hachettespeakersbureau.com or call (866) 376-6591.

ISBN 978-0-316-49209-6
Library of Congress Control Number: 2019954815

10 9 8 7 6 5 4 3 2 1

LSC-C

Printed in the United States of America

For Estelle Parkin
May you find thrilling answers
in the games you play

Contents

A GAME OF BIRDS AND WOLVES

Last Man Standing

23RD MAY 1945

Gilbert Roberts, a retired British naval officer turned game designer, stepped onto the gangway leading up to the ocean liner, then immediately stopped. If he was not mistaken the man making his way down the plank, labouring under the weight of a suitcase, was Karl Doenitz, a German admiral who, twenty-three days earlier, following the suicide of Adolf Hitler, had become Nazi Germany's new head of state.

The men drew close, then stopped in front of one another, suspended, as they had been for much of the war, in a liminal space, neither fully on land nor fully at sea. For a moment, in the mid-afternoon sunlight, the creak and slop of the dockside was the only sound.

Each man looked at least one size too small for his uniform. It was misfortune, not restraint that had helped them avoid the thickening torsos worn by most who reach a high rank and all its associated comforts. For forty-four-year-old Roberts, a violent battle with illness had left him wheezy. At eight stone and five feet eleven, he was also perilously underweight. Doenitz, meanwhile, had spent the month bearing the pressure of trying to broker the surrender of his beleaguered nation. Then there was the unquenchable pain of having lost not one but two sons to war within a year of each other. Moreover, both the boys had died while serving in the U-boat division, which Doenitz had founded and tenaciously commanded at every step of his rise. He had been twice responsible for their lives: as their father, and as their commander.

Catastrophe and a talent for endurance were not all that the two men shared. For the last three years Roberts and Doenitz had also been adversaries in a vast and deadly game of U-boats and battle-ships, played out on the Atlantic Ocean, an arena so treacherous and capricious that it was considered, by all those who fought there, to be the third adversary in their war.

Roberts, having been discharged from the navy in the summer of 1938, the day after his tuberculosis was diagnosed, had been brought back into service seven months into the war. 'Game designer' was not a job description used by the navy at the time, but this was the nature of the role given to Roberts by Britain's prime minister, Winston Churchill. He was to create a game that would enable the British to understand why they were losing so many ships to German U-boat attacks. Teamed with a clutch of bright, astute young naval women known as Wrens, many of whom were barely out of school, Roberts had, in the months that followed, restaged countless ocean battles using his game. Through play he had developed anti-U-boat tactics that, once proven, had been taught to thousands of naval officers before they headed to sea.

Doenitz also knew the curious value of play during wartime. He too had designed games to test and refine tactics that, from his HQ in the bunker beneath an elegant nineteenth-century villa in occupied France, could be issued to his beloved U-boat captains. These would aid the crews in their ultimate aim: to sink Allied merchant ships, thereby preventing food and supplies from reaching British shores, in order to starve the islanders and win the war.

Both men had orchestrated their feints and attacks by shunting wooden tokens around maps of the ocean, known as plots, like pieces on a watery chessboard. The stakes were mortal; many thousands of Britons and Germans had died, including men whom Roberts and Doenitz had each personally known and instructed.

'Good afternoon, Admiral,' said Roberts, who was flanked by a young American interrogator and former FBI agent.[1]

Doenitz, who immediately recognised his rival from a photo-graph printed in a British magazine article the previous year, nodded respectfully.[2] He knew why Roberts had come to the German port of Flensburg: to salvage any evidence that might show whether or not his theories about secret U-boat tactics, deduced via the crucible of his games, were accurate.

In his pocket Roberts, a fluent German-speaker, felt his 'Ike's pass', a document issued and signed by the general of the US Army, Dwight D. Eisenhower, that bestowed on him authority to interrogate anybody related to his investigation. How Roberts longed to quiz Doenitz about the U-boat tactics – the wolfpacks, the torpedo attacks, the underwater getaways – and, moreover, to discover how much the admiral knew about the countermeasures he and the Wrens had designed. But Doenitz was needed in Luxembourg, where he was to join the other captured Nazi Party and SS leaders, army chiefs and ministers and await trial for war crimes.

'We will supply you with everything you need to make your visit pleasant and efficient,' Doenitz said, before continuing down the ramp towards the pier.

As an armed guard led Doenitz past a phalanx of British tanks toward the nearby police station where he was to be searched for hidden phials of poison,[3] Roberts and the FBI interrogator boarded the ship. It was called the *Patria*, the last vestige, as the name implied, of Hitler's crumbled Fatherland.

Aboard the liner, which could accommodate close to six hundred crew and passengers, Roberts was shown to his quarters. It was a first-class suite comprising a sleeping cabin, private bathroom and sitting room, where he planned to interview surrendered U-boat officers. As he walked through the door, Roberts was greeted by a handsome young German naval officer, with slicked hair and a determined brow. The man introduced himself as Heinz Walkerling. He was, he explained, to be Roberts' assistant for the duration of the mission.

Walkerling, who had celebrated his thirtieth birthday just four days earlier,[4] was one of the U-boat captains who, for the past three years, Roberts had been diligently trying to kill. This German had been one of the lucky ones. After successfully torpedoing and sinking five Allied ships – two British, two American and one Canadian – Walkerling had been transferred to a torpedo school at Mürwik, where he had taught trainee U-boatmen how to shoot straight. As the FBI man set up his tape recorder, which was disguised as a suitcase, under Roberts' bunk, Walkerling asked whether his new boss had a gun to keep him safe.

'No,' said Roberts, who had turned down the offer of a weapon before leaving London.

At five o'clock that afternoon, Roberts conducted his first interrogation, with Doenitz's chief of staff, the man responsible for the organisation and operation of all U-boats. After two hours' intensive questioning, Roberts switched off his tape recorder and, accompanied by Walkerling, made his way to the officers' mess for some food.

The atmosphere in the room was confused. The Germans, a mixture of naval captains and dockyard officers, joshed at tables on the periphery of the room. Roberts perceived in their deep and easy laughs an accent of hysteria, a tell, he reasoned, of the relief that follows the lifting of an immense psychological burden.[5] The British officers, by contrast, sat in sombre quiet around a table in the middle of the room, contemplating the gravity of the victor's clean-up task. The ecstasy of the vanquished; the misery of the vanquisher: the curious paradoxes of war.

In almost silence Roberts and the others ate black bread dipped in thin cabbage soup. Still hungry, Roberts retired to his suite. The next day he would begin the task of interviewing and recording U-boat officers in earnest. He was also desperate to visit the plot from which Doenitz had conducted the Battle of the Atlantic, a chance to compare the German nerve centre with that of the British equivalent, in Liverpool, which had been Roberts' home for the last three years.

When Roberts reached his bedroom, Walkerling asked whether he might be able to sleep on the settee in Roberts' cabin.

'I have nowhere else to go,' the U-boat captain said, ruefully.

Roberts refused, but secured his unlikely aide a cabin nearby and ordered that a sign be placed on the door that read: 'German Assistant to Captain Roberts'.

Finally, Roberts lay down in his bunk. He was tired in complicated ways. There were the long-term rigours of the five-year-old war, of course, with its daily rations and, for city-dwellers like

Roberts, its nightly bombings. But he had additional reasons to be weary: the long-term strain of a collapsing marriage and the short-term exhaustion of the previous night, which Roberts had spent in a Belgian hotel, cringing while American bombers thundered over Brussels in one of the final raids of the war.

Roberts fell into the impregnable sleep of the spent. He did not hear the latch to his cabin click. Neither did he see the flickering silhouette of a man caught in the light spilled through the crack in the door. Nor did he see, in the figure's hand, the outline of a Luger pistol.

PART ONE

We have fed our sea for a thousand years,
And she calls us, still unfed
       'The Song of the Dead', Rudyard Kipling

II

As You Wave Me Goodbye

FIVE YEARS EARLIER

Lulled by the creak and sway of the cabin, with a comic book splayed open beside him, Colin Ryder Richardson was dozing when he felt a dull thud somewhere deep beneath his bunk.[1] The clock beside him read 00:03. At home in London, the eleven-year-old would normally be asleep by now. Here on the ship, however, there were no parents to nag about forbidden lights and early rises. When they met for the first time, four days earlier, Colin's Hungarian chaperone and cabin mate, a young journalist named Laszlo Raskai, had decided that the boy with blond hair and intelligent eyes didn't seem to need much adult supervision. Short of toppling overboard, what was the worst that could happen on a transatlantic luxury liner?

Free from adult supervision, Colin had earlier in the week placed a ball bearing he found stuck in the furrow between planks on the ship's deck into the drawer of the writing desk that separated his and Raskai's bunks.[2] The roll and clack the ball made as it tipped from one end of the drawer to the other was soothing and besides, Raskai was never around to complain. Moments after the muffled thud woke him, the ball suddenly clacked loudly, then not at all, as the ship, imperceptibly at first, then in more pronounced terms, began to list. The first strains of shouting drifted into Colin's cabin. Then he noticed the distinct smell of nail polish.

In early September Colin's parents had sat him down after dinner at the family's farmhouse in Wales – a temporary bolthole away from bomb-shaken London – and asked how he felt about taking a trip to America. Colin pictured Hollywood lettering and cowboys keeling from balconies – an eleven-year-old's romantic vision of the country. He responded enthusiastically only to be told that he would be staying not in Beverly Hills, but in New York. Not quite what the boy had in mind, perhaps, but with rationing in full effect, British meals had become monotonous and insipid. To Colin, the 'Big Apple' bespoke a city of food and plenty.

Although his parents did not let on, preparations for Colin's journey were already set in motion. He would travel alone, by ship, to Montreal. From there, the boy would journey south to Long Island, where one of the many well-to-do New York couples who had offered refuge to British evacuee children awaited.

The decision to send their son away had been difficult at first, then less so. The Second World War was a year old. That summer, after a brief six-week stand, France had fallen to the Nazis, removing the last bulwark standing between Britain and the German army and rendering Britain's strategic assumptions obsolete. Like many families, Colin's parents believed the Germans, who had driven the British back from Dunkirk in June 1940, were poised to cross the English Channel, a mere thirty-mile ribbon of sea at its slenderest, in an invasion that would almost inevitably prove successful. In recent weeks the British Ministry of Information had begun circulating leaflets titled 'If the Invader Comes: What to Do and How to Do It'.

Most persuasively, for parents like Colin's, morgues were currently lined with the bodies of children, losers in the grim household lottery of the London Blitz, where, night after night, German planes dropped bombs to topple the city. Families who, a few months earlier, would not have contemplated sending their children off to *who-knows-whom* for *who-knows-how-long*, were now desperate to spirit their sons and daughters away from harm, regardless of the emotional toll.

The Ryder Richardsons' idea to send their child abroad was not unique. In June the British government announced a bold, controversial and, for the parents who applied to it, heartbreaking scheme, to evacuate children from London, Liverpool and other imperilled targets of the Luftwaffe. The response was immense: close to a quarter of a million children applied for just 20,000 places.

The plan was simple, and proven. Since the beginning of the war, merchant ships had been ferrying food, fuel and supplies into Britain, an island nation that, without these imports, would go hungry. Sailors knew from the experience of the First World War that the safest way to cross the Atlantic Ocean was to move in convoys, finding safety in numbers. The Royal Navy sent warships to protect them. The 'escorts', as these ships were known, carried nothing but men and weapons. They encircled the convoy as it plodded its heavy-laden course, and, like sheepdogs facing down wolves threatening a herd, fended off any enemy attacks. First introduced in 1917, convoys were initially centred on the English Channel, but as the efficacy of the tactic was proven, the system was used to protect ships as they crossed the deep and wide waters of the Atlantic Ocean. Colin's evacuee ship was just like any other member of the convoy. Except, instead of wood, coal, oil or pork chops, the SS *City of Benares* carried a cargo of children.

The trip, designed to evade danger at home, would not be without its risks at sea. All year U-boats – short for '*Unterseeboot*', the German word for submarine – had been attacking Allied vessels wherever they found them. These attacks had intensified when, a few weeks earlier, in early August, Hitler had declared unrestricted submarine warfare around Britain.

On 29th August 1940, seventy miles off Ireland's Donegal Coast, a U-boat torpedo struck the SS *Volendam*, the first convoy ship to leave filled with evacuees.[3] The ship was abandoned,* but all 321 children aboard were successfully rescued. While news of the attack made clear the dangers of the scheme, even in disaster, a ship seemed a safer bet than a London bed.

On Thursday 12th September 1940, Colin and his mother took the train to Liverpool. The plan was set: he, along with eighty-nine other children (two of whom had survived the sinking of the *Volendam* a fortnight earlier), would sail for Canada that day.

With a ten-pound note in his pocket – a parting gift from his father – Colin watched the green of Wales smear past the window

---

* The forsaken *Volendam* was towed by HMS *Salvonia*, beached on the Isle of Bute and later refloated and repaired.

of the train. He was raised from his thoughts by a shake to his shoulders, as his mother began to repeat stern lessons he had heard a dozen times already. After counselling her boy on his manners, Mrs Ryder Richardson made her son promise, once again, that he would never, ever remove his scarlet life jacket. She had presented her son with this garment earlier that morning. It was filled with kapok, a buoyant vegetable fibre, and, Colin's mother believed, would provide greater protection than any ship-issued aid. Colin was to wear it day and night. It was a rule to which he mostly kept, a habit that would later earn him among the other passengers the nickname Will Scarlet, after Robin Hood's sidekick. While the boy would not sleep in it, he always kept his lifejacket within reach.

When the mother and her son arrived at Liverpool's docks, with its nodding cranes and furious drills, the reality of separation struck for the first time. Colin presented his gas mask and identity card, his emotions vacillating between the thrill of imminent adventure and the sorrow of imminent separation. Then he spied the liner that would carry him to Montreal in the dock.

The *City of Benares* was an elegant 11,000-ton luxury cruise liner, with two fatly handsome chimney stacks bookended by a cats-cradle of rigging. The hull was painted a light tan colour, not to camouflage it from U-boats, but to reflect the sun's heat in the Indian Ocean, where it routinely carried passengers between Liverpool and Bombay.

Colin bade a brisk farewell to his mother, who didn't want a drawn-out goodbye, and the two parted, leaving the boy standing at the dockside with his single trunk, into which he had packed a clockwork motorboat and his lucky keepsake, a George III penny.

Unlike the other children jabbering on the dockside, most of whom wore name tags threaded on shoelaces around their necks, Colin was not a government-sponsored evacuee but one of ten paying child passengers. The other children were the sons and daughters of policemen, miners and other blue-collar workers, who had been means-tested and selected by the Children's Overseas Reception Board, or CORB, to be sent to North America. CORB had been hastily set up by the government largely to counter indignation in the press about how the sons and daughters of the wealthy were able to sleep soundly in New York skyscrapers while the children of the working class were forced to tremble at night, 'menaced', as one editorial writer put it, 'by the bomber's drone'.[4]

Colin's father was one of those wealthy parents, a barrister who had purchased the ticket in order to guarantee his son's place. This status would afford Colin certain freedoms denied to the majority of other children aboard, who kept an inflexible timetable of lessons.

Once aboard, Colin was allowed free rein, which presented a vision of luxury far beyond the sparse, electricity-less existence of the Welsh farm. An enormous playroom housed an ornate rocking horse, a basket slung over either side, each of which could hold three children. Boutiques selling fine jewellery and trinkets lined one hallway, while the dining room exhibited the soft-carpeted quality of a Mayfair restaurant. Best of all, the *City of Benares* was a ration-free zone; no eking out a few ounces of cheese and bacon over the course of the week's journey.

The majority of the 200-odd crew members were Indians, known as lascar sailors. Some trod barefoot wearing bright turbans and most wore striking blue and white uniforms. Stepping onto the ship was, for Colin, like entering a floating relic of British India; the colours and aromas inspired a fascination that eased the blow of the news that the ship was to be delayed. During a bombing raid the previous night, German planes had dropped mines into the sea, which needed clearing before any vessel could leave port. To the consternation of some of the more superstitious sailors, and with what would later transpire to be the blunt contrivance of a penny dreadful, the *City of Benares* set sail on the afternoon of Friday 13th.

At six o'clock in the evening, while groups of children sang choruses of 'Wish Me Luck As You Wave Me Goodbye', the ship tugged out of Liverpool harbour. In the North Channel, she met up with the seventeen other vessels that comprised convoy OB.213 to Canada, and its contingent of guardians. One of these three shepherding warships was HMS *Winchelsea*, recently returned from the evacuation of troops from Dunkirk three months earlier.

As a private traveller, like the other paying adult passengers, Colin was free to keep his own hours. He roamed the decks while the majority of the other children on board, all aged between five and sixteen years old, had to be in bed by eight, up at half-seven and in the nursery for lessons during the day. When the weather was fair, as it often was for the first two days of the voyage, the boy would sit on the deck and watch as the Indian cooks made their food, placing great sacks of rice and lentils on the aft deck, before mixing it all together with shovels.

Colin and some of the other paying children devised a simple game, whereby they would open a deckchair and let the wind carry it from the port side of the ship to the starboard, slipping through a gangway. Michael Rennie, an Oxford student and promising rugby player, taught some of the children how to lasso deckchairs. Ruby Grierson, a thirty-six-year-old Scottish documentary maker, would often be seen, with beret and lolling cigarette, filming the children on the decks. Grierson was a rising talent in cinematography whose most recent film, *They Also Serve*, had focused on the role of women at home in wartime England. She had been commissioned to record the evacuee programme, and many of the children would trail her around as she framed shots, dawdling in what they perceived to be the director's star presence.

As the journey progressed the weather worsened. Colin split his time between the ship's library and the cocktail lounge, where kindly adults would offer him the cherries spooned from their whisky sours. Unlike some of the adults, Colin was pleased with the squalls. He'd heard about the U-boat threat and figured that, the rougher the sea, the less likely the ship would be caught in a swivelling periscope. Safety was implied by the roll and clack of his ball bearing.

On the morning of 17th September, three and a half days after the *City of Benares* and the other ships in the convoy departed from Liverpool, the three Royal Navy escorts, sheepdogs to the convoy flock, peeled away and began their return journey to British waters, taking their guns with them.

The ship, almost at the mid-point of its nine-day journey, was close to 500 miles north-west of Liverpool and had entered a stretch of mid-ocean water known throughout the war, variously, as 'the Gap', the 'Black Pit' and, to the Germans, 'Das Todesloch', or 'the Death-Hole'. The British believed this area to be safe, beyond the operational reach of the U-boats. As such the *City of Benares* and the other merchant vessels were to cross it alone, before being met on the other side by well-armed Canadian escort ships a couple of days later.

In recent weeks, unknown to the Royal Navy, who were working from outdated information, the Germans had moved their U-boat operations to occupied France's newly captured naval bases. Here, at Lorient, Brest and La Pallice (and, later, Saint-Nazaire and Bordeaux too), U-boats could be repaired and refuelled and sent back out to sea, without having to return to the German ports. And without the need to return to the Baltic Sea to resupply, ten days were added to the amount of time a U-boat could spend prowling the Atlantic. On the surface and while travelling at ten knots the most common U-boat model of the time, the Type VII-C, had a range of nearly 8,000 miles. With six weeks' worth of fuel, a single U-boat could roam the entire Atlantic span, from the panoramic beaches of France to the crags of the North American coastline. The radius of the war now spanned the ocean. There was no longer a safe spot where the convoy flock would be free from trouble. The gap had been closed.

Already, after just six days at sea, the atmosphere inside the U-boat was damp and foul-smelling. *U-48*'s thirty-eight crew members had departed Lorient on the evening of 8th September 1940, believing they were fully prepared for life beneath the ocean. As new recruits, the men, some of whom were still teenagers and almost none of whom were married,[5] had undergone rigorous physical training regimes, followed by specialised schooling in U-boat seamanship and technology. The men who made it to sea were those who could endure the claustrophobia of life inside a metal canister and suffer the bruising indignity of being chained to a lurching deck rail as the vessel spliced along the surface of the choppy water, like a heavy-laden motorboat. Still, there was no way to fully prepare a person for the gloom of U-boat life, with its sweating tables, perma-damp towels and prickling lice.

It was on the water's surface that U-boats were, paradoxically, most at ease, able to travel at their top speeds propelled by churning German-made, air-breathing diesel engines. Underwater, by contrast, the U-boat was slow and vulnerable, forced to switch to electric motors that could do little more than waft the craft through the water, and only for a relatively short amount of time before the batteries needed recharging and the boat was forced to surface.

Inside U-48, there was no space for a crew member to call his own. Each man would hot-bunk, feeling the warmth of the last occupant's body fading in the sheets, a sensation in equal parts comforting and repellent. Light sleepers suffered greatly from the incessant hammering of pistons, the gasps and tuts of inlet valves and the gargling bilge pumps. The slumbering mind had to be trained to distinguish ambient clatter from signs of earnest danger, as signalled by the *Achtung!* klaxon.

There would be days of boredom, dead time filled with games of chess and letter-writing. One crew carried aboard a pet goldfish they called Fridolin to keep them company beneath the waves. [6] In an instant, however, the leisure-time atmosphere could change. If spotted by an escort ship, the U-boat submerged as deep as its safety gauges permitted. It was a delicate manoeuvre; too far and the water pressure could pull a rivet from its socket with the force of a bullet fired from a revolver; too shallow and the vessel was within the blast range of its attacker's depth charges, explosive barrels tossed overboard and timed to detonate at variable depths. Submerged, the U-boat would wait till the threat had passed. When the U-boat was being hunted by one of the Royal Navy's attack-dog corvettes (many of which were named, disharmoniously, after English flowers) or destroyers, the sound was akin to lying between the tracks while a goods train thundered overhead. On these ships, the captain's orders had to be screamed to be heard over the wind. By contrast, as soon as the engines were cut, the U-boat was a whispering realm.

Although they did not know it yet, it was here, in the immense deep, that most U-boat crew members would die. Of all the various forces and divisions of air, land or sea, on both sides of the conflict, the U-boat posting had the greatest mortality rate of any in the Second World War. British planes dropped leaflets over Germany, warning potential new recruits that for every one of the 2,000 U-boatmen who were currently living as prisoners of war in Britain, five more had already been killed at sea. Life-insurance companies in neutral countries estimated the average life of a U-boat sailor to be fifty days.[7] This was not the hyperbole of propaganda. Of the 39,000 men who went to sea in U-boats during the Second World War, seventy per cent were killed in action. By contrast, only six per cent of those who fought in the British Army died in combat.[8] In the early 1940s you were more likely to die on a U-boat than on any other mode of transport in existence.

The Allied code word for U-boat was 'hearse'. The odds against surviving the twelve patrols required of every U-boatman before he could apply to be reassigned to non-combat duties were poor. As they began to realise what they'd signed up to, a kill-or-be-killed mentality hardened in the U-boat crews. Sympathy with the enemy, be they man, woman or child, could be fatal.

Apart from his short, lithe frame, Heinrich Bleichrodt, Kapitänleutnant of *U-48*, was not a natural submariner. Born in Berga, a town close to Leipzig, eastern Germany, in 1909, his father died while he was young, leaving Heinrich's mother and older sister to raise him. His friends called him 'Ajax', a nickname that survived childhood, and followed him into the German navy. At the late age of twenty-nine he made his first tour in a U-boat, and a talent for leadership became obvious to those who fought both alongside and above him.

On 4th September 1940, four days before he left France, Bleichrodt took command of his first submarine. While some of *U-48*'s crew doubted their captain's suitability, this pale, hard-drinking man would come to be well liked by his men. In the pressed confines of a U-boat, not much else mattered.

'On a big ship you are a nobody,' one of Bleichrodt's fellow captains wrote. 'But when you are captain of a U-boat and have the confidence of your crew, you are almost a god.'[9]

Every god needs a domain, and Kapitänleutnant Bleichrodt's was built in 1937 at the German port of Kiel. *U-48* was 218 feet long, twenty feet wide and had a top surface speed of almost eighteen knots, faster than most of the ships it hunted. These Type VII-B U-boats were ideally suited to battle in the Atlantic, quick to dive, and with enviable mobility. They were also impossibly cramped; the entire crew of thirty-eight shared a single toilet – the other bathroom being clogged with stacked cans and preserves for the journey. There were no separate compartments on board, just a long aisle, like that on a train carriage, with constant human traffic and a complete absence of privacy. The changing-room odour was masked, imperfectly, with the scent of a dozen different colognes.

Inside its belly, U-48 carried fourteen torpedoes, or 'eels' as the crews called them. These twenty-three-foot-long missiles, among which the crew lived and slept, were stashed in lockers, tucked beneath floor plates and piled up along the bulkhead. The men would scrawl graffiti on the casing, marking the torpedoes with their signatures, significant dates and doodles. Until one or two eels had been fired, there wasn't even enough room for the occupants to stand upright to change their clothes, adding a further incentive to find and attack an enemy ship at the earliest possible opportunity.

By the end of the war U-48 would have distinguished itself as the deadliest U-boat in Hitler's submarine fleet, sinking no fewer than fifty-five ships before her maintenance crew, aware that the war was at an end, scuttled her. In September 1940, however, she was almost new and untested. Just below the smell of diesel, a talented sniffer could still pick out the fading aroma of fresh paint. Like Bleichrodt, who commanded in the shadow of Germany's trio of celebrity U-boat aces, Otto Kretschmer, Günther Prien and Joachim Schepke, U-48 still had everything to prove.

In the second week of September 1940, just before the *City of Benares* left port, Kapitänleutnant Bleichrodt and his crew slunk around the Atlantic coast of Ireland. Freed by Hitler to now hunt wherever it wanted, U-48 was one of twenty-seven U-boats stalking the British shipping lanes in search of prey.

Reinhard 'Teddy' Suhren had been with U-48 for much longer than his captain, serving as watch officer under Bleichrodt's two beloved predecessors, Herbert Schultze, known affectionately to his crew as 'Dad', and Hans Rudolf Rösing. Suhren, with his experience working under virtuoso leaders, immediately spotted Bleichrodt's weak spots, amply demonstrated one moonless night when, while the lookouts were gabbing on the bridge, *U-48* sidled unawares into the middle of a convoy of British ships. A fox among the chickens, the U-boat came close enough to one of these towering vessels that, by the time the crew realised what had happened, they seemed close enough to reach out and touch its hull. Rather than pull away in order to line up a torpedo, Bleichrodt, who had been shouted awake just moments earlier, instigated a panicked alarm dive,[10] a rookie mistake when so close to such easy pickings.

Bleichrodt's inexperience, however, was compensated for by his seasoned crew, which, alongside Suhren, included Otto Ites, who would go on to receive the Ritterkreuz, or Knight's Cross, one of the highest awards in the German navy, while commanding his own U-boat.

As such, the captain's debut as a submarine commander was auspicious. In the early evening of 14th September 1940, he spied a convoy off north-west Ireland. Just after midnight, having tailed the ships for a while, Bleichrodt gave the order to fire. These volleys sank a pair of midsize merchant ships, the *Empire Soldier* and *Kenordoc*. The torpedo tubes were reloaded, and two minutes later another escort, HMS *Dundee*, was hit. Spotting an incoming destroyer, part of the convoy's armed escort, *U-48* dived to evade detection, sending any men on board who weren't holding on to a secure part of the vessel into a tumbling bundle, in a shower of condoms.

There were, at that time, around 1,500 of these contraceptives on board.[11] They were not intended for the men's use at sea, but rather to be filled with helium, tied to the submerged U-boat and extended up, through the water, into the air, where they could be used as weather balloons or, even more usefully, as antennae extensions, enabling *U48*'s wireless radio to be used underwater to make contact with base. Once any messages had been sent and received, the tether would be cut, and the condom would fly up and away.

That night no moment was spared for the men dozing on board to prepare for such a crash dive. The force of a single depth charge could rupture a U-boat's hull in an instant, sending it bubbling to the seabed. Speed was the essence of evasion. The men crouched in sweating silence.

After he was sure the danger had passed, *U-48* resurfaced and sank two more ships. High on survivor's euphoria, Kapitänleutnant Bleichrodt steered *U-48* west-north-west away from the wreckage and plotted a course into the open Atlantic. Unwittingly, he aimed the U-boat directly toward a luxury liner filled with sleeping children.

III

They Will Come

You aren't qualified to crew a submarine, so the saying goes, until you can successfully carry three cups of coffee from the top of the conning tower, that armoured, peeking fin from which the captain 'conducts' the vessel, down to the bridge in the middle of a storm without spilling a drop. Well, wondered Christian Oldham, as for the fifth time her foot slipped on a ladder rung: what do I get for doing it in an ankle-length evening gown?[1]

The dress didn't even belong to her. After weeks of showing up to parties on the docked submarine wearing the same wardrobe that she'd had room to pack before moving to Plymouth, Oldham and her best friend, Eve Lindsay, had swapped clothes. As the bombs fell and the rations diminished, here was a simple way to rekindle the embers of glamour and break the monotony of war's grey rhythms.

The wardroom, somewhere in the belly of the vessel, was filled with the sound of tinkling glass, the crackle of a record player and that unique heat that hangs in the air when half a dozen human beings giggle and flirt in a confined space. In one corner, a submariner regaled his audience with the story of how, on a recent mission somewhere in the Mediterranean, he was playing cards when the order came down for everyone to be silent. The submarine was being hunted by one of Hitler's U-boats, the captain had explained, and even the jagged sound of a shuffle could betray their position. In the thrumming stress of the moment, this submariner's card-playing buddy had got to his feet and begun to scream. There was no time to stifle his cries, the man explained. Instead, he wound up a right hook, and knocked his crew mate out clean.[2]

Oldham and Lindsay shared a glance. If wars were movies (and this, ultimately, is how most of them end up, one way or another, these days), then every tagline could read: 'Boys will be boys.'

After an hour or so, the women had had their fill of braggadocio. They bade their goodbyes, climbed the ladder into the cool Devonshire night and headed to the local Italian restaurant, where a hassled chef was doing his best to meet the demands of his customers with his dwindling larder supplies.

The German U-boat fleet, which at the time of the *City of Benares'* journey consisted of a few dozen boats, was led and guided by Karl Doenitz, a U-boat ace of the First World War who, in the 1930s, was tasked by Hitler with developing new U-boat designs and tactics.

Doenitz, who for much of the war directed his crews via radio from his base on the west coast of France, was an aggressive commander. Every day that passed without news of an Allied sinking by a U-boat he considered to be a failure. His plan was simple: following the fall of France in the summer of 1940, Britain had been forced to rely on transatlantic shipments for all of her oil, most of her raw materials and much of her food and supplies. In total, a 3,000-strong merchant shipping fleet brought 68 million tons of imports to the country each year, of which 22 million tons was food. If the U-boats could block and sink these ships, Britain, an island unable to sustain its people without imports, would starve. In this way hunger, the blunt, persistent weapon of war, could be deployed against Germany's enemy from a position of remove.

The belief that, if Britain's supply lines were to be broken, national defeat would follow, was not limited to the Germans. After the First World War, the Admiral of the Fleet, John Jellicoe, had stated that the Allies had floated to victory on a wave of oil.* Prime Minister Winston Churchill described merchant shipping as 'at once the stranglehold and the sole foundation of our war strategy'. This

---

* According to the U-boat ace Günther Prien's contemporaneous memoir, Jellicoe's words were well known to the German captains, who used them as motivation to send, as their battle cry went, 'any ship in convoy to the bottom'.

fundamental truth was acknowledged in a chart that took up almost the entirety of a wall in the Operations Room at the Admiralty, the navy's London headquarters. This graph, which charted the number of ships that had been sunk at sea, showed, in the starkest terms imaginable, the stakes at play.

Its top quarter was divided by a thin red line that marked the narrow threshold between victory and defeat: if the rate of ship sinkings stayed below the line, the British people could survive on the amount of food and fuel that was making it through on the convoy ships unharmed. Britain was utterly reliant on imports. Ninety-five per cent of fuel came into the country from trading partners and colonies, while seventy per cent of the nation's food supply was imported. If the graph exceeded the red line, whereby the Germans sank ships at a faster rate than the Allies could build them, the country could no longer continue to participate in the war.

The effects of German U-boats were immediately seen in British kitchens as, in the first four months of the war, they sank 110 merchant ships. Fish became scarce and expensive. From 8th January 1940, butter, bacon and sugar could only be bought with coupons. Onions, which prior to the war were imported from Spain, France and the Channel Islands, vanished from greengrocers.[3] Lemons and bananas, too, disappeared from shops. Farmers expanded their crops and, in doing so, extended the number of days per year the nation could feed itself without imports from 120 to 160 days.*[4] It was not enough. If the U-boat grip tightened to fully stem the flow of merchant ships, Britain could not 'make do and mend', as the slogan went, indefinitely. The government would be forced to impose on the British people an eighteenth-century peasant-style vegetarian diet.[5] After poverty and privation, surrender would soon follow.[6] This was the battle within the battle, a contest known to commanders on both sides of the conflict as, simply, the tonnage war.

To enact his plan, on 1st August 1940, at Doenitz's urging, the German naval high command authorised a total blockade of Britain,

---

* Much of the labour on the growing British farms was provided by the 8,000 'land girls' of the Women's Land Army, whose tenacity in executing their exhausting work was both invaluable and, subsequently, often overlooked.

giving U-boat commanders the mandate to attack ships without warning or prior approval from superiors. Five years earlier Germany had signed a protocol barring this kind of unrestricted use of submarines as weapons of war, but the outbreak of war had, in Hitler's view, nullified the agreement. International shipping law prohibited attacks on merchant ships, but Doenitz's blunt battle orders that 'fighting methods will never fail to be used merely because some international law forbids them' made their commander's position clear to every subordinate.

During the past few days, Kapitänleutnant Bleichrodt had unknowingly but steadily advanced on the British convoy. With a top speed of almost eighteen knots, *U-48* could travel three knots quicker than the *City of Benares*, which, on this particular journey, was already travelling much more slowly than it might. Like a funeral procession forced to match the pace of its eldest member, every ship in a convoy could sail only as fast as the slowest member of the convoy.

After the naval escorts had turned away, some of the *City of Benares'* crew members grew jittery, arguing that, considering its precious cargo, the ship should break away from the rest of the sluggish herd, and make its own way across the Atlantic Gap at a quicker pace. In fact, Admiral Mackinnon, the man in charge of the convoy – shepherd, as it were, to the convoy flock – intended to break up the formation at noon on 17th September. Poor weather had made his plan impossible to execute, however, so Mackinnon delayed the order for the ships to disperse by twelve hours, to midnight.

At 10:02 a.m. Central European Time on the 17th, shortly before Mackinnon had originally planned to break up the convoy, the Germans caught sight of one of the British ships. Moving slowly at around eight knots in a lazy zigzag pattern, *U-48* moved ahead of the vessel, and picked out other ships in the convoy. Bleichrodt soon spotted the *City of Benares*, the largest ship in the convoy of nineteen, and, through his powerful binoculars, picked out the guns mounted on its decks. A sense of bewilderment spread through *U-48*'s crew. The liner was apparently unguarded.

'It makes no sense,' said Rolf Hilse, the U-boat's nineteen-year-old wireless operator.[7]

For Bleichrodt, there was no doubt as to whether or not the *City of Benares* was a fair target: it was the convoy leader, its guns silhouetted on the fore and aft decks. It bore no red crosses, or Christmas-tree strings of lights to indicate its humanitarian cargo.

Not only did Bleichrodt consider the *City of Benares* a fair target, he also considered it a high-value one. To incentivise his U-boat captains to seek out those convoy ships whose destruction would cause the greatest gains in the tonnage war, Doenitz offered the Knight's Cross to anyone who achieved a 'high score' by sinking 100,000 tons of Allied shipping. When the success of a U-boat commander was measured against these hard numbers, a sizeable ship like *City of Benares* represented a valuable prize, especially for a U-boat captain, who, a fortnight into his command, was eager to distinguish himself. Kapitänleutnant Bleichrodt set a west-south-westerly course. The U-boat pulled ahead of the *City of Benares*, and settled into a shadowing that would continue for the next nine hours.

As dusk bruised into night, the weather deteriorated. Thirty-mile-an-hour winds began to buffet the ships, pitching them at wild angles. As the waves grew, swilling the decks with phosphorescent sheets of foam, Admiral Mackinnon sent the order for the convoy ships to halt their zigzag courses, and instead slow and straighten in an effort to ride out the storm as comfortably as possible.[8] At midnight on the 18th a parting in the clouds allowed the moon to momentarily light up the scene. Half a mile off the *City of Benares'* bow, Suhren, *U-48*'s first watch officer, took a bearing through the rangefinder, a pair of binoculars with a graduated scale attached, on the bridge.[9]

With a sharp order for his crew members to remain absolutely still, Suhren estimated the distance to the ship, and its course and speed. From this information he was then able to calculate the angle at which the torpedo should be fired in order to strike its hull. On his command, the torpedo tubes were then flooded with seawater. Suhren waited for the red lights on the dashboard to extinguish and the white one to illuminate, signalling that the system was ready. Finally, Kapitänleutnant Bleichrodt broke the creaking hush with the order to fire.

The range of a German torpedo was considerable; one that missed its target had been known to travel fourteen kilometres before trailing off. But acoustic torpedoes, which could pick out and head towards the noise of a ship's hull and propellers, were still two years away, so, without any homing device, the closer a U-boat could sidle to its intended victim the better. Not too close, however, as there was a risk that a U-boat could be damaged in the shock waves of an explosion; the official manual recommended a U-boat be no closer than 1,000 metres to its target when firing.

The crew of *U-48* felt a slight jolt as the first two torpedoes, expelled by a blast of air, left the U-boat and streaked off through the water. The torpedoes were driven by an electric motor and propellers, designed so that the missile would not release any bubbles that might give away the U-boat's position, a regular occurrence in the previous war.[10]

'Torpedo running,' reported Hilse, listening on *U-48*'s hydrophone.

As he listened on his headphones one of the U-boat's trim tanks flooded to replace the weight of the departed torpedo and ensure the boat remained properly balanced. Hilse waited for the telltale thump of detonation. There was none. Two misses.

Premature or failed explosions were common with the German torpedoes used in the first two years of the war. Nevertheless, misses were costly. Each torpedo cost 50,000 Reichsmarks,* around $20,000. Then, when the U-boat returned to the French port of Lorient, Bleichrodt knew that he would have to fly pennants from the periscope. These were used to mark each successful 'kill', a signal of the crew's success, issued to the crowds watching from the dockside. Every missed torpedo reduced the number of pennants that could be flown and increased the likelihood of embarrassment before the men even disembarked. Bleichrodt ordered a reload.

'We'll risk this one,' he said. 'No more.'

The third missile, fired at two minutes past midnight, flew

---

* Cost of the G7a, the standard-issue *Kriegsmarine* torpedo. The later G7e cost 25,000 Reichsmarks. The cost of an MKVII depth charge as used by the Royal Navy was, by comparison, around £22.

through the water. From the U-boat's conning tower, the captain watched. One minute and fifty-nine seconds passed, an eternity of waiting. Then Hilse pulled off his headphones.

'It's a hit,' he called up to his captain.[11]

From the conning tower the gathered men watched the liner tilt.

In his cabin, having been shaken awake by the noise beneath his bunk, Colin pulled his red life jacket over his pink pyjamas, just like his mother had instructed him to. Then he failed to pull on his dressing gown over that. Next, he picked up his ship-issued life jacket and tried to zip that over the rest of the bulging outfit.

No, he chastised himself: I haven't thought this through. Carrying the life jacket in one arm, and the dressing gown in the other, the boy headed to the assembly point where, a few hours earlier, he and the other passengers had practised lifeboat drill. The whispered rumour in the corridors was that the ship had been struck by another ship in the convoy – the careless mishap of a dozing navigator, perhaps. At a stairwell, someone told him to relax and return to his cabin. But Colin, who recognised the nail-polish-like smell of cordite from the air raids he had survived in London, pressed on.

Upstairs, in the assembly lounge, there was no sign of panic. The ship's captain, Landles Nicoll, had arrived at the bridge two minutes after the explosion. Knowing how difficult it would be to launch lifeboats in a storm, Nicoll dispatched the ship's chief officer, Joe Hetherington, to assess the damage before deciding what to do next.

U-48's torpedo had broken through the ship's port side, tearing through the number five hold to explode directly beneath a row of bathrooms in the children's quarters. Number four hold, Hetherington saw, had also sustained damage. More pressingly, the blast from the torpedo had blown through the watertight door leading to the engine room, turning the corridor into a gulley along which the freezing Atlantic water could flow to greet the ship's burning steel pipes. Hetherington knew that the resulting steam explosions would, in effect, seize the ship's heart. Water was already at ankle height and rising fast. Before Hetherington had made it back to the bridge to report his findings, the ship's chief engineer had already radioed ahead to warn that the ocean was now tickling at his waist.

'Lower the boats,' Nicoll ordered. 'Prepare to abandon ship.'

When the captain's message sounded over the loudspeaker, there were murmurs of disbelief, even indignation, among the passengers who had congregated in the lounge. For those clutching coffees, or tumblers of spirits, it seemed too extreme a course of action. Still, as they filed out onto the cold deck, most passengers felt assured in their belief that there were numerous friendly ships in the vicinity to mount a rescue.

In fact, the opposite was true. In the event of a U-boat attack, convoy ships were instructed to press on, only stopping to aid a torpedoed ship if there was absolute certainty that the attacker had been eliminated or chased off. With no escort ships to hunt U-48, the convoy had panicked and dispersed, not wanting to be next in the U-boat's sights. Fifteen minutes after the eel struck, the City of Benares was utterly alone.

With his ship-issued life jacket slung over one arm, Colin stepped onto the deck, as long as a field, and into a force eight gale. It had been a tempestuous day on the sea and, as the moon wheeled behind the night clouds, the rain had begun to sheet heavy onto the ship's decks. The children, blinking the rain from their eyes, were quietly marshalled by their chaperones onto lifeboats, which began to lower from the stow nests in jerking movements via pulleys, worked by frantic sailors. As boats swayed and pounded against the hull below him, Colin heard the cry: 'Women and children first.'

Immediately on hearing the explosion, Raskai, Colin's Hungarian escort, had left the bar and made his way toward the most damaged parts of the ship to help survivors, before heading to his cabin to collect his charge. When he found the cabin empty, Raskai ran to the pair's designated assembly point at Lifeboat Two. The man greeted the boy briskly, then Raskai clambered into the lifeboat to lift Colin aboard. Great cries of dismay went up from the other assembled adults, who mistakenly believed that the journalist was trying to save himself.

With Colin safely on a cross plank seat, Raskai clambered out of the lifeboat to help others, including the ship's twenty-five-year-old nurse, Agnes Harris Wallace, who moments later sat heavily beside the boy.[12] Finally, Angus MacDonald, the ship's carpenter and assigned pilot of Lifeboat Two, gave the order to lower the vessel into the sea. After a lurching drop, the boat smacked the ocean, and immediately began to fill with water.

More than food and drinking water, the most valuable commodity on a lifeboat, in the short term at least, is composure. This, however, was in short supply. In the chaos of the scene, and before anyone could stop it, one of the boat's oars drifted away. MacDonald shouted at the boat's thirty-seven other occupants to begin bailing, using anything to hand or, if nothing could be found, their cupped palms. Colin, his arms still full of clothing, bobbed in his seat.

Christian Oldham was one of a clutch of Wrens, typically between the ages of seventeen and twenty-five, who had joined the navy to fill slots left by the men called to sea. The navy, an institution resolutely against change for change's sake, had, in its desperation to find workers, turned to young women. It advertised posts in the Wrens with the poster slogan: 'Join the Wrens and free a man for the fleet'. Thousands signed up, out of a sense of duty. Then, Parliament passed a second National Service Act in December 1942 calling up all unmarried women and childless widows between the ages of twenty and thirty by law.[13]

Initially, the women were offered mundane roles as administrators, drivers and cooks. Despite widespread suspicion from members of the establishment (the Civil Service Union fought resentfully against the appointment of Wrens officers) as war progressed, and the Wrens proved their collective value, the women were given greater and more diverse responsibilities. Some became welders, others became carpenters. Some loaded torpedoes onto submarines, others plotted the progress of sea battles on maps hung in clandestine operations rooms.

The Wrens' heroism often matched that of the men they had 'freed' for duty. In 1942, for example, Pamela McGeorge was asked to deliver an important dispatch from one side of Plymouth to the commander-in-chief at the other. She drove her motorcycle through the night while the Luftwaffe dropped bombs on the city. When a bomb landed close to the road, McGeorge was blown from her bike, its wheels mangled. Undeterred, McGeorge ran to Admiralty House with the letter in her hand. On arrival, she offered to immediately head out again with the response.

Oldham's role, when she wasn't visiting submarines, was that of a plotter at Western Approaches HQ, which, during the early months of the war, was stationed in Plymouth, on the south coast of England. It was here, in the Operations Room, that the convoy ships carrying supplies to Britain, and their escort protectors, were monitored and directed. In order to visualise the situation at sea, a huge map of the entire Atlantic Ocean covered one wall of the HQ. This map showed the position of any ship, convoy or reported U-boat. Information to adjust these positions arrived from various sources, but principally from a U-boat tracking room in a complex situated below the Admiralty building in central London. Here all U-boat sightings from ships and aerial reconnaissance as well as the bearings of U-boat wireless transmissions obtained by direction-finding technology were plotted, analysed and sent on to the Wrens in Western Approaches. If no new signal arrived, a ship would be moved according to its supposed speed by dead reckoning.

Plotting was a new role for the Wrens; the first four women plotters were employed at Dover in the summer of 1940.[14] There was no training course available yet, and Oldham arrived without a clue as to how to execute her responsibilities. She learned on the job, by asking questions of the other women, carefully angled to hide her ignorance.

The Operations Room at Mount Wise in Plymouth was divided in half, one side given over to the navy, the other to the RAF. On her side, using coloured wax markers, Christian drew the routes of ships onto the maps. Tiny models indicating convoys, ships, U-boats and aircraft were shunted across the map according to the latest information, which was relayed via four Wrens who stood by the maps, attentively wearing headphones. The Wrens worked watches that lasted either from six in the evening through to nine in the morning, or nine in the morning through to six in the evening: a long day in which emotions fluctuated between deadening boredom or crisp anxiety, depending on the situation at sea.

As the war progressed the system evolved, and white submarine symbols were eventually used to represent the estimated position of U-boats, like 'measles in the green-painted cork', as one of Oldham's colleagues, Mary Carlisle, later put it, replacing them with black submarines when the position of the U-boat was verified.[15] Crimson ships, placed at an angle, represented those ships that had been struck by torpedo.

On a mezzanine floor at the back of the room, facing the wall map, sat the Royal Navy senior officers, who would direct the ships to avoid any U-boats that had been spotted. From their remote, detached vantage point, they could watch the nightly battles of the Atlantic unfold. It was a micro-drama of maps and tokens that carried mortal consequences.

Just after midnight on 18th September one of the plotters at Plymouth received a coded message from Lyness Shore station in Scotland. It came directly from Alistair Fairweather, the *City of Benares'* first radio officer, a man of enviable unflappability, who tapped out the SOS message while drawing on a cigarette, as a scene of chaos played out around him.

Twenty-three minutes later, at 00:29, one of the Plymouth Wrens handed Admiral Martin Dunbar-Nasmith, the current commander-in-chief at the Office of Western Approaches, the decoded message:

'Please send a ship to the *City of Benares*, or her lifeboats, and rescue the passengers.'

A token representing *U-48* was added to the map on the wall, adjacent to the *City of Benares*, the two opposing markers alone in a sea of cork. The officers behind the glass began to consider their options.

Colin watched the adults on Lifeboat Two, which now had around forty people either on board or clinging to its sides, work levers at the stern in order to manually turn a propeller. Having lost its oars, this was the only way for the boat to flee the vicinity, where there was a risk it might be sucked under the waves when the liner finally sank. The oily scent of damaged machinery and cries for assistance hung in the air. Weighed down with water, but suspended by its emergency flotation device, Lifeboat Two sat steady in the water, while Colin watched as other vessels around him were tossed and flipped by the storm.

Around thirty minutes after the torpedo hit, as the storm further intensified, a searchlight swept the waves. Someone cried 'Rescue!' and a tentative cheer went up. The light arced around the scene for a few moments, then clunked off again. It was not, as some survivors believed, another member of the convoy returning to collect survivors, but their attacker, U-48, performing a reconnaissance sweep. After striking the *City of Benares*, Kapitänleutnant Bleichrodt and members of his crew had watched the lifeboats fill with people, then drop into the water. After five minutes, U-48 had moved to target another ship, the 5,000-ton freighter *Marina*. Having sunk the *Marina*, and while the rest of the convoy scattered, the U-boat returned to the *Benares*, moving through the wreckage in order to check whether one of its remaining torpedoes was required to finish the ship.

Satisfied its work was done, U-48 left eastwards, away from the scene of the crime.

Was it, in fact, a war crime? Two years later a captured U-boatman, Corporal Solm, who claimed that he was aboard U-48 that night, was secretly recorded confiding to a cellmate about the sinking of the *City of Benares*.

'We sank a children's transport,' said Solm.

'You or Prien?' His cellmate asked.

'We did it.'

'Were they drowned?'

'Yes, all are dead.'[16]

In this boastful, inaccuracy-riddled telling, the command had come from Doenitz to specifically target the liner and its children. If true, the sinking of the *City of Benares* was indeed an indefensible, immoral act. But the account is contested. Years later, Hilse, U-48's wireless operator, said it was eighteen months before he and Bleichrodt discovered that the liner had been carrying children.[17] The two men had transferred together to a different U-boat. When Hilse heard the news, he took the message to Bleichrodt, who, Hilse claimed, responded with the exclamation: 'Those poor children.' The following year, Bleichrodt reportedly had a breakdown while at sea.

'The deaths of the children played on his mind terribly,' said Hilse. 'He was a decent man . . . an officer and a gentleman who never had any time for the Nazis.'[18]

No victor would emerge from this battle of competing narratives. While Kapitänleutnant Bleichrodt was later charged with war crimes for attacking the ship, he was never convicted. Investigators dropped their case, unable to prove that those on *U-48* knew there were children aboard the *Benares*.

With ice-bath seawater up to his knees, the waves frothing over the sides of the lifeboat, Colin found it difficult to talk. Solidly built, with a double layer of timber, Colin's lifeboat was designed to withstand the muscular waves of the deep ocean. The horror waters of a mid-Atlantic storm were something else entirely. Out here the waves had been known to bend the iron stanchions that carried the guard rail around the deck of a ship into right-angled submission. Sailors would forlornly return to port with accounts of how their ship's deck lockers, where fresh meat was stored to keep it cool, had been cleaved off, leaving only metallic deck scars where they had been once welded in place.[19] During night storms, when it was so dark that, in the words of one coxswain, you'd struggle to 'see a sixpence on a chimney sweep's arse',[20] men would listen as the sea punched the glass clean from portholes. Escort sailors became fond of saying, with the weary wisdom of experience, that the Atlantic weather was a far more formidable opponent than any Nazi.

'Keep hold of the boat,' shouted the twenty-five-year-old carpenter, MacDonald. [21]

In the black of night, there was no way to know when the next wave would hit, and so to brace against its wild energy.

Lifeboat Two had fared better than some of the other twelve semi-submerged vessels on the water, in which one survivor recalled seeing people float as if sitting atop the waves. MacDonald, a carpenter by trade and a merchant navy reservist by circumstance, knew that he had to keep his people both latched on and moving if they were to survive the twin threats of the sea and the cold. For some, the act of shaking with fear and grief was enough to generate some sustaining warmth. Others resorted to rocking the boat vigorously, in an effort to spill excess water over the sides, and to keep active.

Colin could only grip the gunwale, wearing the pair of gloves he'd found squirrelled away in a pocket of his red life jacket. Not for the first time that night, he thanked his insistent mother. He recalled an assurance she had given him the night before she left him at Liverpool: that if the ship was sunk, the Royal Navy would come for him. He noticed that he had lost his slippers.

As the night deepened, with the invincible faith of a child who has been properly loved, the boy repeated her words in his mind like a mantra:

'They will come. They will come.'[22]

IV

Wolves

It wasn't supposed to be like this. The fire, the deaths, even the survivors icing up in half-submerged lifeboats: these were all part of the regretful yet expected cost of doing war. But the instigating circumstance, that of a lone U-boat touring the barren expanse of the mid-Atlantic to happen upon a ship? This was never Karl Doenitz, *Führer der U-boote*'s plan, a plan that was decades in the making.

Doenitz grew up in the Berlin suburb of Grünau where wolves still hunted in the nearby forests. Doenitz's mother died when he was three years old. His father, an optical engineer who worked for Karl Zeiss, the company that would later provide lenses for the binoculars used on U-boats, brought his two sons up as a single parent.[1] Doenitz, who read and reread books describing the exploits of explorers such as Fritjof Nansen, Hermann von Wissmann and Sven Hedin, left school with romantic, novelistic visions of life at sea that led him to join the navy at eighteen. Among the other 200-odd recruits, Doenitz found fraternity, belonging and, in the reassuring strictures of the military, an orderly path toward promotion and success. He had become estranged from his elder brother, and began to view, in ways both practical and psychological, the navy as his surrogate family.

In September 1916, after a brief tour on a warship, Doenitz was ordered to the U-boatwaffe.[2] It was a welcome transfer. Not only did U-boats offer a relatively fast track to positions of command and distinction, but Doenitz's wife was expecting a baby; the extra financial allowances offered to U-boat crew members – a compensation for the suffocating perils and traumas of the work – would help provide for the young family. After completing his training, Doenitz gladly joined the crew of *U-39*, serving under the U-boat ace Kapitänleutnant Walter Forstmann, who a month earlier had received the Pour le Mérite, among the highest orders of merit in the Kingdom of Prussia.[3]

Under Forstmann, Doenitz's generalised love of the navy narrowed and focused on the individual men of the U-boat division. Proximity to one another and proximity to danger knitted crews together far more closely than for those sailing on the ships overhead, where it was possible to go an entire voyage without knowing the name of a sailor assigned to another station. In the isolated desert of the deep ocean, a U-boat crew inevitably became another family. Survival required a total daily investment of one's trust in those around you. You knew their names. You knew their girlfriends' names. The need for constant alertness and self-discipline was a binding agent that turned camaraderie into something approaching love. Years later, as commander of the U-boats, Doenitz would tell new recruits that, if the navy represents the cream of the armed forces, then the U-boat arm represents the cream of the navy; for Doenitz there was no higher calling than that of the life of the submariner.

This was the context in which Doenitz watched Forstmann sink ship after ship. Forstmann had one of the highest hit rates of any U-boat captain in the Great War, a notable achievement considering that the machine calculators used in the Second World War were still years away: every torpedo had to be angled and timed by eye. To narrow the odds, Forstmann would draw closer to his targets than most U-boat captains, who'd prefer to maintain an equitable distance from the enemy's circling escort ships. The technique made its mark on the young Doenitz, who, in September 1917, was given command of a U-boat.

It was a short-lived career leg. Ten months later, Doenitz and his crew were submerged in the Mediterranean, 150 miles south of Malta. Depending on whether you believe Doenitz's official report, his memoir or the testimony of survivors interrogated by the British, *UB-68* either developed a mechanical fault or, during a crash dive, was poorly handled by its engineer, Leumanl Jeschen. Either way, the U-boat ended up almost vertical under the water, an arrow pointed at the seabed. Next, to Doenitz's and his inexperienced crew's dismay, *UB-68* began to involuntarily surface. The vessel broke the surface inside the middle of a fleet of British warships, like a salmon breaching the centre of a ring of patient grizzlies.

Doenitz ordered Jeschen to scuttle the boat, a well-rehearsed action whereby the U-boat was filled with water and sunk in order to prevent the vessel and its constituent technologies from falling into enemy hands. *UB-68* took just eight seconds to disappear, while the crew trod water in a sea bubbling with its final exhalation. Jeschen never surfaced. All but three of the crew were rescued and Doenitz, who had shed his heavy leathers in the sea, was pulled from the water wearing just a shirt, underpants and a single sock.

After a long trip to England, a journey that he spent in a sulk, turning the accident over in his mind, Doenitz spent the next ten months in a British prisoner-of-war camp at Redmires, near Sheffield. There, he began to show signs of insanity. At breakfast he would play childish games with biscuit tins and china dogs. At one point, reportedly, he pretended to be a U-boat.[4] While, in an unpublished diary written at the time, he wrote of how he became obsessed by Jeschen's death – who would appear in his dreams with 'the salt flood' dripping 'from hair and leathers' – Doenitz later claimed all of this was a ploy.[5] Whether his madness was genuine or faked, or something between the two, Doenitz was dispatched to Manchester Lunatic Asylum. In the privacy of his mind however, he remained at work.

Doenitz believed that he had the secret to a tactic that could transform U-boat warfare. The scheme was borrowed from the wolves of his childhood fairy tales. Wolves, Doenitz knew, hunt cooperatively. By working as a pack, they bewilder and run down prey that would be too large to tackle alone. Togetherness also affords the animals the ability to care for wounded pack members, without sacrificing momentum. What better way, Doenitz reasoned, for U-boats to hunt, not as loners picking off stragglers, but as an organised pack, touring the sea with shared focus and intention, able to take down far stronger foes?

'Against the massed ships of a convoy,' he later wrote, 'the only right course is to engage them with every available U-boat simultaneously.'[6]

As a U-boat commander, Doenitz had hoped to test an early version of the concept in battle. The night before he was captured, Doenitz planned to rendezvous with another boat, U-48 (the namesake precursor to Kapitänleutnant Bleichrodt's vessel) and to attempt a joint attack on a convoy under the light of a new moon. It would be more of a pairing than a pack, of course, but in this embryonic sortie, Doenitz wanted to see, first-hand, how much more devastation might be wrought by U-boats working in tandem. U-48, however, was held up for repairs, and missed the appointment. Nevertheless, he wrote in his memoirs 'that last night [at sea in a U-boat] . . . had taught me a lesson: a U-boat attacking a convoy on the surface and under cover of darkness stood very good prospects of success'.[7]

Doenitz was among the first German prisoners of war to be sent home to Germany, in July 1919. In the years that followed, *Die Rudeltaktik*, or the wolfpack tactic, grew into an obsession for Doenitz. In November 1937, two years before the war, he published a paper in which he formally described, for the first time, how it might work.[8] Now, he just had to convince his superiors in the German navy to build him a sufficient number of U-boats to turn the plan into action. For this too, Doenitz had a plan. More specifically, he had a game.

Tangled up in her life jacket, the *City of Benares'* nurse began to slip into the well of the boat. Throughout the night, she had cared for the lascar sailors aboard Lifeboat Two. Wearing little more than sandals and cotton shirts, these men had succumbed to the cold of the Atlantic quicker than the others. Dribbling and incoherent, one had tipped himself out of the boat.[9] Perhaps seeing their crew mate's despair, over the next thirty minutes, three other lascars also slipped into unconsciousness and beyond. Their deaths robbed the nurse of an immediate purpose. After Colin helped the lifeboat's skipper, MacDonald, push their bodies overboard, she cried out: 'I'm going! I'm going!'

The boy held out his arms to embrace the young woman. After a moment's struggle, she relaxed and let him cradle her head, lifting it clear of the water each time a wave broke over the sides of the boat.

'There'll be a ship coming soon, ma'am,' Colin reassured her. 'It won't be long now.'[10]

Colin's calmness belied his true feelings, familiar to anyone who, as a child, has witnessed an intimate crisis of the adult world: the anxiety that there was something more you should be doing, combined with the bewildered sense that it is neither your place nor responsibility to do so.

'I think I see a light, ma'am,' the boy kindly lied. 'It could be a ship.'

As dawn bled onto the horizon, the rain turned to sleet, and the sleet turned to hail. Where, in the early hours at sea, those on the lifeboat had sung songs to maintain their spirits, the relentless weather had enforced a glum silence. Colin – still contemplating the fates of the oil-slicked people in the water who had tried and failed to haul themselves aboard, before sinking away – shielded the nurse's head from the pocking hail.

Agnes Wallace's last words were straightforward.

'Goodbye,' she said. 'I am dying.'

Then, after a pause, she added: 'Are the children all right?'

After a while the man sitting on Colin's other side, a fifty-nine-year-old academic from a Canadian university, who had swum to the lifeboat after falling from a rope ladder into the sea, suggested, as gently as any person might in a storm, that the boy let her body go. She was dead, he said. Colin refused. He feared that, if he released her arm, he might lose his anchoring.

When Angus MacDonald told Colin to push the woman overboard, the boy found his arms stiff and cramped. He was unable to shift the weight. MacDonald made his way to Colin's end of the lifeboat, and together they lifted the body over the side, where it washed away in a swell.[11]

The desperation of the situation on the water was obvious to the Wrens in the plotting room at Western Approaches HQ in

Plymouth. There, in the centre of the map, like a drop of blood in oil, a tiny red ship showed the location of the sunken liner. Admiral Martin Dunbar-Nasmith, commander-in-chief at the Office of Western Approaches, scanned the map for possible candidates to stage a rescue attempt. There were few contenders. The closest ship was HMS *Winchelsea*, the destroyer that had initially chaperoned the convoy of which *City of Benares* was a part. It was now 200 miles away, protecting another flock of merchant ships.

The next best option was HMS *Hurricane*, a Brazilian destroyer that had been bought and rechristened by the Royal Navy at the outbreak of war, which was currently escorting another convoy of vessels from Britain to Canada. This ship was a little over 300 miles from the site of the *City of Benares'* sinking but, thanks to the size of the escort it sailed with, could be more readily spared than the *Winchelsea*.

Dunbar-Nasmith had a difficult decision to make: return the *Winchelsea* to the Gap, and imperil the ships and crew of its new convoy, or dispatch *Hurricane*, a ship that would take longer to reach the survivors, the life expectancy of whom, he knew, was likely measured in hours, but which would place its current charges in less danger.

Pragmatism won the argument. In the early hours of the morning, Peter Collinson, *Hurricane's* twenty-eight-year-old surgeon and code officer, received the message. Once decoded it read, with the brevity forced by the ponderous technology of the era: 'Proceed with utmost dispatch to position 56°43N/21°15W. Survivors reported in boats.' Collinson passed the message to the ship's captain, thirty-four-year-old Lieutenant Commander Hugh Crofton Simms.

'Utmost dispatch?' said Simms, feeling the pitch and roll of the waves below. 'We'll do our best.'[12]

Doenitz hunched over a crumpled map, spread out across a broad table. It was early 1939, eighteen months before Colin boarded the *City of Benares*, and while well-to-do Berliners and their families were skiing the Harz Mountains, Doenitz was set to play a game, not with his immediate family, but with his naval colleagues. Around him, an assortment of German officers bent and peered with an

equal intensity of focus. The map showed the flat expanse of the
Atlantic Ocean, bordered on the east by the tip of Portugal and,
on the west, the toothy coast of North America. The map was
accurate to scale, but its function that day was that of a board, like
chess's chequered battlefield, the squared-off streets of Monopoly
or the rungs and slides of Snakes and Ladders.

The Germans were split into two teams. The Reds played as the
Royal Navy. Their side held a pile of tokens to represent the forces
at their disposal: twelve battleships, five aircraft carriers, twenty-
seven light cruisers and a hundred destroyers.[13] The Blues played
as the Germans. With tokens representing fifteen torpedo U-boats,
two large fleet U-boats, two artillery U-boats, a minelayer, an
armoured raider and a single supply ship, they were impossibly
outgunned.

The rules of the game, which was set four years into the future,
at a time when Germany was imagined to again be at war with
Britain, were simple. The Red team must use their considerable
forces to protect and chaperone five British convoys of merchant
ships heading towards Britain from various countries via the
Atlantic. Using their sorry fleet of U-boats, the Blue team must
stop them.

Why, while the clouds of war thickened above them, would a
group of serious-minded, middle-aged men waste their time on a
board game? Doenitz, at forty-seven, had become a grandfather
for the first time a few weeks earlier. But wargames like this had
been an integral part of the German military for more than a
century, when Prussian officers began to restage recent or forthcoming real-world battles using miniature figures on sand-covered
tables. In this way, wargames assumed an essential role in military
training, enabling high-ranking officers to experience something
of the magnitude of high-level military strategy, in a consequence-
free environment.

Infantry need only congregate in a field, split into two teams,
load their guns and tanks with blanks and start shooting at one
another to experience the disorientating fury of battle without risk.
It is harder for the strategists and tacticians to practise war. Wargames
had come to be used to anticipate battles, as well as review them,

allowing military commanders to test tactical theories in hypothetical scenarios, and gain a degree of experience that is otherwise unavailable outside of war itself.

That day, in Doenitz's game, no restrictions were placed on players. Each side was given the run of the Atlantic, free to select the courses followed by their vessels. The method may have been playful but Doenitz, a keen bridge player, had a purpose of utmost solemnity. Via the game, he hoped to see how the Royal Navy might act at sea during a war, how he might best cut his adversaries' supply lines and, crucially, how many U-boats he would need to do so with any meaningful degree of success.

As the officers nudged the little tokens representing their warships and U-boats around the map, it became increasingly obvious that the Blue team's U-boat fleet was too small to halt the flow of convoys to Britain. They had carefully split their fifteen torpedo U-boats into five groups consisting of three vessels apiece. They positioned the majority of their fleet in the mid-Atlantic along the Canada-Ireland shipping route, where the Red team's ships would be most numerous. A separate group of tokens was sent toward the Canary Islands. So sparse was the coverage that, during the next few turns, three British convoys made it through the U-boats without a single ship being spotted. One U-boat spied a fourth convoy, but the Blue team chose to keep radio silence so as not to give away the vessel's position. The British escort ships found and made short work of the solitary U-boat the moment it attacked.

After the map was folded up and the pieces packed away, Doenitz wrote a report describing what had happened. The Blue team's failure, he surmised, lay not in any particular tactical mistakes but in the 'emptiness of the sea', as he put it. The German fleet was simply spread too thinly. None of this was surprising to Doenitz, who, since becoming the head of the U-boat division in 1935, had been urging his superiors to build more – and better – U-boats. But the game provided evidence to support his arguments. In his written summary, Doenitz drew the conclusion the Germans would require 'at least some three hundred' operational U-boats if they were to form the wolfpacks needed to sink the numbers of Allied convoy ships required to starve the British.[14]

With a sufficient number of U-boats at sea, Doenitz explained that he would be able to form his U-boats into a huge line, perhaps with as much as twenty miles between each vessel. This line would sweep at a right angle to the suspected course of an incoming convoy, intercepting its route. Once the convoy was spotted, the U-boats would converge as a pack, ahead of its route. Finally, when the signal came to attack, the U-boats could attack all at once, confusing and distracting the naval escorts. Without sufficient numbers, however, Doenitz's U-boats would be forced to roam the ocean as lone wolves, hoping to catch sight of something at which to aim and fire a torpedo.

A few months later, in May 1939, Doenitz restaged the Red vs Blue training exercise, this time transposing the scenario from the board to the ocean.[15] In the Bay of Biscay, off the coast of Portugal, he summoned fifteen U-boats to comprise the Blue team's fleet. The Red team, playing as the British, consisted of two helpless merchant supply vessels and two well-armed escort ships, the *Saar* and the *Erwin Wasser*.

This game was intended to be played out on the entire expanse of the sea. Nevertheless, after just four hours one of the U-boats spotted the pretend 'convoy'. Doenitz watched while, as the hours passed, the U-boats congregated and tracked the convoy, first in a group of seven then, by the end of the game, in a pack consisting of no fewer than thirteen boats.

Doenitz's conclusion was foregone. In his report, he wrote that success against the enemy could only be achieved when 'a great number of U-boats can be successfully set on the convoy'. Both the game played on the water and the game played on the board had proven the effectiveness of his tactic.

Armed with his evidence, Doenitz soon found a powerful ally in one of his superiors, Admiral Rolf Carls, who forwarded the paper describing the wolfpack tactics to high command along with a covering note in which Carls wrote that the idea of a U-boat working alone should be 'dropped' and a 'disposition of groups of U-boats striven for'.[16]

The staff at high command, however, were against wolfpack tactics. While it made sense that coordinated assaults would be more effective than lone-wolf attacks, there was an equally logical concern that the radio signals necessary to organise the U-boats into a pack could, if intercepted by British technology, forfeit any element of surprise and aid detection of the vessels by the enemy. Moreover, Grand Admiral Raeder, commander-in-chief of the German navy, wanted to invest in a surface fleet of warships to rival that of the Royal Navy, and diverted funds away from the U-boat construction plan toward surface vessels. Finally, Hermann Goering, Hitler's closest ally and confidant, a former First World War fighter-pilot ace, favoured the Luftwaffe, not only because of personal bias but also because planes could be built more quickly than U-boats and, therefore, could be seen to be having a more immediate effect.

On multiple fronts Doenitz's plan to build a sizeable U-boat fleet was frustrated. By the outbreak of war, instead of the 300 U-boats he estimated that he would need, Doenitz had just forty-six craft available for action, a proportion of which would always be in transit or docked for repairs or resupply.

At the moment at which the *City of Benares* was sunk there were just twenty-eight U-boats active in the German fleet, not enough to organise into wolfpacks. Or so he thought.

In the grey light of dawn, Colin and the other survivors of the *City of Benares* could see lumps of wreckage in the water: deckchairs, shoes, oil clinging to bobbing corpses and other lingering traces of violence, yet to be swallowed up by the sea. The ocean was mottled grey and white as if, like those who had survived its lashings, it too had aged during the night.

Daybreak brought, if not fresh hope, then fresh relief; Colin could see farther and therefore anticipate when the next wave would hit and brace for impact. The atmosphere on the lifeboat was subdued with sorrow, fatigue and concentration. The number of survivors had dwindled, from thirty-eight to fewer than a dozen. Spirits were briefly lifted when MacDonald managed to open a food locker, and fished out a dripping tin of canned beef, biscuits and rum. Using a jackknife, another man punctured a hole in the lid, and Colin ate.

It was the first benison of the disaster and one that, for Colin, raised hopes that there might be another. Many times during the next few hours the boy caught sight of some mirage on the horizon, and felt a tentative, momentary flush of relief that they were to be rescued. Then, soon enough, he realised that he was mistaken.

In fact, Colin's faith was well placed. HMS *Hurricane* had made good time. Driving through the night storms at fifteen knots, it had been a rough ride for her crew, an ordeal made bearable when word reached the ship that many of the survivors to whom they were racing were children. In the early hours, when the weather had eased, the ship's captain, Hugh Crofton Simms, had sped to twenty-seven knots, a pace that had brought the ship into the vicinity of the disaster.

In the early afternoon, Simms began a box search around the *Benares'* last known position, sailing twenty miles due west before turning to port, steering south for one mile, and finally turning again to track another twenty miles due east. Every available crew member stood on the ship's deck, binoculars and telescopes pressed tightly to their eye sockets, searching the horizon in all directions while the ship made its urgent sweeps. HMS *Hurricane* was eighteen miles into the twenty-mile grid before a lookout shouted: 'Boat ahead.'

Even at its slowest speed, the destroyer produced a swell that could easily upturn a beleaguered lifeboat. Rather than risk tipping survivors back into the sea, Simms dispatched a whaler, a narrow open boat, pointed at both ends, to approach the life-boat and report back. Albert Gorman, the ship's whaler, sped toward the first boat, tying a painter rope to latch the craft together. Gorman stepped aboard and, immediately, any sense of hopeful anticipation dissipated. He counted twenty people, all of whom appeared dead. One young woman, wearing nothing but stockings and a torn frock, appeared to be nodding at him. When he checked, Gorman saw that she was gone, her head dipping in time with the waves.

'Should we find ID?' he shouted, through cupped hands, to the *Hurricane*'s deck.

'No,' came the reply. If there were survivors alive on other lifeboats, there was no time to follow procedure. They needed to press on.

The scarlet life jacket was all that was holding Colin's body upright in position when, at 18:00, he caught sight of his rescuers. MacDonald, waving an oar to which he had tied a piece of cloth, stood in the stern singing 'Rule Britannia'. Of the few survivors on the boat, MacDonald, perhaps through his near-constant physical exertion, was still able to move freely, his only injury a gash to the hand, sustained while groping for the submerged supply locker.

As the ship drew close, one of the crew, Reg Charlton, spied the shivering child and shouted: 'Get the boy.'

Colin was unable to move or speak in reaction. His hands, puffy, white and useless through being submerged in salt water all night and most of the day, rested by his sides. He could feel nothing below the waist. There was no way the boy could stand, let alone climb. Only MacDonald was able to make it up the scrambling nets; Colin and a small clutch of other survivors on his lifeboat were hauled onto the ship's deck by lengths of rope looped under their armpits.

Once aboard, the survivors were taken to the galley of the engine room, where the warmth from the engines would dry out their clothes and bones. Colin was given a pair of golfing trousers, the shortest pair on board, in order to allow his pyjama bottoms to dry out. His abiding memory of the rescue was his bewilderment at the youthfulness of the destroyer's crew, many of whom seemed just a few years older than him, and whose thirty-four-year-old captain was considered the grizzled veteran of the operation.

At 11:52 on 19th September 1940, while HMS *Hurricane* was still making its way back to Britain, Rolf Hilse, radio operator on *U-48*, received an unexpected coded message from a nearby U-boat. It came from Günther Prien, captain of *U-47* and one of Doenitz's trio of young U-boat stars. Prien was one of the most esteemed U-boat commanders, having sunk the first Allied merchant ship, the *Bosnia*, two days into the war. After spotting a plume of smoke on the horizon, 'like a dragonfly flitting over a stream',[17] Prien dived, let the freighter pass over his position, resurfaced and, using the U-boat's deck-mounted cannon, attacked the ship. When one of the *Bosnia's* lifeboats capsized, Prien's crew pulled aboard a thrashing teenager, who gave his captors the first account of the war describing what it was like to be confronted by a U-boat.

'You can't imagine what it's like,' Prien recalled the youngster saying in a thick cockney accent. 'You looks over the water and sees nothing, on'y sky and water and then suddenly a bloomin' big thing pops up beside yer, blowing like a walrus. I thought I was seein' the Loch Ness monster.'

Now, on his current trip, *U-47* had expelled all but one of its torpedoes in an earlier battle and, for the past few days, had been acting as a weather boat, a tedious and much-despised beat for a spent U-boat that consisted of signalling intermittent weather reports, often via helium-filled condoms, which German meteor-ologists could use to estimate the conditions over Britain, useful for planning Luftwaffe attacks.

Hilse decoded the message. Prien, it transpired, wanted *U-48*, a newer vessel with superior radio equipment to that of his own U-boat, to relay an important message to Doenitz: he had spied a convoy of more than forty ships travelling east, toward Britain. Prien wanted to know what to do.

When he received Prien's message, via Kapitänleutnant Bleichrodt, Doenitz was at his newly established U-boat headquar-ters (known in German by the mountain range of letters *Operationsabteilung der Befehlshaber der Unterseeboote*, or BdU as it was referred to by anyone who had anything else to do that day) in Kerneval, near Lorient.

Doenitz had moved from Paris with his young Alsatian dog, Wolf,[18] into the requisitioned Villa Kerillon, a handsome, if small, white, late-nineteenth-century building that overlooked the growing Lorient U-boat base of operations, just three weeks earlier, on 29th August. Sensing an opportunity, Doenitz ordered *U-48* to proceed to Prien's beacon signal. Then he sent a similar message to four other U-boats, including *U-99* and *U-100*, captained by the rival aces Otto Kretschmer and Joachim Schepke respectively, to head to the same position too.

As they gathered, the vessels arranged themselves at five-mile intervals ahead of the convoy, HX.72, which consisted of forty-three ships crossing the Atlantic in the opposite direction to the *City of Benares*, carrying thousands of tons of supplies and materials from Halifax, Nova Scotia, to Liverpool. Everything was playing out in precisely the same way Doenitz had practised in the wargame. At dusk Prien signalled the position, course and speed of the British ships. The U-boats lay in ambush, obeying BdU's command to not feed the gulls or throw empty tin cans overboard, tells that might give away their hiding places before the convoy was in the ideal position to be attacked.[19]

Three days after the sinking of the *City of Benares*, and after years of preparation, Doenitz had successfully managed to orchestrate a six-member-strong wolfpack, the first of the war to date. Finally, the line of U-boats broke into a cluster and rounded on the convoy.

At just twenty-eight years old, Otto Kretschmer was addicted to cigars and already the most famous U-boat captain of the young war. In early August he had sailed into Lorient flying seven victory pennants, one for each of the ships that he believed he had successfully torpedoed. The following day, in Paris, Doenitz informed Kretschmer that he was to be awarded the Knight's Cross for the greatest number of ships sunk by a commander in a single voyage. Normally, Kretschmer would have to travel to Berlin to receive his award in person from Hitler. Kretschmer could not be spared, however, and the following day Grand Admiral Raeder, the most senior officer in the German navy, flew to Lorient to make the award himself. After the ceremony Kretschmer and his crew, as gaunt as scarecrows, chugged beer on *U-99*'s deck.

When word of Kretschmer's achievement reached the Propaganda Ministry in Berlin, staff set to work seeding stories in the press about this new, rising ace. A month later, Kretschmer was as famous and feted as a film star. The accolades were appropriate. Kretschmer was a genius submariner who had, in early 1936, been one of the first and most distinguished students at the U-boat school in Kiel, where he was taught by Doenitz himself. For all their competence,

Doenitz's other top students had obvious flaws. Prien was stubborn and quick-tempered, while Schepke, whose considerable charm came, as it often does, with a compulsive need to be liked, was a hard-drinking womaniser.

Kretschmer's flaws included an obsession with naval warfare at the cost of all other interests, an intolerance of those who did not share his focus and a taciturn nature, all characteristics that, in the U-boat realm, became virtues.

Once, while resting between sorties in Lorient, Kretschmer spied four of his petty officers (their names – Bergman and Clasen, Schnabel and Kassel – have the rhythmic quality of characters in a cautionary fairy tale) attempting to drunkenly sneak, on all fours, past the lounge window of his hotel, the Beau Séjour. The following day Kretschmer lined his crew up on the quayside for a blistering lecture, and the threat of disciplinary action should they ever repeat the night's behaviour.[20] It was a harsh reprimand. This kind of exuberant partying was typical of U-boat crews and captains who, after weeks at sea, in 360-degree proximity to death, unwound explosively on shore. But it showed Kretschmer's intolerance for weakness. In peacetime, this would have made him a cruel boss, but, on a U-boat, it merely inspired his crew to work harder and more efficiently through a common eagerness to please.

The recipe, whatever its precise formula, worked. In April 1940 when Kretschmer's newly commissioned U-boat, U-99, left port for its maiden voyage, the dockyard superintendent shouted to its captain: 'Treat her well and she'll sink the whole Royal Navy for you.'

It was an exaggeration, but not by much. No U-boat captain would destroy more Allied ships than Kretschmer. That first day, before setting off, one of his crew noticed a pair of horseshoes hanging from the U-boat's anchor. Kretschmer ordered his staff to paint a pair of horseshoes onto the conning tower. Every time the crew scored a new kill, they'd mark their achievement by daubing another horseshoe on the fin. Luck, however, had little to do with it, as Kretschmer would show that night, during the inaugural wolfpack attack of the war.

Bleichrodt was the first to fire as he loosed a fusillade of his remaining torpedoes. He sank one freighter and damaged another. He then replaced Prien as the convoy 'shadow', radioing signals to the other U-boats, and reports back to Doenitz. In this new role, *U-48* sent a flurry of radio signals to Lorient. Kretschmer, one of whose nicknames was 'Silent Otto', a reference to his aversion to using his U-boat's radio, was furious, fearing that this incautious chatter would give away the wolfpack's position.

Kretschmer set a collision course with the convoy and wrathfully motored along the surface of the ocean, maintaining radio silence. En route he spotted Prien's U-boat on the water. Not wanting to miss a chance to show up his rival, Kretschmer slowed and quietly approached, to within ramming distance, startling Prien's crew, who for a moment believed they were being attacked.

Doenitz encouraged fraternity between his U-boat crews, forbidding the men from shaving while at sea so that, in time, they shared an appearance, as well as purpose. Through a combination of Doenitz's design, and the intimacy that is forged through shared experience of peril and trauma, U-boatmen became a brotherhood. But rivalry and one-upmanship were built into the system too: captains competed on the dehumanising leaderboard of tonnage sunk. As Kretschmer took off, he called witheringly to Prien, now standing at the conning tower: 'You need some lookouts.'

In the light of the moon, Kretschmer closed to attack a freighter. While both the torpedo instruction booklet and the official German *Memorandum for Submarine Commanders* recommended a minimum distance of 1,000 metres* between the U-boat and its target, Kretschmer wanted to see what would happen if he fired from half this distance. *U-99* slipped past the escort destroyer, to sit within the vulnerable columns of the convoy. When the torpedo hit the *Invershannon*'s bows, the explosion revealed, for a few moments, the immensity of the night sky.

Next, Kretschmer headed to the dark side of the convoy, happening across a deep-laden freighter, the 3,700-ton *Baron Blytheswood*. It sank in just forty seconds. Through the gap left by

---

* In the 1943 edition of *The Submarine Commander's Handbook* this suggested range had reduced to 300 metres.

the vanished ship, Kretschmer spied another bulky freighter. The next torpedo struck amidships. With three successful hits, Kretschmer cut U-99's engines to allow the convoy to pull away. His radio operator picked up the distress signal reporting the ship's name, *Elmbank*.

This kind of bold attack from within the columns of a convoy, while new to the Battle of the Atlantic, had precedent. Doenitz, who had seen first-hand its effectiveness working under Forstmann, had managed – or at least, not wanting to be shown up by his young captains, claimed to have managed – on more than one occasion to pass undetected through the prowling escorts, into the columns of the merchant vessels to mount attacks.

Most U-boat commanders knew that, logically, the most effective way to target a merchant ship would be to slip, somehow, past the destroyers, and fire at the flock from close range. Moreover, the Type VII-C U-boats were dressed in a thin outer skin, designed to camouflage the U-boat as a low-lying surface vessel when it came up for air. (This skin was perforated to allow the water to penetrate between it and the pressure-withstanding cylindrical core of the ship, to ensure the disguise was not crushed.) Few U-boat captains, however, had had the gumption to attempt such a move. Uncertainty about the effectiveness of British sonar-detection, known at the time as ASDIC, led many U-boats to fire their torpedoes only from well outside the detection range of the escorts, at a range of 3,000 metres or farther.[21]

In fact, the Royal Navy's anti-submarine tactics were, in the early stages of the war, miserably ineffectual. The British ships had no radar, and only a few were equipped with ASDIC. This formative submarine-detection device was housed in a dome beneath the hull of escort ships, like a great polyp. It sent out pulses of sound waves, which emitted a 'ping' that would produce an antiphonic 'tong' response if and when it struck a solid object within a 3,000-metre radius. This call and response would provide an accurate range and bearing. It was, however, notoriously unreliable in its formative iterations, upset by differing density layers in the water, and would fail altogether if the ship exceeded eighteen knots. Moreover, hardly anyone knew how to work the system properly. One operator described operating ASDIC as like playing the harp, a skill that required dexterity and endurance, and of which those assigned to it had no experience.

Kretschmer had executed, that night, the ideal attack on a convoy: one issued from within the patrolling escort ships, as part of a wolfpack. In his diary entry of 22nd September 1940, Doenitz wrote with a straightforwardness that masked his feelings of *told-you-so* indignation toward the superiors who had frustrated his plans: 'The engagement of the past few days shows that the principles enunciated in peacetime were correct.' The efficacy of the wolfpack had been proven in a board game, then a training exercise. Now it had shown its worth in combat.

V

Pineapples and Champagne

HMS *Hurricane* arrived at Greenock in Scotland on 20th September, while the wolfpack attack was still in progress. It was only during disembarkation that Colin was able to see which of the other children had been rescued, and who among them had not. While the more seriously injured survivors were transferred to the Smithston Hospital via ambulance, Colin and the other walking wounded were led to an assembly shed which served as an impromptu customs office.

Grave-faced, the man at the desk asked for Colin's passport. Before the boy had a chance to scoff at his request, the man added, with the inflexible practice of the humourless bureaucrat: 'Oh, and do you have anything to declare?'

The child produced, from the wallet stowed in his life-jacket pocket, the soggy ten-pound note his father had given him. After offering his statement to Geoffrey Shakespeare, the director of the evacuee programme, Colin was taken by bus into Glasgow and delivered to the Grand Central Hotel, one of the city's loveliest, of which Churchill was a frequent guest. The boy walked into the plush lobby in his dried-out pyjama bottoms, still wearing his red kapok life jacket, his promise to his mother intact.

For a moment, nobody took any notice. Then and all at once, Colin and the others were swarmed by reporters. The cameras began to click, a chorus of grasshoppers.

Kretschmer and his crew, having almost emptied their torpedo tubes, decided to mop up the leftovers of battle for HX.72. Wounded ships did not count toward a U-boat captain's score; they had to be sunk. So, U-99 returned to the Invershannon, and Kretschmer fired a round of bullets from the machine gun mounted above deck, hoping to puncture the ship's hull. When the bullets ricocheted off, Kretschmer sent his first lieutenant, Klaus Bargsten, in a dinghy loaded with explosives. Bargsten, however, promptly capsized and had to be hauled back aboard.

Kretschmer was loath to fire another torpedo to finish the job. His boastful motto was 'one torpedo, one ship'. Yet dawn approached, and with it the risk of being spotted by an Allied air patrol. Aircraft attack was more feared by U-boatmen than that of an escort vessel, as a well-piloted aircraft could mount an attack on a U-boat before it had a chance to dive to the eighty or so metres required to evade an aircraft-hurled depth charge.[1]

Kretschmer sullenly fired another torpedo at the ship's hull. With an elemental yowl, the tanker split in two, from the centre. The ends of the ship rose up, till they were almost perpendicular, locking masts together at the top to form a giant portico. Smoke billowed up in great, sky-scraping columns, while, like a Gothic archway, the wreckage sank, with noble serenity.

As Kretschmer pulled away from the scene, he caught sight of a lone raft. On it stood a man wearing only his underwear. He was leaning against an oar that had been erected as a mast, to which a white shirt was tied, fluttering in the wind. The mournful absurdity of the scene reminded Kretschmer, he later said, of a Punch illustration and, after setting fire to the Elmbank using phosphorous shells aimed at the ship's timber deck-cargo, he pulled alongside the raft. Kretschmer, who had studied for a while at Exeter University, greeted the man in English. After the survivor willingly boarded the U-boat, the German told him to dry off and fetch something to drink.

It was not the first time Kretschmer had aided his enemies in this way. Earlier that summer, he had approached a lifeboat filled with crew of the Canadian steamer Magog. When one of his petty officers appeared at the conning tower brandishing a machine gun, Kretschmer reprimanded him, telling him to get below decks and not to show his face again. Kretschmer gave the survivors a bottle of brandy and a pile of blankets and pointed them toward the Irish coastline.

He was not alone among U-boat captains in aiding the enemy

although, during downtime in the French ports, debate would often rage between the younger sailors on the correct course of action. Many younger men believed it was farcical to shoot at a man when he had a deck under his feet and show mercy when he did not, while the older hands cleaved to the old mariner's credo that concern for the fate of the shipwrecked is the first duty of every seaman.*

Werner Hess, who served on U-530, claimed that Doenitz ordered all of his crews to help survivors. In the first week of war, the crew of U-48, which would later sink the City of Benares, torpedoed and sank the British freighter Firby. The U-boat crew picked up the captain. Close to tears, he explained to the Germans that, against his wife's advice, he had taken their son on the trip.

'Take him with you,' he implored, pushing his boy forward.[2] The U-boat's captain, Schultze, a father of twins and a father figure to his crew, sent out the plain-text radio signal addressed to Churchill himself:

'To Mr Churchill. I have sunk British steamer Firby position 59°40N/13°50W. Save the crew if you will please. German submarine.'[3]

All of the ship's crew, including the child, were duly collected. These acts of benevolence, which became less frequent as the war progressed, were not entirely selfless. 'There was always the chance that our own boat would be sunk one day,' Hess wrote.[4]

That night, U-99's hydrophone operator took charge of the lone man on the raft, who could remember neither his own name nor that of his ship, although he did recall its cargo was iron ore. In fact, the two men, the German Josef Kassel and the Englishman Joseph Byrne, were namesakes. Wrapped in blankets and with a bellyful of brandy, Byrne sat muttering to himself. Kassel assumed he was suffering from concussion. After drifting off for an hour, Byrne awoke and asked for some food. Kassel passed him a tin of pineapples, plunder from the British stores at Dunkirk that had, at Hitler's behest, been distributed among U-boats.

As he ate, Byrne listened to Kretschmer chatting to another crew member in English. In fact, this second man was an Italian submarine

---

* The German journalist Lothar-Günther Buchheim fictionalised one of those wartime debates, on which he had eavesdropped, in his 1973 novel, Das Boot.

captain, shadowing Kretschmer on the voyage to learn how the Germans commanded their U-boats. Kretschmer didn't speak Italian and the Italian didn't speak German, so the pair communicated in English. When Kassel brought Byrne some coffee, he was astonished when his captive said: 'Thanks mate. A bloody U-boat torpedoed the ship, but those blasted Nazi swine didn't get me.'

Suffering from mild concussion and confused by the officers' conversation and the tin of pineapples, Byrne had assumed that he had been rescued by a British submarine. Rather than disabuse his captive of the idea, the German bandaged Byrne's head in order that he might be transferred to another lifeboat of survivors that Kretschmer had spied on the horizon. Byrne protested, saying that he was comfortable enough on the submarine.

Exasperated, Kassel told Byrne to look at the swastika on Kretschmer's cap when he next climbed the conning tower. Carefully enunciating each word, he finally said: 'We are a German U-boat.' Byrne laughed at the suggestion. It was only when *U-99* pulled alongside the lifeboat, and Byrne climbed the ladder to stand alongside Kretschmer, ready to protest, that the sailor saw the captain's cap, its insignia and his mistake.

'I hope you feel better,' said Kretschmer, holding out his hand. In pale-faced silence, Byrne shook it, before tripping into the lifeboat, filled with survivors from the *Invershannon*.

Kretschmer handed bread rolls and water down to the men whose ship he had destroyed a few hours earlier. Then he set the ship's boatswain on a course for Ireland. Before pushing the lifeboat away, the boatswain reached down and threw a carton of 200 cigarettes up to Kretschmer as a thank you.

The battle for HX.72 was finished. The Germans had won a decisive victory. Over a period of three days, the pack of U-boats had sunk eleven ships and damaged three more, robbing Britain of tens of thousands of tons of vital supplies. The victory vindicated Doenitz, who for more than two years had pleaded with his superiors to grant him the assets he needed to execute wolfpack attacks. And the battle had also proven the usefulness of Kretschmer's high-risk tactic of penetrating the convoy to attack from within. Ten of the eleven Allied casualties were sunk by Kretschmer and Schepke alone, pioneers of the tactic.

The next day, while en route to France, the crew of *U-99* tuned their radio to the German news. They listened with hot indignation as a Berlin news announcer credited the sinking of *Elmbank* and *Invershannon* to Kapitänleutnant Bleichrodt, who was, at that moment, also heading back to Lorient. In a job where one's effectiveness was measured in the cold, irrefutable numbers of tonnage sunk, a miscredit affected not only one's ego, but also one's status. Still, Silent Otto, true to nickname, chose to not issue a correction to U-boat headquarters, assuring his men that he would clear up the misunderstanding when they returned to port.

On 25th September 1940, while Colin was being reunited with his family,* his assailant, Bleichrodt and Kretschmer sailed into Lorient, their respective crews standing on the upper decks of *U-48* and *U-99*, pale and hollow-eyed, in their salt-crusted fatigues, with caps askew and thickening beards. Seven white pennants fluttered on each U-boat's raised periscope, each one representing a ship sunk and a further blow to Britain's food supplies and, in the case of the *City of Benares*, families.

Seventy-seven of the ninety children who sailed on the *City of Benares* did not return home. How they must have wondered, in their final moments, why they were being made to die. How might any of us answer their question, then or now? Our adult wars are incomprehensible from anything but the stratospheric vantage point. There, where the grotesque detail of war's human impact – the blitzed nursery, the mother's hysterical phone calls, the lifeboats filled with slipper-less corpses – can no longer be made out, a war can be viewed as a conflict of ideas. Close up, however, war is senseless. For civilians, life becomes a series of overlapping scandals and outrages, each one

---

* Shortly thereafter Colin was sent to St Andrew's school, near Pangbourne, Berkshire, where he studied alongside David Cornwell, better known as the novelist John le Carré.

a reaction to some new capricious tragedy. Even so, the loss of so many children caused outrage at a universal scale. The sinking of the *City of Benares* belongs to that rare category of disaster able to alter not only the national mood, but also the national stance.

Prior to the sinking of the *City of Benares*, the U-boat had not been an entirely foreign entity in Britain. In fact, many people had seen the inside of one. Two decades earlier, on 2nd December 1918 a captured U-boat, the *Deutschland*, had been towed up the Thames and docked, provocatively, next to Tower Bridge. Part trophy, part morbid attraction, hobbling veterans and inquisitive day-trippers alike could pay a shilling to poke around its confines. Squat and tubby, the *Deutschland* began life as a cargo carrier. It immediately distinguished itself as the first German submarine to cross the Atlantic. In its maiden voyage in 1916, it carried $1.5 million worth of gemstones, valuable dyes and pharmaceutical drugs from Europe to Baltimore (much to the protestations of the panicky British, who beseeched the Americans not to classify U-boats as merchant ships, arguing that submergible vessels cannot be easily stopped and searched for illicit munitions).

In February the following year the *Deutschland* was transformed into a wartime vessel with a refit that added six bow torpedo tubes and two naval guns borrowed from a battleship. It was sent to war, where it sank a harbour's worth of forty-two Allied ships. Then it was surrendered to the British at the Armistice. The *Deutschland* was one of a hundred or so German U-boats that were towed to England at the end of the First World War to be scrapped for metal, and the reliable, German-made diesel engines removed and used in industrial factories.

Even in peacetime, the *Deutschland* continued to wreak havoc both major and minor. While being towed up the Thames, it collided with a passing steamship. (This was the second accidental impact the U-boat had been involved in; when departing the port of New London before the war, it rammed a tugboat, killing all five crew members.) Then, after its stay in London, the decommissioned vessel conducted a tour of the UK for exhibitions in Great Yarmouth, Southend, London, Ramsgate, Brighton and Douglas on the Isle of Man, further raising the U-boat's profile in the national consciousness. In September 1921, the vessel was finally towed to Birkenhead, just outside Liverpool, to be scrapped. During the process of breaking up, an explosion killed five young apprentice fitters, a final act of devastation by a submarine much of whose brief existence had been characterised by wanton destruction.

In more recent times, too, the British civilian had been made aware of the U-boat menace. It was a U-boat that had made the primary attack on the first day of the war. A few hours after Britain declared war on Germany at 11:00 a.m. on 3rd September 1939, Lieutenant Fritz-Julius Lemp, captain of *U-30*, sighted the transatlantic passenger ship SS *Athenia* north-west of Ireland, en route to Canada from Glasgow. Lieutenant Lemp sank the liner. The attack, in which 117 passengers and crew members died, violated the Hague convention, which prohibited attacks on unarmed passenger vessels, and ensured that the start of war was marked by national awareness of the lethal U-boats stalking British shipping lanes.

In the early months of war, Winston Churchill, then First Lord of the Admiralty, had sought to allay these fears. (Later he famously wrote that the U-boat terror was 'the only thing that ever really frightened me'.) In a speech at Mansion House on 20th January 1940, at a moment when British forces had sunk just nine of Germany's fifty-seven U-boats, Churchill claimed to have sunk 'half the U-boats with which Germany began the war'.

To arrive at this dishonest conclusion, Churchill had added sixteen U-boats that the Admiralty believed *may* have been sunk to the nine U-boats known to have been sunk. To this number, for good measure, Churchill also added a further ten U-boats of his own imagining, to bring the total to more than half of the U-boat fleet as British intelligence understood it to be.

This exaggeration of gains and suppression of losses, be it by accident or scheme, had, as the author of a classified inquiry into publicity around the Battle of the Atlantic wrote immediately after the war, 'a heartening effect on the British public'. The political advantage apparently justified the damage caused to truth.[5] Arguably, had the full miserable extent of the Allied performance in the Battle of the Atlantic to date been fully known, it may have had an invigorating effect on the coordination of efforts to find an urgent solution. The author of the inquiry, Admiral V. Lt. Godfrey* concluded, however, that Britain 'never came quite clean about the progress of the war at sea'.[6]

There was, however, no possibility of maintaining public denial when news of the *City of Benares* broke, the discussion of which dominated newspapers and pubs alike. Speaking at the House of Commons, Geoffrey Shakespeare, the director of the evacuee programme who had interviewed Colin when he landed, spoke of his sense of 'horror and indignation' that any 'German submarine captain could be found to torpedo a ship over 600 miles from land in a tempestuous sea'. This deed, he said, 'will shock the world'.

Shakespeare's outrage was echoed and amplified in every headline that week. 'Nazis Torpedo Mercy Ship, Kill Children', read the front page of the *Daily Sketch*. The *Daily Mail*, which only a few years earlier had offered fascism its full-throated support, ran an editorial that urged readers to dwell on every 'dreadful' detail of the story, so that they might be 'burn[ed] into our minds as proof of the character we are sworn to defeat'. Still unaware of the Holocaust, an editorial in *The Times* went so far as to argue that no Nazi brutality would stay 'longer graven upon the records than the sinking of the *City of Benares*'.

While Kapitänleutnant Bleichrodt unwound at the U-boat hotel in Lorient, British propaganda began to depict the U-boat captains as fanatical Nazis, and their crews as pitiless killers. On the latter count, the reputation was often earned. In the five months from June to October 1940, during which the *City of Benares* was lost, U-boats sank 274 merchant ships and sustained just two losses. By the end of the year the U-boats had sunk more than 1,200 ships, about five years' worth of construction work in typical peacetime conditions, and more than the rest of the German navy and Luftwaffe combined.

The numbers told, if not the whole story of the 'Battle of the Atlantic' – as, with characteristic flair, Churchill had memorably christened the front – then the salient point: the British were losing catastrophically.

★   ★   ★

---

* Ian Fleming, author of the James Bond novels, is said to have based the character 'M' on Godfrey, who was Fleming's boss during the war.

After weeks at sea, the U-boat crew members' first steps ashore were faltering, a clumsiness that betrayed the cramped conditions they had laboured under, and the need to acclimatise.

A so-called *Marine Helferimen*, the German equivalent of a Wren, greeted Kretschmer with a fat bouquet of flowers. It was the German's first taste of the VIP treatment that was to come. While Colin and the other survivors of the *City of Benares* had returned to a country of thrift and rations, the U-boatmen landed in a country of wine and plenty. Lothar-Günther Buchheim, a war correspondent who travelled with a U-boat crew, later described France as 'a kind of paradise' to the crews who had, in the first year of war, become grimly accustomed to German shortages.[7] The exchange rate for the occupying forces was fixed at twenty francs to the Reichsmark[8] – three more than the rate quoted on the Berlin stock exchange – a favourable discrepancy that enabled crew members, who received a U-boatman salary on top of their service pay, to spend their downtime living the high life.

Beak-wetting went all the way to the top. When he first arrived in France, Doenitz promptly commandeered a hotel and requisitioned all of its supplies, including its stocks of champagne, bottles that he made available to his U-boatmen for a token sum. Many of these men would destroy themselves with booze, numbing the harrowing reality of their position.

Some crew members took the BdU Zug, an express train reserved for U-boatmen that ran from Nantes through Le Mans and on to the German cities of Bremen, Hamburg and Flensburg, and would be home within two days. Those who chose to remain in France were sent to the *U-bootsweiden*, luxury hotels or chateaux that had been commandeered to be used as rest camps. These safe havens were far from the ports targeted by Allied bombers, where people were routinely forced to seek shelter, either from bombs or from falling debris from downed planes, whose pirouetting wings seemed as harmless as falling feathers, till their weight was felt through the ground.

In Lorient, relationships between the Germans and the locals varied. In the week after the Germans marched into Paris, and before they arrived in Lorient, on 21st June 1940 the port's *préfet maritime*, Admiral Penfentenyo, prepared to resist the impending German arrival. He ordered all Lorient ships to sail, some of which, like the *Victor-Schoelcher*, were loaded with crates of gold and money. Warehouses and oil depots were torched, unseaworthy vessels scuttled. Two platoons of French naval riflemen held back the German advance for two hours, till a false report that Admiral Penfentenyo had died resulted in a French colonel ordering a ceasefire and the raising of a white flag of surrender.

The next day a notice, signed 'WELCKER, commander-in-chief of German troops' and printed in the local newspaper *Le Nouvelliste du Morbihan*, called for 'calm and order'. Welcker warned against 'thoughtless acts', and assured citizens that the mayor and police would be held responsible for maintaining order. The sale of spirits was forbidden, and a ten o'clock curfew implemented, during which residents could no longer drive or assemble unless they were doctors, priests or midwives.

'Resistance and acts of sabotage . . . [were] pointless,' Welcker wrote.[9]

From the first week of occupation, the Nazi flag flew above all public buildings. Road signs were rewritten in German in black Gothic lettering, and residents were warned that for every German soldier killed by the Resistance, ten Frenchmen would be shot in return. Tuning in to British radio was punishable by death.[10] Yet an uneasy peace developed between the French and their occupiers, who had been ordered to make a good impression on the locals, distributing chocolates and cookies to the children, and staging parades and concerts for the adults.

Life ashore was comfortable. The German crews were allowed to visit the local cinema Rex in rue de la Comédie, where the films changed every five days or so, for free. Some U-boatmen used brothels, which all German soldiers were permitted to frequent, providing they cleared out before half-past ten each night.[11] While the Germans established quasi-official bordellos in France, there were not enough workers, and some Frenchwomen, all of whom were in desperate need of money, joined. Some of the women passed information to the Resistance, who then relayed it to London.[12] Other crew members took local girlfriends, relationships that came at a significant cost when, after the war, 189 women were tried for so-called 'horizontal collaboration' and deprived of certain civil rights.[13]

On their first night ashore, Kretschmer and his crew dined at the Beau Séjour hotel. After toasting their successes, the crew was told that in the morning they were to be sent to a *U-bootsweiden* in Quiberon for a week's recuperation. Most of the men headed out into the night. Kretschmer, ever studious, joined Prien to discuss the nascent wolfpack's successes, and Prien assured his friend and rival that he had sent a signal to command correcting the miscrediting of *U-99*'s kills to Bleichrodt. Neither man was yet aware of a kill that undeniably belonged to Captain Bleichrodt: the *City of Benares*.

Just then, another captain from the wolfpack – the third famous ace of the young war, Joachim Schepke – clattered into the lounge, haggard from two days partying in Parisian clubs. Kretschmer made his excuses and retired to his room and began to write up his standing orders for *U-99*, a document that laid out the rules for the efficient and successful running of a U-boat. This twelve-point plan covered everything from the need for an effective lookout (the ease with which Kretschmer had managed to sneak up on Prien a few days earlier was fresh in the mind) through to the need to set aside time for cleaning dishes.

Most of Kretschmer's instructions were commonsensical. Point nine, however, went against the written advice that U-boat captains maintain a minimum distance of 1,000 metres between the U-boat and its target. Kretschmer countered, plainly, that at every given opportunity, torpedoes should be fired at extreme close range.

'This can only be done', he wrote, 'by penetrating the escort's anti-submarine screen and, at times, getting inside the convoy lanes.'

Having scored three kills in quick succession, Kretschmer knew that there was no more efficient way to cause havoc on a British convoy, causing the escort captains to flounder.

'This should be the objective of all our attacks,' he added.

In two sentences Kretschmer had outlined a tactic that would, in the months to come, lead to the deaths of thousands of Allied sailors and raise the line on the chart of shipping losses at the Admiralty in London perilously close to the red threshold of starvation. It was a tactic so effective that it would lead to the formation of a British unit staffed by a ragtag crew of women, led by a captain with a life-changing disability, dedicated to its uncovering.

VI

Never at Sea

Madge Barnes ran along the Edinburgh cobbles and, with a flutter of adrenaline, dropped the envelope into a postbox. It was not the first time the teenager had applied to join the Wrens. A year earlier, on the eve of her seventeenth birthday and less than a week after the outbreak of war, she had sent much the same application letter to London. The eventual reply, that Barnes was, alas, too young, had stung, but at least the rejection was temporary. A year later, a week or so before the *City of Benares* left Liverpool, Barnes promptly re-sent her application. It was timed to arrive at Wrens headquarters in London on 5th September 1940, the day of her eighteenth birthday.

Barnes was one of tens of thousands of young women who sent off similar applications for, initially, one of just 1,500 vacancies in the Wrens. Christian Oldham was another. Having attempted to bandage her step-grandfather's bald head as a try-out, Oldham had decided that nursing was not for her, and chose the Wrens instead. Oldham had a twin advantage in securing one of the hotly contested spots. Not only was her father an admiral, but her bridge partner was Colonel Frank, brother of Vera Laughton Mathews. And Laughton Mathews, or VLM as she was often called, was the newly appointed director of the Wrens.

Vera Laughton Mathews had joined the first incarnation of the Wrens, formed in 1917 to support the First World War effort, in her late twenties after reading an advertisement in *The Times* under the headline: 'Women for the Navy: New Shore Service to Be Formed'. Like Barnes, it was not the first time that she applied. Three years earlier, in 1914, long before there was any talk of allowing women to share the work of naval men, she strode up to the imposing Admiralty building and asked for a job. The man on the front desk looked her up and down and replied, curtly: 'We don't want any petticoats here.'

The rejection bounced off Laughton Mathews, who since the age of twenty had been involved with the suffragette movement, fighting for women's right to vote, and who often boasted that she was descended from pirates on both sides of her family.[1] Principled, idealistic and usefully confrontational – the necessary characteristics for any young activist – Laughton Mathews felt the full force of society's prejudice just as she was entering the adult world. While standing at the side of the road handing out issues of the *Suffragette* newspaper, on which she worked as a journalist, passers-by would spit in her face.

With characteristic eagerness, Laughton Mathews showed up at the first temporary Wrens office on the same day that she read the advertisement in *The Times*. Three women in plain clothes – including the inaugural director of the Wrens, Dame Katherine Furse, a 'tall, handsome, athletic woman who, despite her youth, had the quiet, determined authority that accompanies a natural leader – conducted the interview. Laughton Mathews volunteered the nugget that she had been a suffragette. As her interviewers' faces darkened, she tried to make amends with mention that she also had a brother in the navy.

'Ah,' said one of the women, witheringly. 'Does that mean you also have lots of boyfriends in the service?'

Despite her fears, Laughton Mathews had not in fact thrown the interview. She was told to enrol on the first Wrens officers' course, scheduled for the end of December. The next month, she arrived at an old naval training facility in Crystal Palace – the only naval establishment at the time that was willing to receive a woman officer – wearing a bottle-green coat and beige hat (an official uniform was some way off, and the stylish haute-couture cut of the later Wrens uniform decades away). The Wrens' motto at the time was 'Never At Sea', a pledge that also carries with it a sort of negative space assurance: *we know our place.* What other organisation is defined by what its members are forbidden from doing, rather than what they hope to achieve? Nevertheless, 7,000 women joined the Wrens in the First World War, more than double the anticipated number. In addition to cooking and clerical work, they performed an array of duties. At the Anti-Aircraft Defence Corps, Wrens worked as telephonists calling up gun stations during air raids to pass on orders for gunfire and barrage. At the Battersea Experimental Workshops, Wrens were employed in drawing, tracing and preparing designs for new machinery and weapons. Seventy Wrens worked as drivers for the Admiralty.[2]

Then the war was over. Just a year after Laughton Mathews had read the advertisement in *The Times*, the training depot at Crystal Palace became an Army Demobilisation Centre. Before the last of the recruits had been demobbed, Laughton Mathews fell victim to influenza, the great plague spread by the Great War in France, where men fought in trenches that flowed with blood, rats and urine, before returning in their infected millions to their home countries around the world. By the time the virus had run its course, almost three years later, as many as 100 million people had died – a higher toll than that of both world wars combined.

The pandemic's symptoms were like spells cast by a cruel yet imaginative witch. Most commonly, hands and faces turned a pale shade of lavender, the result of a condition known as heliotrope cyanosis. After a few days, some victims' skin turned black, before their hair and teeth fell out. Others gave off a curious smell, like musty straw. One medic described seeing men choking to death, 'the lungs so swamped with blood, foam and mucus that . . . each desperate breath was like the quacking of a duck'. The American novelist Katherine Anne Porter survived, but the disease permanently turned her ebony hair pure white.

Laughton Mathews suffered a milder form of the flu. But her younger brother Hubert, who had been wounded and gassed in the Battle of Le Cateau in northern France, died of it two weeks after the Armistice. Laughton Mathews, who was closer to Hubert than any other member of her family, went to Edinburgh to grieve and recuperate. By the time she recovered, the Wrens had been disbanded. Without war, there was no need for women to take the jobs of men. Despite its brevity, the impact of the service was great, not only on the war effort but also on women's liberation. The first incarnation of the Wrens had managed to crack, as Laughton Mathews once put it, 'the ice of age-old prejudice.'

Between the wars, Laughton Mathews married and, for a time, moved to Japan. The friendships she made during her brief stint in the Wrens persisted and soon blossomed into a formal alumni group. Laughton Mathews edited its monthly magazine, the *Wren*. Dame Furse, one of the women who had interviewed Laughton Mathews, looked at this nostalgia with scepticism, believing it to be an indulgent invitation to live in the past. Rather than turn her back on the movement she pioneered, however, Furse established a naval-themed branch of the Girl Guides, which eventually came to be known, with a *Boy's Own*-style flourish, as the Sea Rangers.

The Sea Rangers attracted naval super-fans, young girls who dreamed of learning to tie complicated knots, deliver signals and of, just maybe, one day going to sea. Nautical terms were used for everything, and drills were directed with a bosun's whistle. The first company, like all those that would follow, took the name of a famous ship, in its case the 'Golden Hind'. Laughton Mathews ran the second company, which she titled 'Wren' after the new destroyer HMS *Wren*. She would take the girls camping, rowing and swimming, and taught them signalling and first aid. After a brief stint in local politics, Laughton Mathews took over leadership of the 'Golden Hind', a crew that consisted mostly of young London working girls, including a bright insurance clerk named Jean Laidlaw.

Laidlaw, short, pretty, with a dark, Tinkerbell-pixie-bob, grew up in Scotland, where her father was an electrical engineer working on the tram system. She left the fee-paying High School of Glasgow when the family ran into financial difficulties and moved 400 miles south to Maida Vale, London.[3] The Sea Rangers offered Laidlaw – a lonely young woman living in an unfamiliar city, who, at a time when homosexuality was still treated as a crime by the state and a sin by the church, was confronted with the unthinkable yet inescapable fact that she was attracted to women – the chance to make a new group of friends, some of whom she would keep up with for the remainder of her life. In the dim, misty hours before the working day began, Laughton Mathews took Laidlaw and the other girls boating on the lake at Regent's Park, where they learned to sail as, in the encircling roads, the day's traffic gathered.

With age, experience and the roomy perspective that comes with having travelled, Laughton Mathews' guiding conviction – that 'at the root of much that was wrong with the world' lay the lack of equal partnership and opportunity for women – deepened. She gave evidence before the House of Lords on a bill to raise the legal age of marriage to sixteen, to prevent the exploitation of girls and, later, on the question of whether or not to allow women to apply to become diplomats. Still, as war loomed it seemed as though the Admiralty had no intention of reforming the Wrens until, in 1938, with the navy facing widespread staff shortages, the government issued a booklet to every British household explaining how men and women might offer themselves to national service. As well as advertising positions for women to serve as air-raid wardens, ambulance drivers and first-aiders, this *Handbook for National Service* explained that there was a position for around 1,500 women to serve as secretaries, accountants, cooks and waitresses in naval establishments. Fifteen thousand women responded, but there was no one to sift through their applications.

On 22nd February 1939, Laughton Mathews walked through the tunnel that leads from what was then Trafalgar Square tube station toward the Admiralty, her heart thumping as she approached the doors from which, twenty-two years earlier, she had been turned away on account of being a 'petticoat'.

This time, the experience was quite different. Laughton Mathews was led into the salubrious room of the secretary of the Admiralty, Sir Archibald Carter. The room filled up with distinguished men and other ex-Wrens officers. Seated at an expansive round table, the gathering's discussion was halted when the grander of the two doors into the room opened and Laughton Mathews saw, framed in the doorway, Charles Little, the Second Sea Lord, standing 'like a god'. Little sat quietly, listening to the discussions, as the group began to pick over the question of what this new women's service might be called. Unanimously, the conference members agreed that the old name of Women's Royal Naval Service was not only unimprovable, but also now carried with it the traditions and glories of the First World War. A. S. Lemaitre – head of the Civil Service and a man with, as Laughton Mathews later put it, 'a sparkling brain' – suggested officialising the colloquial acronym 'Wrens'.

There was silence. Then, all at once, the crowd agreed on the brilliance of the branding. Laughton Mathews did not know it but throughout the meeting the other attendees, who believed that she might be a suitable candidate to lead these Wrens, were observing her. A few days later she received a phone call inviting her back to the Admiralty. Once again, she sat at the round table in the imposing room, this time across from Sir Archibald, who promptly offered her the job. It is one of the twentieth century's great curiosities that a branch of the British naval establishment, one of the most conservative organisations in the world, should come to be led by a battle-scarred activist and self-identifying feminist, and should prove so astonishingly successful.

Late one evening at the end of December 1940, Laughton Mathews was passing the deserted offices on her way home when she saw a light from beneath one of the doors. Inside she found Laidlaw, her former Sea Ranger, who, at twenty-one, had become a chief Wren, poring over a stack of papers. Laidlaw, a keen statistician who was also one of England's first female qualified chartered accountants, had been calculating the number of Wrens currently in service. At war's outbreak in September 1939, there had been 1,600 recruits, more than half of the number that Laughton Mathews had estimated would be required.[4] Now, a little over a year later, Laidlaw ran her finger down the columns to rest on the final total, which read, implausibly, 10,000 recruits, exactly.*

Madge Barnes, who received her letter shortly after her eighteenth birthday, and Christian Oldham were among these early recruits. Both women were asked to report to London for a medical

---

* In June 1944, when the organisation was at its height, 74,620 Wrens were in active service, more than ten times as many as served in the First World War.

examination. Next, they were interviewed by a very senior and, at just five feet, very short Wren, Nancy Osborne, who assessed their potential suitability for one of the vacancies in the service.

Osborne, an Australian polymath, had come to England in 1932 after being rejected for a job with one of Sydney's top newspapers ('A woman?' the editor had exclaimed. 'On my newspaper? Never, never!').[5] With a letter of recommendation in her pocket, Osborne met a recently retired principal of a Cambridge college, who advised her to take a shorthand-typing course, obtain a job in an office, then 'lose the typewriter'. ('Oh, Perfidious Albion,' Osborne recalled murmuring under her breath.) Osborne nevertheless took the advice, joined the National Council of Social Service and, after a brief stint working as a typist, earned a promotion to oversee an arts programme, building local village halls, then furnishing them with high-quality music and drama events. Osborne was one of the first women to join Laughton Mathews' Wrens, first building up the headquarters staff to a hundred, then dispatching young Wrens like Oldham and Barnes around the country.

Oldham, who spoke fluent French and wrote faltering Latin, was sent to a former London University building in Campden Hill Road, where she reluctantly attempted to learn to touch-type. To break the monotony, she would spend the evenings tearing around Hyde Park on a motorbike, riding pillion with an old school friend who was also on the course. Barnes, meanwhile, was sent to Greenwich, to be trained as a cypher officer decoding signals that, among other things, would report the positions of U-boats in the Atlantic, positions that, in months to come, Oldham would pin to the plots.

At the Wrens training college in Greenwich, Madge Barnes joined a cohort of other young recruits to learn not only nautical terms and naval traditions, but also, in that nobly stifling British way, the rules of civility and decorum. In the Painted Hall, a room of tear-jerking beauty designed by Christopher Wren and Nicholas Hawksmoor as part of the Restoration palace for Charles II and his heirs, Barnes ate breakfast, lunch and dinner from long, silver-candlestick-laden tables each day. Naval staff waited on the Wrens, treatment that contributed to Barnes's blushing sense that she had passed into a new and elevated world, a place where it was quite reasonable to suggest that there was a right way and a wrong way to eat a pea.

During the ten-day training course Barnes, along with dozens of other bright young women, was trained in deciphering naval signals – secret work that demanded quick wits and tight lips ('Be like Dad, keep Mum' read one handout, now painfully of its time), memorising cyphers that would report the position of British ships and, if they had been spotted, that of any U-boats in their vicinity. On graduating, she was sent to Scarborough where, as the war continued, more and more Wrens would congregate in a secret underground hall on Irton Moor, today inhabited by Government Communications Head-quarters (GCHQ), intercepting and decoding U-boat radio signals.*

For all the wolfpack's power and menace, it had one key weakness. In order to organise their U-boats for an attack, the captains needed to communicate at regular intervals, initially to report the sighting of a convoy, and then to invite other boats to join. Even in the midst of battle, requests often came in for U-boats to announce the result of specific attacks, fuel and torpedo stocks and, thanks to those helium-filled condoms, to issue weather reports. These signals, when picked up by Allied shore stations, acted as clues to the U-boats' whereabouts. By triangulating the signal from two sources, a fairly accurate location could be determined, and the estimated position of the U-boat pinned to the plotting maps around the navy's various premises.

Many U-boat captains, suspecting that their radio signal was being used to find them, refused to answer more mundane requests from Nazi command for up to three days, the threshold after which the U-boat crew's families would be informed they were missing, presumed sunk. There was one notable exception to the rule. Occasionally, after a fortnight's cavorting while on leave in the French ports, news would arrive via the U-boat's radio that one of the crew had got a girl pregnant. The man would be expected to ask the woman

---

* GCHQ Scarborough is now the largest continuous serving site for signals intelligence anywhere.

to marry him. The U-boat's patrol, however, could not be interrupted or cut short. As such, the exchange of wedding vows would be organised remotely, over the radio. Each party would exchange the words 'I do' at the appropriate moment in the proceedings, which were conducted by a priest.[6] Any Wren who decoded the message, usually sent from Scarborough to Station X, the code name given to Bletchley Park, would have been bewildered by the exchange.

The Hotel Cecil became Barnes's home in Scarborough, a so-called Wrennery, where all of the cypher Wrens were housed. It was a tall, comfortable building overlooking a park and, beyond that, the sea. Only a few of the young women shared rooms; most were given the luxury of their own space and, in the warm summer evenings, would congregate on a knoll in the park to read or chat in the flattering light of the golden hour. The young Wrens came from across the country, typically from middle-class families. The work was tiring, and the Wrens kept unusual sleeping hours, making different friends at different times, according to the watches they were asked to keep.

For all of war's great horrors, service in the Wrens offered these women an unexpected freedom from the strictures of their previous lives, where they were subject to the rules of their Victorian fathers. For many young men the Second World War wiped out a multitude of possibilities. For many young women, however, war obliterated previously impenetrable barriers. In assuming an active role in the war effort, Wrens slipped the expectation to marry early, remain at home and bear children at the earliest opportunity. Joining the Wrens was something akin to setting off for university, a profound loosening of the centuries-old constriction of female prospects. For these girls – and many were still girls – war's secondary effects had to do with liberation, excitement and possibility.

'It gave me my first taste of freedom,' wrote one Wren after the war. 'Before the Wrens, I'd had to account for everything – where I was going, who with, and what time I'd be home. You didn't really think about it until you had a chance to be much freer.'[7] Even in war, when a young person's range in the world expands, thoughts of death retreat. As well as the long hours, the endless drills and the burdensome stakes, there was also freedom to be young. The women sang. The women tried out falling in love. And when news came that the Wrens were looking for volunteers to form a delegation of cypher officers to sail for sunny Gibraltar, Barnes and all the other women excitedly applied.

This was an important posting for Vera Laughton Mathews, one of the first delegations of Wrens to represent the service abroad (the first had left for Singapore a few months earlier). Moreover, the signals officer at Gibraltar didn't want women. He pleaded for the navy to send men instead, only accepting the Wrens when he was told it was women or nothing.[8] The posting felt like a micro-cosm of the wider world's resistance to women in spaces typically occupied by men. As such, Laughton Mathews personally selected the ten chief Wrens and twelve cypher officers from a long list of keen volunteers. These women were, in Laughton Mathews' esti-mation, the most promising young officers of the service.

On 12th June 1941, nine months after the sinking of the *City of Benares*, twenty-one-year-old Phyllis Bacon, one of Barnes's friends and another incumbent of the Hotel Cecil, wrote to a friend, incredulous with the news that she had been hand-picked by Laughton Mathews to sail to Gibraltar.[9]

'I can't THINK how we did it,' Phyllis wrote. 'Except perhaps they approved of my skirt, specially lengthened about four feet for the occasion, and my thick – very thick – stockings.' The women were given coupons with which to acquire light, cotton clothes and 'bright sandals' appropriate for the Mediterranean climate. The trip, however, was to remain a secret. The Wrens were told not even to mention that they were going overseas, a source of consid-erable frustration for Phyllis, who feared her friends and family would think 'nothing ever happens in the Wrens except leave'.

Before Gibraltar, a number of the Wrens were sent on a more modest delegation to Liverpool. In early June they arrived at Derby House, the newly located Western Approaches HQ, which had been built, at great and controversial expense, in the basement of the Exchange Flags building, close to the water. They were to provide expert help to the cypher Liverpool Wrens. Roxane Houston, a new Wrens recruit, had arrived in Liverpool just a few weeks earlier. She marvelled at the 'remarkable ease' with which the Gibraltar-bound Wrens sped through the mound of incoming signals. In the few days they were together, Houston struck up a friendship with twenty-three-year-old Isabel Milne Home. In down-time the pair would speak about Isabel's visions of Gibraltar, as well as her anxieties about the journey.

As the date of embarkation approached, these private worries were expressed more regularly. After the sinking of the *City of Benares* and all those other ships that followed, the Wrens were aware of the risks of the journey, especially as the route would take their convoy along the French coast.

The day before she left for Liverpool in early August, Barnes sent another letter, this one to the skipper of her Sea Ranger unit in Leith, Scotland. 'If anything should happen to me,' she wrote, 'I want you to know that the happiest moments of my life were when I was at a Sea Rangers muster . . . I am crazy on the sea, and it gave me my first connections with it.'

Barnes's letter has the quality of prose written by someone wanting to set things straight in her life, to repay a debt of gratitude. That night, ten of the twelve chief Wrens, along with a young naval nursing sister who was to accompany the delegation, posed for a photograph on the steps of the Hotel Cecil.* The young women are frozen in a moment of uncomplicated joy, without the filter of self-consciousness usually found in posed group photographs. Despite the uniforms, and private anxieties, the unmistakeable spirit of youthful anticipation pulls all focus.

Women were forbidden from stepping aboard Royal Naval ships. As such, the Gibraltar Wrens were assigned to one of the merchant ships in the convoy. The SS *Aguila* was an ageing trading vessel that, since the 1890s, had delivered tomatoes, bananas, potatoes and cruise-goers from Liverpool to the Canary Islands, with stop-offs in Spain and Portugal. Each passenger paid £21 for a twenty-one-day cruise accompanying the ship's crew while they collected their cargoes. The ship was one of five vessels run by the

---

* The faces of the two missing chief Wrens, who joined the delegation at Liverpool, were later superimposed.

Yeoward brothers, each named after a different bird (*aguila* is the Spanish for 'eagle'), whose Liverpool offices had been so badly bombed they had been forced to take up a temporary residence. The *Aguila* was fitted with deck guns, and, under the long-term expert captaincy of Arthur Firth, had already survived a brush with a U-boat. Still, it was old, lightly armoured and certainly no warship.

The restriction was, in part, due to the fact that the Wrens were considered a part of the Civil Service rather than the navy proper. It was a classification that forced Laughton Mathews into endless administrative scuffles, from difficulties in securing training premises down to arguments about whether, for example, Wrens' lodgings should be referred to in military terms as 'quarters', or in civilian terms as 'hostels'. Patronisingly, some naval officers argued that classifying Wrens as civilians was intended to protect them from the possibility of court martial, and the upsetting image of a young woman 'trembling in the dock'.

This classification was also responsible for a considerable hold-up when it came to the design and manufacture of the women's uniforms. In fact, for the first few months of war they had no uniform at all. Detractors argued that if Wrens were technically civilians, why should they be given a uniform? To Laughton Mathews' dismay, a representative for the director of victualling, responsible for the allocating of uniform materials, told her that he could see no reason why the women should wear a uniform, but if they absolutely had to, why not wear something, anything, khaki? Then, in early 1940, just as Laughton Mathews obtained approval to award a contract to design and manufacture a Wrens uniform, the Naval Stores depot in Deptford was hit by a German bomb, destroying both the materials and the officer in charge.

During the First World War, Director Furse played down the importance of uniform due to 'anxiety . . . that the usual remarks should not be made that women think only of dress'.[10] But like Doenitz, Laughton Mathews knew the psychological power of a uniform. The right cut could create a sense of shared purpose, pride and identity. Just as Doenitz tried to encourage a sense of fraternity between his submariners, instructing captains to cock their caps and unbutton their leather jackets, so Laughton Mathews wanted to encourage sorority between the Wrens through the clothes that they wore (and, indeed, the way that they appeared: the wearing of jewellery was forbidden when Wrens were on duty, while hair had to be worn off the collar[11]). She commissioned the fashion designer Edward Molyneux to design a couture uniform that wouldn't look out of place on a Parisian catwalk. Molyneux, a captain in the First World War, later mentored Christian Dior and dressed not only European royalty but also Hollywood stars such as Greta Garbo, Marlene Dietrich, Gertrude Lawrence and Vivien Leigh.

'Clothes must make us look our best,' Molyneux once said. 'Better than we really are. Your tailor must make a suit that does something for you. A woman's dress should do even more.'[12]

Joining the Wrens gave young women the opportunity to be styled by a designer whose work was, for most, beyond reach. The writer of Molyneux's 1974 obituary in the *New York Times* claimed that the designer's clothes either reminded women of their breeding or provided them with it. In war, duty called first. Even so, many young women reasoned that if duty demanded that they must join the war effort, why not apply to the best-dressed service? The Wrens cap became a fashion item even among civilians, and was sold in high-street shops in a variety of colours. At a meeting at Buckingham Palace, the queen admitted to Laughton Mathews that to the delight of her children, the princesses Elizabeth and Margaret, she had even tried one on. (When the director of the Wrens received her CBE in 1942, the king leaned in to ask: 'How's the hat?')

So it was that, at 14:00 on 13th August 1941, twenty-one Wrens stood on the above deck of the *Aguila* in buttoned-up uniforms and tricorne hats as it pulled steamily out of Liverpool.

As western Ireland faded on the rear horizon, and the convoy broke the latitude of the Bay of Biscay, the weather was the best that many of the ship's 161 passengers had seen all war. The sun shimmered in an unclouded sky. The sea was still and kind, allowing the ships to carve their precautionary zigzags with ease. The route to Gibraltar had been calculated to take the convoy in a great arc, down from gloomy Liverpool and far enough away from the French coastline to avoid any questing German air patrols. At the last minute, the route was altered and tightened, so as not to take the ships quite so deep into the Atlantic. But they remained far enough from land that, over the quarterdeck guard rail, sightseers could spot whales, basking sharks, flying fish and, to the great delight of the gathering crowd, a plucky, lone turtle, making its long journey toward Florida, some 4,000 miles away.

In the easy breeze, ship-hands took turns to sunbathe, the sun baking their tattoos and bronzing their calves till they were lulled or irritated into wakefulness by the sound of the ship's stoker, on a break from his duties in the engine room, wheezing into a mouth organ.

The novelist Nicholas Monsarrat was a lookout on HMS *Campanula*, one of a handful of flower-class corvettes deployed as chaperones to the *Aguila*. One hundred and thirty-five of these chunky, hardy warships were made during the war, thirty-five of which were lost,[13] and each was named after a different and equally delicate English garden flower (*Bluebell, Zinnia, Hyacinth, Aubretia, Coreopsis*). They were notoriously uncomfortable ships but doggedly seaworthy (their sailors were rarely lost overboard[14]) and, most usefully, presented only a small target to U-boats. The *Campanula*, Monsarrat later wrote, was a miserable ship on which to serve, but nevertheless the journey to Gibraltar had the soft-focus quality of a sunshine cruise, the sort advertised in the back of upmarket magazines. It was a welcome change, but one that came with peculiar risks. On ships, sunny comfort, just like cold routine, can easily dull a sailor's vigilance.

At the outbreak of war Monsarrat was a freelance journalist who wrote regularly for the *News Chronicle*. Just as the Wrens was composed of students, journalists and cooks, so the men who made up the Royal Naval Volunteer Service, of which Monsarrat was a member, had left behind mundane jobs that had done nothing to prepare them for life at sea, let alone battle. Men need men they can look up to, and men they can look down upon, never more so than in the military. Members of both the 'proper navy' and the

'Wavy Navy'*, the professional merchant seamen of the Royal Naval Reserves (RNR) felt the sting of mild irritation whenever they spied the letters RNVR – Royal Naval Volunteer Reserve – stitched at the bottom of a sleeve. These volunteers were seen, as one observer put it at the time, as 'playing at being sailors'. Monsarrat's captain, a long-term professional in the RNR, described Monsarrat, a member of the RNVR, as a 'pink-faced amateur'.

The jibe was not entirely without grounds. Like Laughton Mathews, Monsarrat had joined the war effort after replying to an advertisement in *The Times* that, intriguingly, invited 'Gentlemen with yachting experience'. A few months later, he was a temporary probationary sub lieutenant in the RNVR, initially earning £20 a month (almost enough for a peacetime cruise on the SS *Aguila*), a figure that increased to £26 following a swift promotion to lieutenant.

Monsarrat's trip from journalist to lookout was, in fact, typical. One fellow officer was a former car salesman, another a gas-company cashier, another a barrister. Not only did war throw a kink into the professional trajectory of many young men, it also booted them firmly from the dawdling plains of adolescence. Those five martial years, as Monsarrat later wrote, 'made a man out of me and a corpse out of my brother'.[15]

It also, unexpectedly, made a physician out of the journalist. Monsarrat's father was an eminent surgeon and Monsarrat's captain believed that mere proximity to the profession was enough to qualify the young man to care for the wounded and dying who were hauled on board. If anyone had told Monsarrat of the horrors coming his way – the need to stitch up a man's throat without the benefit of anaesthetics, or to coax a dangling eyeball back into its socket – 'I might have kept my yachting experience secret,' he wrote, 'and settled for prison.'[16] It was a skill, or lack thereof, that Monsarrat hoped he wouldn't be called upon to use on this journey.

On Monday 18th August, after being sighted by a long-range German plane the day before, two Junkers 88 bombers appeared suddenly, and dropped bombs at the convoy. All eight missed, and

---

* A reference to the wave-like bars displayed on an RNR cuff.

the two bombers retreated, chased off by curtains of fire from the ships. In an instant, the lazy, cruise-like quality of the journey vanished. The *Aguila*'s rigging was damaged, either by one of her own overenthusiastic gunners or by stray bullets fired from another ship. Then, at 18:51, a signal arrived from the Admiralty in London warning that, based on U-boat radio signals received and triangulated by the Wrens' colleagues in Scarborough, there appeared to be a wolfpack of four or five U-boats in the vicinity. The commodore, who was in charge of all ships in the convoy, ordered the vessels to trim their boiler fires in order to eliminate any telltale smoke, and, as day turned to night, to extinguish all lights.

While the weather remained warm and calm, the atmosphere among the ships' crews was more fraught. On board the *Aguila*, the commodore's yeoman spotted a Wren leaning over the guard rail.

'Put that cigarette out,' he shouted, worried that the smallest prick of light might give the ship away to a shadowing U-boat.

On the *Campanula*, where there were no women present to encourage decorum, sailors in search of sport and gossip to take their minds off the situation joined Monsarrat on his lookout. One of the men pulled out a little tin box, a keepsake, he said, to lift his spirits on just such a dark and lonely night. The men crowded around as the sailor cracked open the box to reveal a solitary pubic hair, plucked, he claimed, from a distant lover. The men laughed like schoolboys. Then, after a moment, another pulled out a tin of his own and, with a knowing flourish, clicked back the lid to show not one hair, but three.

As Monsarrat walked away, he heard one of the men quip: 'They're probably all different colours.'

On the *Aguila*, the captain, Arthur Firth, left the bridge to go to dinner. On his way, he stopped at the bar to chat to a steward. While they spoke, Firth invited a passing Wren officer to have a drink with them. As she finished her glass, she held out her hand.

'I would just like to say goodbye,' she said.

'Goodbye?' said Firth.

'This is goodbye from me,' she replied, as if having received some premonition of their imminent fates. 'I wish you all the luck in the world, but you don't need my good wishes. You'll survive.'

Firth finished his drink and went to dinner alone.

The combination of fine weather and jittery success in repelling the German bombers had led to an impromptu singsong around the saloon. One of the sailors sat at the piano, and the diners, loosened by wine, sang in unison together. For the finale, Second Officer Christine Ogle lined up her company of Wrens. Wearing their Gibraltar whites, the young women, their faces as clean as cherubs, sang the hit of the day: 'The World is Waiting for the Sunrise'.

Everyone retired to their cabins with the song's lyrics – 'While the world is waiting for the sunrise . . . my heart is calling you,' a perfect expression of the longing that follows parting, and the hope of reunion – sounding in their ears.[17]

At 03:00, from the dark sea, Kapitänleutnant Adalbert Schnee, a U-boat officer who served five commands under Otto Kretschmer before being given captaincy of his own vessel, U-201, fired two torpedoes at the Aguila.

Both struck, and the ship sank in ninety seconds.

At Western Approaches HQ, Roxane Houston deciphered the first signal to arrive from the Gibraltar convoy. For two hours she and the other Wrens, 'sitting in the warmth and comparative safety within the four walls of our room', fought the battle second-hand. They were the first to hear news of hard-pressed escorts dashing to the aid of torpedo-wrecked stragglers. The convoy's constant signals told of the desperate evasive action being taken while the wolfpack, now twelve U-boats strong, fired from within the convoy's columns, just as Kretschmer had instructed.

A smothered gasp from the table next to her told Houston that which she had been dreading. All twenty-one Wrens – including Madge Barnes, who had twice applied to join the Wrens, Phyllis Bacon, who had carefully adjusted her outfit before her interview for a place on the delegation, and Isabel Milne Home, who had been so helpful deciphering signals at Derby House – died that night. A twenty-second woman, Kate Ellen Gribble, a nursing sister who was also aboard the Aguila, perished too. Houston dropped her pencil, transported, she wrote in her diary, to 'that thunderous darkness,' with her friend Isabel somewhere in its middle.

Laughton Mathews, who had hand-selected the women for the trip and who had known some of them (including Mildred Norman, a former member of her 'Golden Hind' Sea Rangers), since they were children, was in Plymouth at the time of the sinking. Laughton Mathews later wrote that the scent of honeysuckle, which hangs heavy in the Devonshire summer air at the time she received the news, became forever associated in her mind with the tragedy. Close to a quarter of all the Wrens who died on service during the Second World War were lost that night.*

As the Wren had predicted, the ship's captain, Arthur Firth, survived the torpedoing, and was rescued (miserably, he was again torpedoed and again survived on his return journey to England). When he finally arrived in London, a broken man, Firth met Laughton Mathews.

'I have never forgotten my talk with him,' she recalled, 'nor the intense impression he gave me of what it means to go down into the bowels of the sea with the superstructure of the ship on top of you.'

Just as the sinking of the *City of Benares* had brought an end to the CORB programme to send British children overseas, so a change to policy immediately followed the sinking of the *Aguila*. Wrens proceeding on duty overseas were now permitted to embark on Royal Navy ships.

Rather than act as a deterrent, news of the tragedy spurred young women to join the Wrens. Scores volunteered to travel to Gibraltar in place of the lost Wrens. A fresh delegation was immediately organised. A few weeks after these women arrived in Gibraltar, the sceptical signals officer who had pleaded with Laughton Mathews to send men wrote to the Admiralty. 'In every way I am most fortunate, and I am jolly proud of my team,' he wrote of his new Wrens. 'I would not swap them for anybody.' The message provided Laughton Mathews with vindication and, in some small way, a moment's respite from grief.

Monsarrat later said that this battle, more than any other, was

---

* The name of every Wren to have died in active service is recorded in a book of remembrance, held in central London at St Mary le Strand, the official church of the Women's Royal Naval Service.

the one to which he would return in his nightmares. Mortality is a theme, sometimes explicit, often lurking, for every writer who has survived combat. But Monsarrat is one of the few who explored, in his fiction, the loss of women's lives at sea. In *The Cruel Sea*, his 'forlorn last try' to make it as a writer, and the book that subsequently made him a millionaire, one of his characters falls in love with a Wren. The pair's marriage pledge is thwarted when she is killed after a ferryboat capsizes in a storm, a tentative prodding of his darkest memories of the war at sea.

After the war, Monsarrat sailed the 'loathed' Atlantic to a posting in South Africa. The glow of a peacetime sun did nothing to salve his psychological scars. As he peered over the deck, he imagined the water to be strewn with dead sailors, some blown up, others burned to death, their bodies 'shredded' and, finally, 'sucked down'. The jetsam of human bodies could not be forgotten by those who saw these scenes. It was seven years before Monsarrat could bring himself, when visiting the beach – where children squatted by rock pools, their spades nosing the air like bayonets – to touch the water with his toes. With the misaligned rationale of the traumatised, he considered the lapping water to be 'poisoned forever'.[18]

Eight of the convoy's twenty-three ships were lost, along with two escort ships, one British and one Norwegian. The *Aguila* was one of five kills that went to Kapitänleutnant Schnee, whom Doenitz considered to be an 'exceptionally brilliant captain',[19] success that totalled more than 9,000 tons.[20] To write of sunken ships in these numerical terms is to be somehow complicit with a dehumanising tactic used by warmongers. How much easier it is on the psyche to measure kills not by the number of lives lost on board, but by weight in steel.

'If it's only one man you imagine it could be you,' says one of the characters in Lothar-Günther Buchheim's *Das Boot*, a fictionalised account of the author's time spent with U-boatmen as a war correspondent in 1941. 'But no one can identify with a whole steamer. That doesn't strike home.'[21]

For German captains, a quota of tons focused the mind on the task at hand: to sink more ships than Britain could build. It turned war into a scoresheet, a game in which the winner would be declared in points, not on merit. It also helped to dull or perhaps even neuter the distress associated, for most people, with proximity to death, especially death caused by one's own hands.

Teddy Suhren, U-48's first watch officer who had fired the torpedoes at the *City of Benares*, later wrote of how he focused not on the men in the ships, but on the cargo on which 'Great Britain was dependent if she was not to starve or bleed to death'.[22] On scoring a ship, Suhren would look it up in the *Naval Handbook No. 123*. This book contained not only the names and particulars of every merchant vessel, but also their silhouettes, which made identification easier for the U-boatmen who attacked mainly at night. Besides, Suhren wrote, 'names were completely irrelevant; it was their tonnage that mattered'. They were all 'just ships', he added, 'whose wakes stretched from one horizon to another'.

Doenitz actively encouraged this blinkered focus on numbers. Every U-boat captain who achieved 40,000 tons earned a mention in the dispatches. Still, occasionally the crimson horror of what was involved in this competition was made human. In late July 1941, a few weeks before the loss of the *Aguila*, the cruiser HMS *Manchester* docked in Gibraltar carrying the remains of thirty-eight crew members who had been trapped below decks when it was hit by a torpedo fired from an Italian aircraft. The captain had been forced to leave what was left of the men in their watery, sealed-up grave till, a week later, the ship made harbour. Junior sailors wearing masks to cover their noses and mouths carried the remains, which had to be washed clean of oil, on pushcarts, before they were transferred to another ship for burial at sea. The job took close to eight hours and, in the Gibraltar heat, the dockside began to hum like an abattoir, a sensual horror that became familiar to many who fought in the Atlantic.

It is awful. But, for a moment, stand on the dockside as the carts quietly trundle past. Here comes one. And another. And another. As much as war is, in our contemporary imagination, Churchill pounding his points home at the Dispatch Box in a dimly lit House of Commons, as much as it is the chisel-jawed pilot breaking the clouds in a Spitfire with strains of Elgar swelling in the background, this too is the substance of war.

Technology has a distancing effect on combat. The fist becomes a sword. The sword becomes an arrow. The arrow becomes a trebuchet. The trebuchet becomes a torpedo. The torpedo becomes a nuclear missile. The ICBM becomes, maybe, a clandestine social media campaign, designed to undermine and topple democracies. With each step change the attacker is removed yet farther from the material effects of his actions. At a distance it is harder to properly count the cost. It is, surely, our obligation to count the cost.

'I thought how we all cheered when a German battleship was successfully sunk with the loss of almost 2,000 men,' Houston, the Derby House cypher Wren who mourned her friend Isabel's death on the *Aguila*, wrote in her diary of the sinking of the German battleship *Bismarck*. 'And we congratulated ourselves on a great victory. How could we? What was the war doing to us?'

Exactly three weeks after the sinking of the *Aguila*, Winston Churchill, who had replaced Neville Chamberlain as prime minister the previous year, addressed Parliament to announce that the government would no longer be playing by the rules of the German's so-called tonnage game. The publication of official monthly figures reporting shipping losses to U-boats would cease. To justify the information blackout, Churchill argued 'it is not desirable to give [the enemy] too precise or, above all, too early information of the success or failure of each of his various manoeuvres'. He added, for reassurance, 'the public, and indeed the whole world, have however derived the impression that things have gone much better . . . I cannot deny that this is so.'[23]

In private, however, Churchill knew the truth. Close to 3 million tons of shipping had been destroyed in the first six months of 1941. The prime minister's order to the minister of information, Duff Cooper (who had, like Colin's parents, sent his son to America as an evacuee), to discontinue the publication of monthly losses was not only motivated to hide this information from the Germans, but also to hide it from the British people.

That autumn, imports to Britain had fallen to two thirds of the pre-war level, mostly thanks to the success of the U-boat campaign. Even with ever more stringent rationing (in March 1940 the meat allowance was cut to one shilling's worth, around a pound of meat per person a week), the Ministry of Food was questioning how it could continue to provide British citizens with sufficient calories each day. The British diet had been forced to move away from fat-rich foods, which made up thirty-eight per cent of the average calorie intake pre-war,[24] to a carbohydrate-rich diet of wholemeal bread and potatoes. The shift not only flattened the variety and taste of the typical Briton's diet, it also had negative practical consequences. For a manual worker to obtain the 4,000 calories they needed for a day's work from carbohydrates alone, they would have to spend almost the entire day eating. Fatigue became widespread in the workforce.

In his memo, Churchill warned Cooper that the press would accuse the government of attempting to 'cover up the size of our most recent shipping losses'. When responding to journalists, the prime minister advised Cooper to say: 'Well, that is what we are going to do anyway.'[25] After all, Churchill added, 'We shall have a lot worse to put up with in the near future.'

Questions hung heavy over the naval command as well. Captain George Creasy had been appointed the new director of anti-submarine warfare in the month of the *City of Benares'* sinking. Creasy spent months poring over reports of U-boat attacks on convoys, and from the patterns established by these accounts had begun to sketch out what he believed to be the U-boat tactics. He knew that the Germans preferred to attack at night, using daylight hours to shadow their prey. He knew that U-boat captains preferred to attack from the bow of the convoy, before falling back to fire torpedoes on the convoy's beam, finally withdrawing to a safe distance to reload the tubes. He did not yet know, however, about the technique pioneered by Kretschmer, of attacking from within the perimeter of the convoy, at point-blank distance.

So Creasy and all the rest at the Admiralty were left pondering what tactics the U-boats were employing that enabled them to continue to achieve such disproportionate success over the Royal Navy. What might be done about it, and who, for that matter, was the person to do it?

PART TWO

Play so that you may be serious.
Anacharsis, (*c.* 600 BC), quoted in Aristotle's
Nichomachaen Ethics

VII

Roberts

At 22:10 on 12th September 1940, the night before the *City of Benares* set sail from Liverpool, Gilbert Roberts was dozing in the basement of his rented home in West London when he felt a dull thud somewhere high above his bed.[1]

The Blitz, the Luftwaffe's persistent bombing campaign on Britain's major cities, was only five days old, but those who had picked their way through London's streets, newly seasoned with shards of shopfront glass, glinting shrapnel and lunar hollows, knew that the routine of city life had instantaneously changed. For Roberts, this had meant sleeping below ground.

Roberts had taken the mattresses from the upstairs bedrooms in the white-fronted town house in Courtfield Gardens, near London's museums in South Kensington, where he and eleven other tenants had lived on the top floor since April, and shunted them together to make a sea of the basement floor. At night he instructed the two children among the group to lie down in the broom cupboard, so that if the house collapsed they might have a rubble den in which to await rescue. Finally, with the assistance of the house's other tenants, Roberts built a heavy wooden hatch, adding another line of defence against the choking dust and sleep-skewering noises of siege outside.

Now, listening out for the sound of falling debris, Roberts eyed the hatch. It was not the first bomb he had felt land that night, but it was the closest.[2] Three years earlier, Roberts had been forced out of the navy – 'invalided', as per the term of the time, with all its cruel connotations – following a bout of tuberculosis that had brought him close to death, then left him gaunt and breathless.

Still, having reached the rank of commander, he had spent more than two decades in active service and could instinctively estimate his distance from a falling explosive, and what, if anything, he needed to do about it. While the adults crowded in the basement whispered assurances to the children, Roberts opened the hatch with a creak and a clack, then climbed the stairs into the hallway.

Considering the hour, the hallway was oddly bright. Over the past week residents had been instructed to extinguish every light source in order to make it harder for the German pilots to place their bombs. There were severe penalties for anyone who breached the rules. That night, however, brilliant flares dropped from the German planes had, like lilting stars, exposed London's harried streets. Roberts looked through the sitting room window. There, outside and half-buried in the pavement, sat a bent bomb, a 250-pounder, dripping with oil. Roberts went outside and saw that the oil had covered most of the front of the houses on his side of the street. Mercifully, there were no fires.

He took a closer look at the bent device on the pavement. There, on top of the bomb, sticking out of the casing at a cartoonish angle, quivered a smouldering fuse.[3]

Twenty-seven years earlier, and a few miles away, the twelve-year-old Roberts, wearing his school uniform and with a puffy black eye, sat at a polished mahogany table in a high-ceilinged room in the Admiralty, and stared into the severe faces of six men. Outside it was a summer's day, but the meeting room was dark and oppressive. A series of papers, written tests that Roberts had been asked to take as part of his application for entrance to the Royal Naval College, were laid out on the table.

The men stared at the boy. The boy stared at the men. Finally, a bewhiskered admiral, the most senior member of the group, leaned forward.

'Roberts,' he said. 'How the devil did you get that black eye?'

An explanation spilled forth, of how during a recent cricket match Roberts had dived to stump one of the batsmen, only to receive a club to the face.

'And I didn't even stump him,' he added, with a sorrowful flourish.

It was 1913 and applying to naval college was Roberts' rebellion: his father was an honorary colonel of the London Irish Rifles and his elder brother a horse-gunner in the army. Securing a place at naval college was going to be a challenge, however. At school, Roberts had opted to study German instead of Latin, and Latin was still a prerequisite of the navy at the time.

Next the interviewers asked the boy to locate the town of Dingle on a map of Ireland. Roberts confidently placed his finger on the chart, only to be told that he was mistaken. Not so, said Roberts, whose father had mentioned visiting Dingle during a recent fishing trip to the area at which he was pointing. Holding his nerve, the boy requested a more detailed chart be brought to the table. After a moment's scrunch-nosed searching, he triumphantly stabbed his finger at a label that read 'Dingle', a diminutive namesake to the better-known town on the south-west coast of Ireland. Roberts' pluck and determination made its mark on the panel. Alongside a clutch of other promising pubescent boys, he was accepted into the college two months shy of his thirteenth birthday.

At naval college, as well as distinguishing himself academically, Roberts proved to be a championship swimmer – a talent he was called upon to use during the summer of 1924. After serving at sea as a midshipman, he had returned to Portsmouth to train as a sub lieutenant. During a short leave break Roberts, who was by now in his early twenties, travelled with friends to Polzeath, Cornwall, a town that at the time was no more than a single row of houses sitting in front of a YMCA hut.[4] In the gaps between 'loafing, swimming, rock-climbing, surfing and loafing', as Roberts later described the group's summer preoccupations, he took himself off to study the *Magazine Handbook of Regulations*, a 'boring book' that he nevertheless had to learn in order to pass his final exams.

On a rounded hill above hundred-foot cliffs between Pentire Point and The Rumps, close to where the poet Laurence Binyon wrote 'For the Fallen' with its famed stanza about those who will not grow old as we grow old, he would sit in the buzzing grass, back pressed against a rock, reading and rereading the handbook. On 5th August 1924, from over the top of his book Roberts spied a group of five young holidaymakers making their way down the 'rough and imperfect' rock stairs on the east side of the bay.[5] He assumed they wanted to peer into the mouth of a cave where seals were known to often swim.

'They seemed, wisely, to be roped together,' Roberts recalled. 'But it also seemed to me a very unwise thing to do.'[6] The end of a strong westerly gale was blowing. The sea was 'only now a little ruffled', Roberts wrote, 'but it still had a high swell which was springing up the west-side cliffs and falling back in a great smother of spray'.

Twenty minutes later he heard chatter and saw four people traipsing back up the hill. Roberts called over to ask what had happened to the fifth person. The answer came back that he wasn't a member of their party and they weren't sure where he had got to. Roberts descended the hill and clambered down the cliff face toward the frothing sea. On a low-hanging ledge, he removed all his clothes except his underwear and a pair of gym shoes.[7] Fearing that he might be swept off and 'smeared down the cliff in the backwash', Roberts picked his moment and leaped into the broiling water, swimming under the surface a few yards to clear the rocks.

The currents were stronger than he had expected, but now Roberts had a clear view of Seal Cave, which, he reasoned, the man must have climbed into for a better look. Roberts swam towards the cave, diving to avoid its craggy roof, just as a wave lifted him into its mouth. Roberts grasped a rock and, in the seconds before the next swell hit, looked around for the man. He lingered a moment too long, and the next wave clattered him around the rock walls like a shoe in a washing machine. Wincing under the water, Roberts spied a body. When he reached the man 'there was no mistake at all; it was unnecessary to try to tow him out'.

Tiring fast, Roberts realised that he was now fighting for his own life. On the clifftop, a group of bystanders peered down. Roberts had lost track of time, and the light was beginning to fail. He began to swim out of the cave into clear water, leaving the body behind. He could see Pentire Head, around which he believed the water would be calmer, and set off at a steady pace.

'But after some time, I saw I wasn't moving at all,' Roberts wrote. 'What an ass: I had forgotten the tide.'

As the sky turned to dusk, Roberts realised that he was 'water-logged and very tired'. As he trod water, bleeding and exhausted, he heard voices then felt himself being wrenched from the sea. A group of French fishermen had seen him and hauled him aboard. Within moments they had given him a revitalising swig from a bottle. The Frenchmen were headed to Penzance so, when he had regained his strength, Roberts requested that they first deposit him back into the water, half a mile along the coast, within swimming distance of the broad sands of Polzeath Beach.

Roberts had lost his canvas shoes in the sea, and he climbed the cliffs on numb, lacerated feet, worried that he might strike his head on a rock in the dark or lose his footing.

'Anxiety took me clear of trouble,' he wrote.

He made it to the top of the cliffs and found his way to his abandoned handbook and sweater.

'There was nobody around,' he wrote. 'They'd all gone home.'

Roberts made his way back to the house. The next morning, he awoke to find his sheets soaked with blood and, in the local newspaper, a report that he was missing, presumed drowned. A few days later, Roberts and one of his friends, Sandy McKillop, were towed by the coastguard in a rowing boat to the cave. They retrieved the man's body, which was taken to St Ives for an inquest, which Roberts attended.

Roberts was awarded the Royal Humane Society's bronze medal by the Prince of Wales for his efforts to save the man, later identified as James L. Wainwright of Henley.[8] Roberts wrote of the incident in the plain, pragmatic prose of the wizened sailor, who sees in the sparkling ocean not serenity, but a sleeping monster.

Roberts' naval career continued on a promising, if unorthodox trajectory when, following sorties to fit out Australia's first aircraft carrier and a trip down the Danube, he was made a game designer for the Royal Navy. In July 1935, a few days after he was promoted to the rank of commander, Roberts joined the tactical school at Portsmouth. Here naval captains and their senior staff played wargames, hyper-evolved military-themed board games staged on floors painted to look like giant chessboards. Distant cousins to commercial board games such as Battleship and Risk, these wargames were intended to explore and rehearse lifelike combat situations, a crucible in which tactics could be tested, analysed, and refined. It was work to which Roberts took an immediate liking.

The use of games to represent the manoeuvres of warriors on stylised boards can be found throughout the historical record; archaeologists have unearthed sets of miniature soldiers that represent Sumerian and Egyptian armies. Many of the earliest board games that, like chess and go, are still played today are either military-themed, or explore military concepts of strategy and tactics. Games establish consequence-free realities in which we can explore and experience situations that in actuality are too dangerous, rarefied or consequential. This makes them the ideal sphere in which to experience war.

In his 1913 book *Little Wars*, H. G. Wells captured the allure of the wargame that captivated his interest as a boy, and held his attention into adulthood:

> Here is the premeditation, the thrill, the strain of accumulating victory or disaster – and no smashed or sanguinary bodies, no shattered fine buildings, nor devastated countrysides, no petty cruelties, none of that awful universal boredom and embitterment, that tiresome delay or stoppage of embarrassment of every gracious, bold, sweet and charming thing, that we who are old enough to remember a real modern war know to be the reality of belligerence.[9]

For similar reasons wargames have proved themselves of supreme value to professional militaries, who are able to use the board as a kind of divination pool in which they test tactics and strategies in fictional fronts. H. G. Wells perceived this usefulness, arguing in *Little Wars* that 'the British Empire will gain new strength from nursery floors'.* One of the earliest known games, *wei hei* (meaning

---

* This line appears only in the UK edition of the book. The American edition reads: 'The men of tomorrow will gain new strength.'

'encirclement'), was designed by the Chinese general Sun Tzu for this purpose.

In the seventeenth century, recognising the limitations of abstract wargames like chess in preparing to lead an actual army into battle, more complex variants such as *Koenigsspiel*, or king's game, emerged. Invented in Germany in 1644 by Christopher Weikhmann, *Koenigsspiel* added units such as colonels, captains, couriers, bodyguards and private soldiers to chess's traditional roster of kings and knights. Weikhmann claimed the game was a 'compendium of the most useful military and political principles'. Wargames continued to evolve in complexity, size and realism till, by the 1850s, '*Kriegsspiel*' were widely used by the German military.

Around this time, John Clerk, a Scotsman who had never been to sea, designed a game to represent combat between warships with the aim of devising more efficient tactics.[10] Clerk wrote up his findings and suggestions in a book titled *An Essay on Naval Tactics*. In the preface he explained how he, a man with experience of neither combat nor sea, might presume to correct those naval officers and commanders who had spent their life fighting on the ocean.

> As I never was at sea myself, I have been asked, how should I have been able to acquire any knowledge in naval tactics, or should have presumed to suggest my opinion upon that subject . . . I had recourse not only to every species of demonstration, by plans and drawings, but also to the use of a small number of models of ships which, when disposed in proper arrangement, gave most correct representations of hostile fleets . . . and being easily moved and put into any relative position required, and thus permanently seen and well considered, every possible idea of a naval system could be discussed without the possibility of any dispute.[11]

Clerk's assertion that it was possible for admirals to become experts from the comfort of armchairs was contentious but, eventually, accepted. The Germans were first to accept and embrace wargaming as an imperfect yet instructive mirror of reality. Then, in the late nineteenth and early twentieth centuries, the growing size of armies made it impractical and often foolishly provocative to practise full-scale mobilisation. Other nations began to adopt wargames to simulate deploying to a range of potential locations.[12]

Tactical schools, such as the one that Roberts joined in Portsmouth in 1935, became an essential component of every force. In doing so, officers could evaluate their previous decision-making, and perceive potential pitfalls in future encounters. Games, which employ logic and rules to create scenarios in which a player can evolve strategies, simulate perfectly the perspective and problems that naval captains face in combat. The board is indistinguishable, in functional terms, from the commanding officer's map. Game-player and officer tactician alike have a bird's-eye view of the theatre of war, pushing a unit forward here, making a retreat there.

Wargames also proved their worth to the military in the civilian sphere. Not only did they allow amateurs such as H. G. Wells to experience, vicariously, the scale of challenge that faced commanders in a real battle, they also attracted young men to join the services. In his 1930 autobiography, Winston Churchill admitted that his decision to enter Sandhurst, and thereby pursue his chosen career, was influenced by his childhood passion for staging imaginary battles with toy soldiers, a hobby that 'turned the current' of his life.[13]

The best-known sea game is undoubtedly Battleship, variants of which were published by various companies under various names, initially as a pad-and-pencil game in the 1930s. The board-game manufacturer Milton Bradley published its first Battleship-style game in 1943, under the title Broadsides: The Game of Naval Strategy, a title that was distilled to Battleship in 1967. MB Games claims it has no record of who designed or named the game,[14] but there were clear commercial precedents.

L'Attaque was a French board game designed by Mademoiselle Hermance Edan, who filed a patent for a '*jeu de bataille avec pièces mobiles sur damier*' ('a battle game with mobile pieces on a game board') on 26th November 1908. Produced in Great Britain from the 1920s by H. P. Gibson & Sons, players moved pieces that represented different classes of soldier around a board measuring nine inches by ten. Each piece has a numeric value, hidden from the opponent and only revealed when an attacking piece moves onto a square occupied by an opponent's piece. In most cases, the piece with the highest value wins and the losing piece is removed from the board. Play continues until one player finds and takes the opponent's flag piece.

H. P. Gibson & Sons designed a number of follow-ups to L'Attaque, including a naval-themed variant called Dover Patrol ('Easy to learn,' states the blurb in the September 1932 *Games and Toys Journal*, 'but reaches the skill of chess') and Aviation, an air-force-themed version. In 1932 they ran an advertisement with the slogan: 'War Without Tears!!'[15]

The company also published a game titled Jutland, similar in rules to the modern game of Battleship. Two players each mark out the position of their warships on a ten-by-ten grid, hidden to their opponent. Once their ships are positioned, each player takes turns to fire a salvo of six missiles at their opponent's grid, hoping to strike a ship rather than the sea.

'A lot of skill can be exercised in finding the position of one's opponent's ships,' states the game's manual, reassuring the reader that this is no game of mere chance. The progenitor of the wargame on which Roberts based his games in Portsmouth was Fred Jane, a failed novelist who, in 1898, published the rules of a boardgame-style naval wargame in the *Engineering Journal*.[16] Later that year, his books, *Jane Naval Wargame* and *Fighting Ships*, provided a formal set of rules, scorecards and ship diagrams, which were subsequently adapted by the navy. The game, which used scale ship models, a squared board and even some ping-pong-like bats to fire projectiles, was notable for its flexibility and realism. Jane tested the game aboard warships docked in Portsmouth Harbour and, four years later, a modified version was issued to HM Ships for training. It was a version of the *Jane Naval Wargame* that Roberts adapted at his posting in Portsmouth, more than three decades later.

Chance played its role in Roberts' games at Portsmouth, which, on a board painted across the entire floor of a room, on which ships of various sizes were manoeuvred, bore a passing resemblance to Battleship, but the aim was to reduce serendipity's role in sea battle by incrementally refining naval tactics.

The technique may have been sound, but the focus of Roberts' wargames was misplaced. Despite the fact that during the First World War the Germans had used submarines to great effect to disrupt the convoys bringing food and supplies to Great Britain, neither U-boats nor convoys featured in the wargames of 1935.

'All the information about the lessons from the First World War was available for anyone who wanted to read it,' said Peter Gretton, a commander who repelled numerous U-boats while escorting convoys in the war. 'But I'm afraid no one bothered.'[17] The vital lessons of the Great War, when Britain had faced starvation by German sea blockade, had been forgotten.

'Submarines were not mentioned,' Roberts wrote of the games he was tasked with designing. 'Nor were convoys and attacks on them. Nobody connected Hitler's rise . . . to the possibility of another Battle of the Atlantic. Nor did I, to be absolutely fair.'[18] *

(In fact, a wargame to test convoy protection was designed and played at the naval college in Greenwich in January 1938. This game, of which Roberts was seemingly unaware, correctly estimated the time of war's outbreak but assumed that the threat to convoy ships would come not from U-boats, but from German raiders disguised as merchant vessels.[19])

Despite this consequential oversight, Roberts worked with his colleagues for two years to develop new naval tactics via these wargames. Roberts' keen interest in the push and pull of tactical manoeuvring, and his bright imagination, which enabled him to add an engaging layer of fiction to the wargaming, made him the perfect leader for such a course.

'What an astonishing two years,' he wrote. 'I loved it, absolutely.'[20]

Eventually, however, Roberts' talent on the tactical table earned him a role on an active ship. In the autumn of 1937, he was appointed captain of the lithe destroyer *Fearless*, and dispatched to the seas of Gibraltar. Here began one of the happiest times of Roberts' life, patrolling the seas around the Spanish coast as commander of his own destroyer, a 'lovely little ship'.

---

* Neither did the Royal Navy players anticipate the fall of France, and its effect in expanding the German operation range.

During downtime, Roberts and his crew partook in athletic competitions held on the rock, including the Windsor Baton, an exhilaratingly complicated relay race unique to the island. This started with a sack race at the Spanish border, running and walking sections, a bicycle leg raced by each ship's postman carrying a full sack of letters on their back, a climb up the harbour crane and scrambles over docked ships, followed by a swim across the harbour and, finally, a hundred-metre sprint to the finish line.

During these halcyon days, Roberts developed a wheezing, whistling cough that turned him into a sweating insomniac. A prescription of linctus, a thick, syrupy medicine designed to coat the throat, alleviated the cough but none of the other symptoms. Roberts endured the rest of the sortie, which included training exercises off Portland, and a visit to Scotland. There the commander-in-chief Sir Charles Forbes showed Roberts, who was bravely trying to conceal his sickness, around the battlecruiser *Prince of Wales*, which was still under construction.

As the pair surveyed the new ship, Forbes turned to Roberts and said: 'That would do just for you, wouldn't it?'

It was not to be. Roberts' ship *Fearless* departed Glasgow and made for Devonport on the south coast of England. He arrived into port in abject pain and, on disembarkation, was escorted to the battleship *Resolution* to see the surgeon commander. The doctor delivered his diagnosis on the spot: tuberculosis.

'That was the end,' Roberts wrote in his diary.

Roberts was summarily relieved of his command and, with the bruising efficiency of an organisation that requires its members to be fighting fit, discharged from the Royal Navy before the day was out.

After two nights in Stonehouse Hospital, Roberts was provided with a chit that admitted him to a private nursing home in Camberley, Surrey. The fees would be covered by the navy for just ninety days. Roberts would also receive ninety days' pay. Thereafter, if he survived his illness, he would be on his own. Equally troubling was the news that Roberts would not receive a pension. His heiress wife was profoundly rich, but he felt the natural obligation to provide for his two young children. Where would he go? What would he do?

At thirty-eight years old Roberts had spent his entire adolescence and adulthood in the navy. 'The navy was his life,' said one officer who served under Roberts. Beyond the distant, misty plains of young childhood, it was the only thing he had known. Of the 180-page unpublished memoir that Roberts wrote later in life, just a single handwritten page relates to his pre-naval childhood. Moreover, the war that he had spent so many months preparing for via tactical wargames was unquestionably on its way.

Anxiety is malleable; it contorts to fit the shifting shapes of our lives. A few weeks earlier Roberts' preoccupations were the common worries of the professional approaching middle age: of being passed over for promotion, of spending too much time away from his family. Now, like black treacle, his fears adapted to fill the new circumstances of his world. To be removed from this moment of great and deep history delivered an existential blow. What man was left, when the uniform was taken away?

Without a travel warrant, Roberts made his own way to the convalescence home. There, in a sunless bungalow wing, a doctor X-rayed Roberts' chest. The infection was extensive in his left lung and spreading to the right. The prognosis, the doctor said, was poor. Tuberculosis, he explained, was 'a curse', one that usually led to death. Reeling from the double blow, Roberts asked the doctor for a radio, a cricket scorebook and a pen. A Test match was due to start the next day. If Roberts was to die, he would go out keeping score.

He did not die. While the war raged in his lungs, Roberts, forced into a blanketed wheelchair, spent the next year fighting on a second inner front: a battle to hold onto his identity and purpose. Those memories associated with his physical virtues – the cricket match, the cave rescue attempt, the heroic running races – became keepsakes, a reminder for the life vanished and hope for the life to come.

During those months of tristesse, Roberts was not entirely abandoned. A visit from Surgeon Captain Ingleby Mackenzie reassured him that there were those in the navy who still cared for him. Then, following a visit from a concerned rear admiral, Roberts received the news that he was to receive a pension; the Treasury had conceded that his illness had been contracted as a result of his service. The financial news was as nothing to the warm sense that Roberts had not been disowned by his naval family, in whom he had invested his best years. After a stint at the King Edward VII sanatorium in Midhurst, Sussex, in July 1939 a brighter, fitter Roberts was moved to Yelverton, Devon, where the clean air of the moors would, everyone hoped, salve his deeper wounds.

Eager to offer himself, once again, to service of his country, Roberts answered a newspaper advertisement asking for men with experience of guns, searchlights and ammunition. His application was rejected. Hoping to leverage his connections, Roberts wrote to the Second Sea Lord in search of a role. A dispiriting response followed: write again in a year's time. When Roberts successfully wheedled his way into the labour battalion of the Duke of Cornwall's Light Infantry, he immediately found himself standing in front of the colonel, Willie Buckley, who also happened to be his cousin. Buckley, knowing all about the health difficulties Roberts was facing, ordered him to stand down.

The illness that knocked him from his career trajectory was, for Roberts, a source of if not private shame then at least profound self-consciousness. Later in the war he lied to a newspaper journalist from the *Liverpool Daily Post*, claiming that he was invalided not through illness but 'as a result of an accident' in 1938.

Chronic illness, like war, arrives uninvited and inexorable. And, like war, it too disrupts and transforms the lives of those it touches. Bewildered by the sudden, dizzying change in circumstance, Roberts came loose from the other anchor points in his life. Cracks and valleys appeared in his marriage to Alice Brooks, known to all as Margot, heiress to a family fortune made manufacturing bicycle saddles, who, with an absent husband, spent more and more time with her horses. For now, his marriage endured, even if the relationship around which it was built began to collapse.

In November 1939, Roberts received a letter from the Admiralty. Any hope he felt was soon extinguished when he read its contents: 'I am commanded by My Lords Commissioners of the Admiralty to inform you that you will not be accepted again for general service in the Royal Navy. In view of the nature of your illness . . . it is very unlikely that any suitable service could be found for you.'[21]

With the matter closed, Roberts, who was bright but not an intellectual, and whose educational efforts had been focused entirely on preparing for a naval career, finally found somewhere that would take him. He joined the local police force as a special constable, serving the local farming community in the early months of war, before becoming a local defence volunteer, a member of the so-called Home Guard, the anti-invasion force that would later gain – not unfairly – a reputation for being a rather hapless organisation of ragtag individuals and hangers-on, via the sitcom *Dad's Army*.

In March 1940, a few months before the fall of France, Roberts' telephone rang. The call came from the Admiralty. After a slew of firm rebuttals, Roberts was asked to return to duty as a retired commander, on full pay and in uniform. He was ordered to leave Devon and find a place to live in London, before reporting to the duty captain at the Admiralty, close to where Vera Laughton Mathews was busily assembling and organising her Wrens.

The newspaper classifieds were full of vacated houses and apartments available to rent. Roberts picked Courtfield Gardens due to its useful proximity to Gloucester Road Tube station. He reported for duty at Admiralty House wearing his old uniform, now at least one size too large for his devastated body, a civilian gas mask in hand and, over his shoulder, a tin helmet with the word 'Police' daubed in white paint. His job was dull but vital: ensuring the resupply of ammunition to the escort ships fighting the U-boats in the Atlantic. Estimating how many shells each ship might need on return to port may have been a desk job, but it nevertheless allowed Roberts to live vicariously through his calculations.

Then, five months after arriving in London with his family, Roberts found himself face to fuse with a real German bomb.

VIII

Oak Leaves and Christmas Trees

The self-effacing Otto Kretschmer, great ace of the German fleet, had come to hate the ceremonious homecomings that welcomed his U-boat each time it chugged into Lorient. The grinning girls with their bouquets of flowers, the tooting brass bands, the scribbling journalists – it all seemed to Kretschmer a corrupting indulgence. This time, however, he knew that he would be unable to avoid the inevitable fuss. In the weeks following the embryonic wolfpack attack on convoy HX.72, Kretschmer had carried out two further patrols, during which he sank no fewer than eleven Allied vessels.

Kretschmer had continued to develop his pioneering technique of firing on targets at point-blank range, sinking the British armed merchant cruiser HMS *Laurentic* from a distance of just 250 metres. So compelling was the news of these winter victories that Joseph Goebbels, the Nazi minister of propaganda, described them in a radio broadcast as 'the greatest adventure story of the war'. Then, on 4th November 1940, while Kretschmer was still at sea, Hitler awarded him the Oak Leaves to the Knight's Cross, the highest decoration a German could receive for valour in the face of the enemy.

Four days later *U-99* slunk into harbour at Lorient. Kassel, the petty officer who had given the concussed Briton, Joseph Byrne, a tin of pineapple a few weeks earlier, took down an incoming signal from Doenitz, notifying Kretschmer of the award and the order that he was to travel to Berlin to receive it from Hitler in person. On his previous return to port, and much to the consternation of his crew, when Kretschmer had spied the waiting crowds he had pointed *U-99* toward a little-used Lorient jetty, unpopular with

U-boat crews as it was such a long walk from town. Having tied up, Kretschmer was preparing to disembark when a launch sped up alongside the submarine.

'Commander Kretschmer, there has been a mistake,' cried the officer aboard. 'Admiral Doenitz and the military command have turned out to greet you. You are to take your ship over to the main berth now.' Having been caught out, Kretschmer decided to give the onlookers a show, and, in a wide, frothing arc, made toward the main jetty at full speed, before slamming the engines into reverse to come to a shuddering halt a few feet from the quay.

Today, fearing more of Kretschmer's self-effacing tricks, Doenitz had his ace captain escorted from *U-99* to a waiting plane, to take him directly to Paris for a face-to-face debrief. There, after providing a rundown of the ships he had sunk on *U-99*'s most recent sortie, Doenitz asked Kretschmer to select five other members of his crew for decoration. With characteristic magnanimity, Kretschmer argued that it was an unfair request: all of his crew, he said, were deserving of recognition. Finally, when pressed, Kretschmer conceded that his petty officer Kassel should be the first in line for an Iron Cross.

That night Kretschmer sat in the corner table in the Parisian club Chez Elle. He had enjoyed little sleep during the past week, and the emotional bends caused by the lurch from the Atlantic battlefront to the clubs of Paris were only heightened by the knowledge that tomorrow he was to meet with the Führer. In this psychic anteroom, caught between the depths of the ocean and the heights of political power, Kretschmer drank his champagne in lusty, nerve-quietening gulps.

The following morning, 12th November 1940, Kretschmer arrived in Berlin and disembarked the five-seater plane on which he was the sole passenger. It was the first time the twenty-eight-year-old had stepped onto German soil since moving to France, but any warm sense of homecoming ran cold from Kretschmer's mind the moment he saw the car waiting to escort him to the luxurious Kaiserhof Hotel. There he bathed and, after a brief meeting with Grand Admiral Raeder, leader of the *Kriegsmarine*, was escorted

200 yards to the Reich Chancellery by car, an extravagance that, considering the shortages of oil and petrol in France, rankled the U-boat captain.

Hitler's naval aide, Captain Puttkamer, whose job was to drill Kretschmer for the day's ceremony, led him into the Chancellery, past a giant eagle, through the lobby into the high-ceilinged reception room. Four and a half years later this room was where Berlin's soldiers would make their final stand, in a mesh of fallen crossbeams, the frail walls pocked with shrapnel. It would be a scene of utter destruction, one that the Soviet foreign minister, who visited shortly after the fighting ended, described as an illustration of Dante's hell. That day, however, it was pristine and palatial, the walls hung with tapestries of pastoral scenes, the floor thick with miles of yielding Persian rugs.

At noon Kretschmer's chaperone, Puttkamer, left the room. After a few nervous minutes, Kretschmer watched the tall swing doors open. Hitler walked into the room, Puttkamer at his side, holding a small, gold-edged box in his hands. Kretschmer stood and greeted the Führer, who offered his leading U-boat ace a few words of praise before presenting him with the box, inside of which nestled the Oak Leaves.

The brisk ceremony complete, Hitler motioned Kretschmer to the settee. For a while the U-boat officer listened while Hitler spoke of the campaign, boasting of how the fortuitous taking of the French ports had been his plan all along. Kretschmer did not let on, but in private he was weary. A few months later a secret recording of a conversation between the captain and one of his crew was made by the British in which Kretschmer admitted: 'For a long time I have felt no enthusiasm for the war.'[1]

It was this fatigue that motivated Kretschmer, when Hitler asked how the U-boat war was progressing, into a mode of courageous forthrightness. There were too few U-boats, Kretschmer said, pointedly. Since the beginning of the war, neither Doenitz nor Grand Admiral Erich Raeder had been able to convince Hitler to fully back naval economic warfare. As such, Kiel's shipyards had insufficient steel and labour to build the fleet of 300 U-boats that Doenitz estimated he required to deal a critical and sustained setback to Britain's imports. Kretschmer was surely aware of Doenitz's frustration, and took the opportunity to reaffirm his superior's appeal.

'The quicker they build them,' he said, 'the more possible it will be to press home night surface attacks and produce wolfpacks large enough to wipe out convoys.'

Boldness begat boldness and Kretschmer, warming to his subject, moved on to the urgent need for large-scale air reconnaissance in the Atlantic. With a squadron of planes searching for convoys, and a large number of U-boats waiting patiently at sea, the Germans' current advantage in the Battle of the Atlantic could be pressed, he said. Hitler nodded, rose to his feet.

'Thank you, Commander,' he said. 'You have been admirably frank, and I shall do what I can for you and your colleagues.'

Before he left the room, Hitler informed Kretschmer that they were to take lunch together. A guard escorted Kretschmer to the dining hall. There, around a large round table, a dozen or so aides stood behind their chairs, awaiting Hitler's arrival. Kretschmer was shown to his chair. It was the seat of honour, at Hitler's right-hand side. Kretschmer had no experience of stately meals, and realised that neither meat nor alcohol, which Hitler despised, was to be served. Worse still, as he looked around at the other guests he correctly guessed that smoking was forbidden, a realisation that only heightened his pangs of nicotine withdrawal, after weeks chain-smoking cheroots at sea.

While lunch was served by wide-set SS guards, Kretschmer listened as talk turned to the subject of the arrival in Germany of Vyacheslav Molotov, the Russian premier. Molotov and his entourage, one adjutant explained, had arrived at the German border by train from Moscow, then changed trains. Once aboard the Berlin-bound train, they had refused to eat the German food, and had instead brought their own breakfast baskets.

'Wise,' said Hitler, 'if a little theatrical.'

Finally, the adjutant noted the number of women that Molotov had brought with them. The rumour was that the delegation feared that German women might stab them while in bed. Not wanting to sleep alone, the Russians had brought their own companions.

'Are they pretty?' asked Hitler.

When the adjutant failed to hear the question, Hitler repeated, more sharply: 'Are they pretty?'

The Nazis believed the role of women was, as Goebbels put it, 'to be beautiful and to bring children into the world'. One hand-drawn propaganda poster at the time showed an Aryan woman in a blue dress, framed by a yellow sun, breastfeeding a plump baby. Guidelines for how German women should live were issued, urging them never to wear trousers, make-up or high-heeled shoes, or to dye or perm their hair.

Hitler believed women's lives should revolve around three Ks: 'Kinder', 'Küche' and 'Kirche' – 'children', 'kitchen' and 'church'. The party systemised this belief in society in various ways. The Law for the Encouragement of Marriage presented newlywed couples with a loan of 1,000 marks, of which they were permitted to keep a quarter for each child the woman bore. Women were further incentivised by the Mutterkreuz, the Mother's Cross, a matronly equivalent to the Oak Leaves that was awarded to those mothers who bore a large number of Aryan children. Single women were permitted to have a baby for a member of the SS.

Further financial incentives were offered to those women who chose not to work. While female auxiliary staff had been used in the German army for decades, there was no provision for the recruitment and employment of women to the war effort until after the fall of France in the summer of 1940, when the demands of occupation and prolonged war made Hitler's position on women untenable. Even then, women's roles were broadly limited to the menial.

Members of the Wirtschaftshelferinnen, for example, worked as cleaners and kitchen staff. The Stabshelferinnen, staff auxiliaries, were women between the ages of eighteen and forty who served as clerical workers in army administration posts.* While the German navy had a long history of employing female auxiliary staff, the

---

* The German command eventually permitted the Stabshelfesinnen to engage in tactical analysis in 1944. In this task the women proved skilful, albeit too late in the war to be effective.

Marinehelferinnen, the closest German equivalent to the Wrens, wasn't founded until July 1942.[2] Unlike the Wrens, who were encouraged to feel a sense of belonging and sorority from their clothes, a *Marinehelferinnen*-specific uniform was not issued till September 1943; prior to this the women wore Luftwaffe pattern uniforms.

While, with historical distance, the British might feel proud of the progressive way in which women were welcomed into the services, the German attitude was matched in Britain by a robust institutional resistance to the allocation of Wrens into senior roles of responsibility during the early years of the war. One naval captain later articulated this pervasive attitude as 'Wrens can't do this, can't do that; can't go here, can't go there; what – send them abroad? Never!'[3] While conscription for women came to Britain sooner than in Germany, there was widespread opposition to the idea, which some argued strongly would undermine the role of women within the home.

'War is not a woman's job,' said Agnes Hardie of the Labour Party. 'Women share the bearing and rearing of children and should be exempt from war.'[4] (Hardie, it should be noted, also campaigned for sexual equality, and recommended equal compensation for war injuries, which at the time favoured men by seven shillings.[5])

In Germany, however, the resistance sprang from a sterner form of ideological misogyny, rooted in the corrupt soil of Nazism. Moreover, there was no German equivalent to Vera Laughton Mathews, a leader quietly yet determinedly campaigning for women to be included in all strata of the war effort.

'I have not seen them myself,' replied the adjutant, in reply to Hitler's enquiry about the women. 'But I will find out this afternoon.'

'Do that before Molotov comes to see me,' said Hitler. 'I should like to taunt him with some of our beauties.'

The meal finished, Hitler rose to his feet, shook Kretschmer's hand for what would be the final time and wished the captain good hunting at sea. Kretschmer returned to his hotel. A few hours later he was driven to the state opera for a staging of Wagner's *Tannhäuser*. He was shown to the state box, typically only used by Hitler or visiting representatives of foreign powers. Beneath him, audience members whispered to one another: was that really the U-boat ace?

There Kretschmer sat, among cascading blooms and bouquets, peering down at the stage. From his enviable vantage, he was free to contemplate both the contrast of this week compared to the last, and the fact that here, as at sea, he remained both the focal point of everyone's attention, and utterly alone.

The bomb wedged in the concrete outside Roberts' front door, smoke curling from its fuse, was one of the latest yet most unreliable weapons in the Luftwaffe's arsenal. A bloated incendiary device, the oil bomb was known to the Germans as the *Flam* or *Flammenbombe* and contained an oil mixture and a high-explosive bursting charge. Many of the forty-two oil bombs that were dropped during the Blitz on the borough of Kensington and Chelsea, where Roberts was staying, failed to detonate, splitting the case open to spill gallons of fuel.[6] As such, in January 1941, just a few months after its introduction, the *Flam* was withdrawn from widespread use.

While 244 people were killed and 770 houses demolished by bombs in Kensington during the Blitz, Londoners were at a greater risk from rounds fired by the British high-calibre anti-aircraft guns; when the bullets missed their targets, they would fall, like coins spilled from a purse, back toward the city at deadly velocity.

Right now, however, Roberts knew that he and everyone else in the vicinity was in grave danger: should the spark from the fuse reach the casing, the oil would catch fire and set the entire street ablaze.

War inevitably brings provocations to bravery, tests that allow no room for considered thought, forcing individuals to act on character and instinct. Roberts grasped the fuse in his hand and pulled hard. It came free, and as the pain from its heat lit up in his hand, Roberts threw it into the road before kicking it into the gutter, where a bystander ran to stamp it out.

With the sounds of planes still screeching in the sky, his shoes covered in oil and three of his fingers burned, Roberts returned to the house and climbed up to the room he had previously used as a bedroom. After he had washed the oil from his hands, and bound his burned fingers with cloth, he returned to the basement.

Moments after he closed the hatch, ten minutes after the first bomb landed, there was a thwomp and Roberts and the others listened as part of the front basement ceiling collapsed. In the dark, as he listened out for the telltale hiss of a leaking gas pipe, Roberts felt not only curiously calm but also curiously exhilarated. After the past few years of feeling like a discarded cog, with no place in the machinery of his country's war effort, he was back where it mattered, in the middle of the action, even if, right now, that meant spending the night half-buried in a basement.

Across London, on the other side of the River Thames, Christian Oldham arrived at Greenwich to begin officer training. At her previous digs in Campden Hill Road, having failed to learn to touch-type, Oldham had spent much of her time under the direction of the strict and disapproving Hilda Buckmaster, scrubbing floors as punishment for her various misdemeanours. Inside these insalubrious premises, she would duck through a coal hole to reach the canteen, where she and the other Wrens would race to be the first to finish their meagre plates of food in order to claim one of the few second helpings. She had shared a room with three other Wrens, at least one of whom never removed her vest and, as a result, hummed with the vinegary sweet smell of body odour.[7] During a chance meeting with Nancy Osborne, chief officer of the headquarters staff of the Wrens, who had first interviewed Oldham, the young Wren pleaded for a transfer.

Osborne took pity on Oldham and invited her to join the team at Wrens HQ, where she took up residence in an office next to Diana Churchill, Winston's eldest daughter, who, in her early thirties, seemed implausibly ancient to the twenty-year-old. After a stint running the degaussing range on the Thames, where ships would be fitted with wire coils designed to foil German magnetic mines, Oldham was put forward for promotion to officer.

Oldham arrived at Greenwich via ferry, disembarking at the same pier that kings, queens and many of Britain's most accomplished naval commanders had journeyed to for centuries. Nancy Spain, who, like Monsarrat, had been an up-and-coming freelance journalist before the war (and who, after the war, became a celebrated newspaper columnist), wrote of her arrival at Greenwich, of the astonishing feeling of being cosmically reconnected to her country's past, seeing 'like a conception of God . . . all English history spread before my eyes'.

The Painted Hall was a place for which, as Nancy Spain put it, 'no contemporary eulogy, nor nineteenth-century engraving had wholly prepared me'. Here, Oldham and the other scores of Wrens would eat in the flattering light of a thousand candles, from tables carved from the timbers of ships that had fought at the Battle of Trafalgar, as the sound of jingling cutlery was joined by the sotto bass rumble of London's flak cannons. During the Blitz, the Wrens at Greenwich slept down in the deep stone cellars. When the arrangement became too uncomfortable, balancing risk with the need for comfort they moved to the games rooms, where the women slept beneath the billiards tables.

Oldham quickly earned her promotion to third officer and was informed that she was to be transferred to Plymouth as a plotter. It was, she thought, the pick of the limited selection of jobs available to Wrens in the early months of war, not least because plotters had access to the so-called Pink List, a document that listed the whereabouts of every ship within the navy, an invaluable resource for any young Wren who, as Oldham put it, wanted to keep tracks on her 'latest young man'.[8]

At Plymouth Oldham learned the art of plotting by surreptitiously watching her fellow Wrens, and soon began working watches, shunting tokens to represent the convoys and U-boats. The hours were long and the work demanding. After a few nights of being awoken from her on-site mattress by a frantic admiral, wanting her to retrieve some sea chart or another from the chart cabinet, Oldham took to dozing and reading novels in a plotting-room chair. Her watches would sometimes last for two days at a time, with little opportunity for sleep. Thereafter, the Wrens plotters would enjoy two days to recuperate and attend parties on the ships and submarines docked nearby.

For Oldham, the submarine crews were the elite of the Navy, and had a certain romantic appeal. Technology's distancing effect on all forms of warfare, including that waged at sea, had removed the fighting sailor from the nexus of battle. As Donald Macintyre, one of the three most famous and successful U-boat hunters, later put it in regretful tones, sea warfare had become 'largely a matter of mathematical computation, of aiming guns accurately at a barely visible target some dozen miles away'.[9]

Submarining was similarly work defined by gauges and read-outs, but something tactile and immediate remained to the art, which, as a result, attracted men of a certain dauntless temperament. It was during a party in the cramped wardroom of the minelaying submarine HMS *Rorqual*, docked in Plymouth harbour in between sorties to the Mediterranean, that Oldham met one such man, its captain, Lennox Napier.

Napier was a bright character, bristling with verve and anecdotes, who ran his submarine with equal vim. HMS *Rorqual* spent much of the war supplying fuel and food to the beleaguered island of Malta, while simultaneously laying mines for the encircling Italian and German ships. On one occasion he attempted the pioneering act of sending a kit of carrier pigeons from the submarine's conning tower, only for the birds to refuse to leave the vessel. Christian and Lennox became increasingly close, taking long walks across the wuthering Dartmoor in the gaps between war work.

As they strode and chatted, the young Wren felt the frisson of feelings. Later she wrote that she considered Napier to be 'from that rather romantic genre who would not commit himself to any course of action he could not be sure of carrying out'. Whatever his reasons, if Napier felt an equivalent attraction toward Oldham, it was left unacknowledged. Still, after departing Plymouth, he wrote to Oldham regularly. A lively writer and cartoonist, who drew scratchy, humorous illustrations in the margins of his letters, Napier signed off each of them 'with love' to Oldham. These documents sustained and deepened her feelings toward Napier.

On the long nights of her watch, Oldham pondered not only the question of whether or not Napier would return to and for her, but also the question of whether or not she would wait for him. Then, before the matter could be settled, Oldham received the news that, once again, she was to be moved on. After brief stints in Edinburgh and Newcastle, Oldham was told she was to be moved a third time. Would she prefer to return to Plymouth, or to go elsewhere? By now, Oldham's friends had all been re-deployed, and, with Napier back at sea, she decided to undertake a new adventure. Oldham left for Belfast and began working the plot there, shunting the little ships across the panoramic map in an almost real-time representation of what was occurring at sea.

From the walls of her new base in Belfast Castle, she could watch the ships in the Irish Sea below, slicing to and from Liverpool.

The morning after the bomb, Roberts moved out of Courtfield Gardens, and relocated to Dolphin Square. His new home in Frobisher, one of the estate's thirteen blocks, each named after a famous navigator or admiral, was hit no fewer than twelve times. One incident on 5th November, 1940 involved a two-and-a-half-thousand-pound bomb and left Roberts with a splinter in his neck that had to be surgically removed. Despite the ongoing risks, it provided him with a haven for the remainder of the year.

Three months later, in December 1940, Londoners were preparing for their first hidden Christmas since the Blitz began. Not wanting to provide the Luftwaffe pilots with a twinkling target, there would be no lights strung up on Regent Street this year. In the fields outside London, the Norwegian pines were kept small; there was no room for the six-foot trees in the Blitz basements and bunkers; it was to be, as one American commentator put it, a Christmas of contrasts, of 'holly and barbed wire', of 'guns and tinsel'.[10]

In central London, windows usually filled with baubles were shattered, and stock ruined, many customers dead or departed. The ground, covered in the confetti of war, crunched underfoot. Streamers hung damp in blackened shopfronts. The toys reflected the new martial reality of life in Britain: model Spitfire and Messerschmitt fighter planes, little tin hats and miniature soldiers' uniforms so that children might dress as their serving sisters, brothers and fathers.

There was no ringing of church bells in England that Christmas. In war, their meaning had changed: a toll no longer issued a call to worship, but rather a warning of overheard dangers, a ringing intended not to pull the community into pews, but to drive it underground. Similarly, no Londoners prayed for a chance to see the stars. All they wanted for Christmas was a cloudy night, the weather turned ally, to keep the enemy planes at home.

One night, Roberts' friend Bernard Stubbs asked whether the pair could visit South Kensington underground station. Stubbs, a former BBC correspondent, was, like Monsarrat, compiling notes for a war book. That night he hoped to see the blanketed crowds, shifting and snuffling on the tracks, which had been switched off in order to turn the station into a mass bunker.

'He wanted to grasp the silence,' Roberts wrote in his diary.[II]

When they reached the platform, Roberts counted twelve little Christmas trees. The two men stood by one of the trees, watching the children 'sitting on the bunks in amazement' while their mothers knitted; leaning against the tiles, moustachioed men slept on their backs, still in their caps, upon piles of blankets.

After a while, Roberts spied through the branches a face he recognised, and blanched. The man, wearing plain clothes and cap, and carrying a walking stick, circled the tree. The trio stood in silence till the man asked, in a quiet voice, whether the uniformed Roberts and Stubbs could accompany him back to ground level. At the base of the silent, frozen escalator, the man was recognised by others too. 'There were no cheers,' Roberts wrote. 'But they bowed as he climbed up the middle row of stairs [while] saying "Happy Christmas, Your Majesty."'

At the top of the stairs the king turned, looked back at the crowds and murmured: 'Aren't they wonderful?'

Outside, George VI shook hands with Roberts and Stubbs, climbed into a grey Hillman car and drove away. The two men stood at the entrance to the station, 'quite overcome', until a policeman ordered them to move on. It was to be one of the last nights either man spent in London. Stubbs was posted to the battlecruiser HMS *Hood* and, five months later, along with all but three of the 1,400 crew members, was killed when the ship was sunk during action with Germany's doomed battleship the *Bismarck*. He never completed his book.

On the last day of 1940 the Second Sea Lord sent for Roberts and informed him that he was to be posted to Portsmouth, where there was a shortage of ships and a surplus of men with little to do. Roberts was to train the men as an anti-invasion force. Of leaving London, Roberts wrote in his diary: 'I shall never forget the attack on London, and the unprovoked cruelty let loose on those without weapons, the children, and the aged.'

For the next twelve months Roberts drilled the men in Portsmouth, training them in close combat (how to strangle a man in the dark using a fifteen-inch length of degaussing wire, for example) as well as stalking, infiltration and techniques of nature-craft survival.

'It was better than I expected,' Roberts wrote, 'coming back from the Retired List.'

While Roberts busily turned a ragtag band of men into something approaching a Home Guard force, consternation at the Admiralty in London grew. The grand chart showing losses in the Atlantic loomed like a calendar outlining the schedule of a death sentence. Throughout 1941 Allied shipping losses steadily increased from 2.5 million tons in January to an average of 4 million tons of food, fuel and building materials a month by the autumn. Successively, meat, tea, jam, biscuits, breakfast cereals, cheese, eggs, lard, milk and canned and dried fruit were subject to rationing. The Ministry of Food's Department of Scientific and Industrial Research developed techniques to spray-dry eggs, converting them into a powder that took up just twenty per cent of the shipping space required for fresh eggs. Powders and pastes were designed to approximate scarce or vanished foodstuffs such as bananas and cheese. Hotels and restaurants were limited to offering meals that cost no more than five shillings, and which consisted of no more than three courses, of which only one could contain meat, fish or poultry.[12]

In December 1939, researchers from the University of Cambridge had tested whether Britain could survive with only domestic food production if U-boats forced an end to all imports. After subjecting themselves to a tough regime of work and a minimal diet, the researchers and their volunteers found that they could survive, while noting a 'remarkable' increase in flatulence and a 250 per cent increase in the volume of stools.[13]

If the gassy nation could survive, for a time, on only home-grown produce, clothing and fuel were another matter. On 1st June 1941 clothing was rationed and, by the following summer, Allied shipping losses had led to the abolishment of the basic civilian petrol ration. Thereafter fuel was available only to official users, such as the emergency services, bus companies and farmers.

The majority of the 1,300 merchant ships sunk in 1941[14] were attributed to U-boats and, in this fight, the Allied score looked pitiful: just twelve U-boats were sunk in the first half of the year, with none at all in January, February or July. As such, naval commanders continued to contemplate how, in the face of devastating losses in the Atlantic, they might improve the training of escort-ship crews. Lacking a coherent set of effective tactics, the ships remained woefully unprepared for encounters with U-boats at sea.

During a Trade Protection committee meeting in autumn 1941, one member suggested the idea of a game that could be played aboard ships during training exercises, to simulate a U-boat sighting, and the ensuing cat-and-mouse hunt. A discussion followed on how a game might specifically improve the cooperation of the bridge team, from where a vessel is commanded by the ship's captain, watchkeeper, lookout and pilot so that 'the commanding officer and his anti-submarine control officer were left free to attack the submarine, and relieved of the necessity of attending to details such as the housing of the correct signal'.[15]

At a training facility in Londonderry, the development of a game with precisely this aim was already underway, led by Lieutenant Commander I. M. Carrs, an anti-submarine officer. By early September 1941, a few weeks after the sinking of the SS *Aguila* and its cargo of young Wrens, he had completed a prototype.

His invention was designed to be played not on the floor, like those which Roberts had run prior to the war, but aboard an anchored ship. The crew would take their usual stations while a U-boat sighting and attack was simulated. They would have to respond exactly as they would in a genuine U-boat encounter. The only difference was that the ship would remain stationary; the players would merely imagine it was moving around the water, with its position and the suspected position of the U-boat denoted by tokens on a map. In this way the captain and crew could picture the hunt in their imaginations, while using a 'small device' that worked much like a gyro compass, to help everyone envision what was happening at sea.

The game would come with a box of pre-written orders that the commanding officer on the ship would need to follow, a celluloid protractor engraved with time distancer scales and various turning circles. Lastly, there would be a transparent sheet covered in lines and markings that acted as a 'master plot', to show how the hunt, ideally, should play out. This would be placed over the ship's plot at the end of the game, to allow players to check how closely their actions correlated to the optimal course of action. The exercise was designed to test the commander's tactical ability, as well as to expose any weaknesses in the crew's capacity to work effectively together in the stress of battle.

Unlike previous training exercises the pieces for the game would come in a box much like a board game, mass-produced and sent out to every escort ship in the navy. Its development, Carrs' commanding officer explained in a letter to the director of anti-submarine warfare at the Admiralty, would require the cooperation of various anti-submarine departments. In his letter, the CO requested the loan of young game designer Lieutenant M. E. Impey to join the project for a month from his current posting in Portsmouth, where Roberts was then working. Lastly, the captain wrote, 'The Director of A/S Warfare is requested to obtain provisional approval for six gramophone records.' Carrs' and Impey's game, it seemed, was to have audio accompaniment.

A month later, on 15th October 1941, Impey flew from Londonderry to Liverpool and on to London, arriving at the Admiralty the following day carrying under his arm a prototype of the game. After he outlined its workings, he explained that the gramophone record, which was to be played during the game, was needed to help increase the sense of realism for the ship's crew. This was not to provide a stirring soundtrack, but rather the 'ping' and 'tong' of the ASDIC apparatus, the early form of sonar used to detect submarines, which would be synched up with periods of the game in order to provide participants with an accurate reading of the simulated U-boat's position. For those playing in the plotting room of the ship, away from the portholes, any differences between playing the game and hunting a real-life U-boat would be almost imperceptible.

Six days after Impey's presentation, the game, plainly named 'A Portable Anti-Submarine Trainer', was green-lit for production. Three variants would be produced, one for destroyer crews, one for corvette crews and a third for trawlers, at a cost of £5 per set (not including the extra reels of paper rolls and traces that would be required for any subsequent play-throughs). Such was the expense of manufacturing the ASDIC gramophones that only a few select crews were issued with these. In all, fifty-two sets were made for destroyers, thirty-eight for corvettes and sixty for the trawlers, at a total cost of £750.

Just as Doenitz had used games to prepare for the tactical and operational challenges of the U-boat war in the Atlantic, now games were being used to prepare the Allied crews hunting down those very same U-boats. Carrs' and Impey's game proved a useful resource, revealing snags and pitfalls in the consequence-free arena of play, so that they might be avoided in the consequence-rich arena of battle. But while 'A Portable Anti-Submarine Trainer' was able to improve and perfect an escort crew's procedures, it did nothing to expose the tactics being so effectively deployed by the U-boat captains. And neither did it train escort ships on how to work together. A well-trained crew could only do so much while working as an individual unit. True effectiveness, as the wolfpack had so clearly demonstrated, required teamwork. And for that, a different kind of game was needed.

The spectre of scepticism that hung over the use of games in wartime, even after the success of Carrs' and Impey's work, could not withstand the desperation of the situation at sea. Anything and, indeed, anyone that might give Britain an advantage was worthy of consideration.

★   ★   ★

On the first day of 1942, Roberts was told to report to the Admiralty offices with an overnight bag. On arrival he met two of the navy's most senior officers, the Second Sea Lord, Sir Charles Little, and Admiral Cecil Usborne, the former director of naval intelligence, now an aide to Winston Churchill. Usborne was responsible for overseeing the development of anti-U-boat weapons. To Roberts' astonishment, the men began to describe, 'most clearly', the true extent of Britain's ongoing losses in the Atlantic, and the Allied force's miserable performance in battling the U-boats.

The clues were there, at a granular level, in every bare larder and forsaken storeroom.

'We are not starving,' wrote freelance journalist Maggie Joy Blunt in 1941, 'but our usually well-stocked food shops have an empty and anxious air. Cheese, eggs, onions, oranges, luxury fruits and vegetables are practically unavailable . . . Housewives are having to queue for essential foods . . . Prices are rising . . . the outlook really seems very grim indeed.'[16]

Still, the true picture was, at the time, known to only a clutch of senior naval officers and those who had access to the portentous chart of shipping losses, with its thin red line that showed the upper limit of cost to food and supplies that Britain could afford. Even some senior members of the Cabinet were ignorant of the desperation of the collective situation that Britain faced.

The truth was, Sir Charles Little told Roberts, that German U-boat losses had been gravely exaggerated, and Allied convoy losses equally downplayed. Next Little offered a glimmer of hope. Britain's fortunes in the Atlantic, he said, were poised to change. The capture in May 1941 of an Enigma machine – one of the contraptions used by the Nazis to encode their communications – had hastened the breaking of the code that underpinned the cryptic messages that passed between U-boats at sea and Doenitz at his headquarters.

Messages intercepted by Wrens in Scarborough were passed to Bletchley Park. There a staff of Wrens led by the genius cryptographer Alan Turing would decipher the U-boatmen's messages. Once translated, information was passed to the commander-in-chief of Western Approaches, who could then more intelligently direct his escort ships in the Atlantic either to avoid U-boats when in convoy, or to pursue them. Prior to the breaking of the Enigma code, the position of U-boats could only be added to the plots once they were spotted at sea; now the maps were pocked with U-boat markers, based on messages intercepted as they passed between Doenitz and his captains.

Procedures at Western Approaches had improved too, following the move to Liverpool, and the promotion of Sir Percy Noble to commander-in-chief. Noble was a battleship commander who had served in the Grand Fleet during the First World War. Prior to his arrival in February 1941, officers such as Donald Macintyre, captain of the destroyer HMS *Walker*, had been frustrated by what they viewed as the 'mistaken tactics' issued by Western Approaches command, which often resulted in 'exasperating, futile days'.[17] Like Doenitz, Noble was a brilliant, experienced sea captain, well respected by his fellow officers and someone who, despite his seniority, would readily seek the opinion and insight of his subordinates.

One of Noble's first acts in his new role was to sail the Atlantic aboard an escort ship, HMS *Veteran*, to see for himself the interplay between shore command and those at sea who had to act upon the orders. Noble watched first-hand the way in which command sent conflicting or confusing orders, forbidding senior officers from using their own judgement, and the way in which the set-up often led to vain chases, fragmenting the convoy till, at one point, Noble's was the only escort ship guarding the merchant vessels. He returned to Western Approaches determined to 'bring this nonsense to an end'. The promise was upheld.

'A new feeling of intelligent purpose was in the air,' wrote Macintyre. 'Our sudden dashes across the ocean were not so aimless and each time we returned to harbour it was evident that head-quarters was more on its toes.'

Despite these improvements and advantages, Britain remained at high risk of undernourishment. In many households, hunger had become the dominant sensation of war. While the British could see from intercepted radio transmissions that U-boats were increasingly working together, providing the German vessels with safety in numbers, the specifics of their highly effective tactics could only be guessed at. The Admiralty graph that showed the number of merchant ships the U-boats had sunk each month was drawing close to the threshold of defeat. Pre-war Britain was the recipient of 68 million tons of imports. Usborne revealed to Roberts that this number had now more than halved, to just 26 million tons.[18]

Desperate to find ways in which to reduce the tonnage of inessential imports, and thereby free up space in the holds of merchant ships, Cabinet Office economists frantically noted that animals were being allowed to 'eat shipping space . . . at a rate comparable with the rate at which submarines are destroying it'.[19]

'Unless something was done in the Battle of the Atlantic,' Roberts was told, 'we were going to lose [the war], merely because vital food and war supplies would not arrive.'

Moreover, ships were being sunk by U-boats at a faster rate than they could be built,* and the U-boats were now operating principally at night. Churchill was fretfully preoccupied with the situation. A few months earlier he had set up the Battle of the Atlantic Committee, which had focused its attention on the inefficient running of the docks, where weary and disenfranchised workers had been causing those imports that successfully made it to port to pile up on the dockside. Forty thousand men from the armed forces had been released to work in shipyards repairing a vast backlog of weather- and torpedo-damaged ships. Despite these logistical improvements, Churchill had come to question the efficiency of Allied weapons and technology, as well as the tactics that were being employed whenever a convoy was attacked.

Usborne motioned Roberts out of the office, and the two men went to the canteen to eat. There, over the course of two hours, Usborne explained what was needed of Roberts. He was to take the train to Liverpool, and report to Noble at the new Western Approaches HQ, which had been established in a building called Derby House, nicknamed 'the Citadel'. He was to take charge of a large room on the top floor. Roberts would be assigned a group

---

* The British shipbuilding industry entered a recession in the 1930s from which it had not emerged by the time of war's outbreak.

of young staff. Then, using any and every means necessary, he and his staff were to get to work on the U-boat problem.

Churchill's aide believed that Roberts, who had shown himself to be a talented strategist in Portsmouth and an enthusiastic proponent of games as a way to prepare for war, was the ideal person to evolve anti-U-boat tactics. Moreover, as a gifted communicator he was qualified to train escort commanders in those tactics.

Roberts' new boss, Percy Noble, Usborne warned, was under tremendous pressure and would likely not take kindly to the presence of an officer commandeering part of Derby House who was both his junior and, to make matters worse, retired. Noble had agreed to the formation of the unit, but had told Usborne: 'Don't bother me with it.' You are, Usborne told Roberts, going to be 'unpopular'.

'Plan very quietly,' Usborne advised. 'And correct mistakes later.'[20]

Roberts would command this unit, but would remain on the 'retired list', a distinction that placed him beneath those in active, ongoing service. When the war ended, Roberts was in no doubt that his role would end with it; it was to be a temporary posting. Before Roberts left for the train station, he was led into a nearby office room. Inside, sitting at a desk in harrumphing contemplation, he met Churchill. The prime minister looked up at Roberts.

'Find out what is happening and sink the U-boats,' he said.

Roberts left the building, his mind swirling, and almost missed the midnight train to Liverpool.[21]

IX

The Aces and the Note

In November 1940, just over a year before Roberts caught the train to Liverpool, in a salubrious restaurant in a tiny village outside of Lorient, Germany's trio of U-boat aces gathered to celebrate Kretschmer's recent decoration by Hitler. The restaurant, frequented by German officers, had, it was said, the best food on the Atlantic coast. There was certainly plenty of champagne, subsidised to the officers, who paid soft-drink prices for bottles that in peacetime would be far beyond their budget. By the time coffee and brandy were served, alcohol had played its party trick of exaggerating the personality traits of each man.

At thirty-two, Prien was four years older than the others and keenly disliked by his crew. He would drill the men for hours during shore leave, and piously forbade them from cursing in all but 'the most exceptional circumstances'.[1]

'When a man joins the forces . . . personal liberty is reduced to a minimum,' Prien had written in an autobiography published in Germany during the early years of the war. 'Its place is taken by the word of command, the iron discipline of service under arms. The sailor is always on duty.'[2]

War had hardened Prien's support of Hitler's ideologies, leading him to look down on other U-boat captains, whom he judged to be holding back in their attacks on British convoys. Twenty-eight-year-old 'Silent Otto' Kretschmer was more educated than the others and revered by the men who served under him. One of his crew members told a German newspaper that Kretschmer's 'coolness' gave the crew a feeling of 'absolute security'.[3] Nonetheless, the rigours of war had led Kretschmer to further retreat into brooding.

By contrast, the physical and psychic pressures of combat had only heightened Schepke's boisterousness. Alcohol further inflated the performance of the lithe and striking philanderer, whom Doenitz once described as 'a real thruster',[4] to something approaching the theatrical. The bravado was surely a carapace. The German press wrote regularly and adoringly about the three aces (Kretschmer was once forced to fend off an overbearing Berlin publisher who, mid-war, repeatedly implored the U-boat captain to write his memoirs[5]), which added the burden of celebrity to the already considerable pressures of war. There were whispers among U-boat staff that Schepke had been overstating his reports, claiming that every vessel sunk was a 10,000-tonner, while failing to provide the ship names required to verify the claims.

That night Schepke proposed a bet, designed to settle the pecking order between the three men.

'Let us wager on which of us reaches 250,000 tons first,' said Schepke, all consideration of the devastation to life and families behind the number absent from his mind.[6] If Schepke lost, he continued, he would buy the others as much champagne as they could drink. If he won, however, the others would buy him as much food and wine as he could stomach. The trio shook hands. As Doenitz's first protégées, rivalry, not friendship, had united the men. But if rivalry characterised their time together, it was character that would define each man's destiny.

The three commanders left the restaurant and returned to the Beau Séjour hotel. In the lounge, they drank more coffee. Kretschmer chose the moment to once again try to persuade his rivals of his tactic: sneak past the escort ships in order to attack from within the convoy lanes.[7]

Kretschmer's boat, U-99, was due a refit. The commander was given three weeks' leave, during which Doenitz tried to convince him to give up operational command and instead become chief instructor at the U-boat training school. Doenitz was desperate not to lose his favourite ace. He also wanted Kretschmer to pass on his knowledge and expertise to the next generation of U-boat crews. Kretschmer forcefully rejected the idea. He had neither the political nous nor the ingratiating social flair for shore work; he was at peace only at sea, beneath the realm of politics.

'No man can take what you are doing without a rest – if only for the safety of his crew,' admonished Doenitz, while the pair drove to Paris from Lorient. 'A tired captain is a menace at sea.'[8]

Kretschmer would not relent and, on 22nd February 1941, three days after Prien left port, U-99 departed Lorient harbour. Behind the refitted U-99 a river steamer sailed. On the decks, a brass band played a new composition titled, simply, 'The Kretschmer March'.

On 25th February, Prien spotted a convoy of thirty-nine ships in the North Atlantic, guarded by seven escorts. After being driven off by Allied air patrols, Prien signalled Doenitz in Lorient with a fix on the convoy's location.

Doenitz dispatched three Condor bombers from Gruppe 40 – planes transferred from the Luftwaffe to the U-boat arm following Kretschmer's successful appeal to Hitler during lunch. The planes sank seven merchant ships. Under the cover of darkness, Prien, ever truculent, sank three more. Two days later, Kretschmer arrived on the scene.

A mist had settled on the ocean, and Prien and Kretschmer took advantage of this cover to pursue the badly wounded convoy as it limped toward Halifax. As suddenly as it had descended, the mist lifted to unveil two destroyers, one of which turned and, with great frothing wake, tore toward them. Prien and Kretschmer dove, and the captains and their crews listened as the muffled rumblings of depth-charge explosions sounded overhead.

The depth charge was a rudimentary piece of technology, unchanged since its invention in 1917: a drum filled with explosives that was dropped over the side of a ship with a timer that could be pre-set to explode at a specified depth. It was an imprecise tool in a skirmish that required precision within three-dimensional space: the explosion needed to occur within twenty feet of a U-boat to have any effect on its intended target.*

---

* Problematically for the British, the noise of a depth charge explosion would temporarily 'blind' the ship's ASDIC officer.

Experienced U-boatmen would be able to listen to the smacking sound of a depth charge hitting the water and, based on the assumption that the bomb sank at a rate of four metres per second, use a stopwatch to calculate the depth-setting. Even if they got lucky, it was difficult for the navy to confirm a 'kill', although the smell of oil in the air and the sound of bubbling on the headphones implied success. If they could be spared, two escort ships would sit over the site of the suspected hit for forty-eight hours, a sufficient amount of time that, if the U-boat was merely playing dead, its air supply would run out, forcing the crew to resurface.

That day the two aces evaded the depth charges and, after waiting for the escort ships and the convoy to pass, continued on their Atlantic prowl.

Seven days later, on 6th March, Prien spotted another huge convoy, OB.293, heading westwards. After shadowing the forty-one ships, in the early hours of the next morning Prien led a small pack of four U-boats in an attack. Kretschmer employed his preferred technique, manoeuvring into the centre of the convoy. Once there, he sank two ships. While Kretschmer executed his attack, two of the escort ships, HMS *Camellia* and HMS *Arbutus,* spotted one of the other U-boats, *U-70,* captained by Joachim Matz. For four hours the corvettes hunted Kapitänleutnant Matz and his crew, who had executed a crash dive, dropping fifty-one depth charges, the last of which hit the U-boat, causing it to sink to more than 650 feet.

Matz, realising his U-boat was mortally wounded, blew the ballast tanks and rose to the surface. Such was the pressure inside that, when the hatch was opened, he and a number of his crew were blasted onto the deck. Twenty-six of the crew managed to disembark to await rescue. The other half of the crew were trapped inside as the U-boat sank.

U-70 was not the only victim of the night's action. Kretschmer's *U-99* was pitched and thrown about by the force of the volleys of depth charges, but evaded damage. Prien's *U-47* was, apparently, less fortunate. At some point in the night, Prien's radio went quiet. Doenitz, feeling 'great anxiety', radioed *U-47* asking for a situation report. There was no response.

In the days and weeks that followed Doenitz struggled to

relinquish hope of Prien's survival, choosing to believe that his ace's radio had merely broken and that, any day now, he would surely reappear in Lorient. Understanding the effect that the news would have on public morale, Hitler reportedly forbade the announcement of Prien's death. It was not until 26th April 1941, two months later, that the three stars denoting a loss were placed beside *U-47* on BdU's logs. Then, on 23rd May, the news of Prien's death was formally announced to the nation. The announcement, issued by the high command of the *Wehrmacht*, read:

'The U-boat commanded by Korvetten-Kapitän Günther Prien has failed to return from its last patrol. The vessel must be presumed lost . . . He and his brave crew will live forever in German hearts.'[9] The first of the aces was gone from the fight.

At the time of Prien's death, Captain Donald Macintyre was in Liverpool. Ever since the outbreak of war Macintyre – whose face, with his eyes squeezed into a squint by chubby cheeks, earned him the nickname 'Bulldog' – had longed to hunt U-boats, a showdown that he considered to be 'the perfect expression of a fighting sailor's art'.[10]

As a junior commander Macintyre had been consigned to a fleet destroyer, 'aiming guns at a barely visible target some dozen miles away'. But at the start of 1941, Macintyre was transferred to the Atlantic battlefield as commander of the destroyer HMS *Hesperus*. Early frustrations at the 'wild goose chases' he and his crew were sent on by command at Western Approaches had been quelled by the arrival of Sir Percy Noble at Derby House, who, in Macintyre's view, brought a sense of 'intelligent purpose' to the organisation of convoy escorts that had been previously lacking.

In early March 1941, Macintyre was told he was to be moved to a new ship, HMS *Walker*. The decision was a 'rude shock', and one that he deeply resented. Not only did this mean he would have to leave his experienced crew, which had become 'an efficient fighting team', but his new ship was a 'battered veteran of the First World War'.[11] *Walker* had sustained serious damage in September 1939 when it collided with another vessel 200 miles south-west of Ireland, killing fourteen men. (The first lieutenant shot some of his injured men, who were trapped in the wreckage.[12]) *Walker* had been fitted with a new bow of which Macintyre had grave misgivings.

'I could not have the same confidence in her,' he later wrote.

Nevertheless, in the first week of March, Macintyre departed Gladstone Dock in Liverpool in HMS *Walker* as leader of the newly formed 5th Escort Group, pleased to discover that the majority of the ship's officers were 'experienced and professional' and 'accustomed to searching dark horizons in search of the low-slung silhouette of a U-boat'. *Walker* made its way into the Atlantic, where the remaining two of the U-boat aces lay in wait.

Shortly before midnight on 15th March 1941, Fritz-Julius Lemp, the U-boat captain who had sunk *Athenia* on the first day of the war, sighted Macintyre's ships before they spotted him. Kapitänleutnant Lemp, piloting one of the new Type IXB U-boats, which had greater range and speed than the Type VIIs, reported the sighting to Doenitz in Lorient, then torpedoed the 6,200-ton tanker *Erodona*. Macintyre watched in 'shocked silence' as the tanker exploded, the first of this kind of 'appalling night disaster' that he had seen. He gathered his pack of escort ships, the destroyers *Vanoc*, *Volunteer*, *Sardonyx* and *Scimitar*, and the corvettes *Bluebell* and *Hydrangea*, and staged a haphazard search for the U-boat, to no avail.

Frustrated and fearful, Macintyre ordered a drastic alteration of course. For a while the evasive tactic worked. Then, at 22:00, Kretschmer and Schepke found the convoy. Kretschmer again penetrated the convoy's columns to attack from point-blank range, scoring direct hits with seven of the eight torpedoes he fired, sinking five ships and damaging a sixth. It would be the single most destructive salvo of the war.[13] In the dense smoke issued from the burning tankers, Kretschmer hid, plotting a course back to Lorient.

As the ocean lit up with the fires of devastation, Macintyre was 'near to despair', fumbling for some kind of tactic to 'stop the holocaust'.[14] The escort ships frothed to and fro, dropping so many depth charges over suspected U-boat positions that the ASDIC operators were unable to distinguish barrel from boat.

Two hundred feet below, Schepke and his crew waited. The men counted thirty-four explosions, each one a little closer than the last, ratcheting the tension. The thirty-fifth was a direct hit. As the vessel rocked with shattering force, the lights went out and whistling leaks sprang along the length of the boat. *U-100* began to sink, stern first, to a depth of 750 feet – deeper than any surviving U-boat had gone before.

Schepke, afraid not only that the sound of the hissing would be picked up by the destroyers, but also that the U-boat's hull might be crushed like a tin can under a jackboot, shouted for his crew to surface, in the hope that they might slink away in the chaos. As *U-100* broke the waves, Schepke opened the hatch and took the U-boat's deck gun in his hands.

Just after three o'clock in the morning, the ASV operator on HMS *Vanoc*, which was equipped with one of the first seaborne radar devices, reported contact 1,000 yards on the starboard side. *Vanoc*'s captain, Jim Deneys, judged his speed to be sufficient to attempt to ram the stricken U-boat. He steered the destroyer hard toward the target, cutting the engines five seconds before collision.

As he spotted the incoming destroyer from the conning tower Schepke called for full power, but neither *U-100*'s diesel nor electric motors would spark. After a cold moment, he called down to his crew: 'It is all right, the destroyer is going to pass under our stern.'[15]

It was a miscalculation. At 03:18 the destroyer struck *U-100* midships. Schepke was crushed between the U-boat and *Vanoc*'s bow. In the years that followed, the ace's death was embellished with gruesome, outlandish detail: cleaved legs, a torso arcing through the air. Indisputably, Schepke's body sank into the ocean, and did not surface. Just six crew members, including Lieutenant Siegfried Lister, a torpedo officer who before the war frequently went yachting with English friends, survived the attack to record his commander's final words.

While *Vanoc* began to pick up survivors from the water, *Walker* circled protectively. Kretschmer remained close by, on the surface, trying to sneak away. From the bridge, Kretschmer's lieutenant Heinrich Petersen spotted *Walker* a few yards away. Petersen, believing the U-boat must have been spotted, ordered a crash dive. In fact, none of *Walker*'s crew had seen the Germans, who likely could have escaped had they remained surfaced.

Instead, shortly afterwards Macintyre's sonar operator shouted 'Contact! Contact!', having detected a 'ping'. Walker dropped six depth charges over Kretschmer's U-99, at least one of which was close enough to damage the vessel, breaking the crucial main depth gauge, which indicated the U-boat's position in the water. With both lights and gauges out, Kretschmer was double-blind in the dark, and sinking. At a depth of around 700 feet, the oily water rising inside the U-boat, Kretschmer blew all of the surviving ballast tanks, and with ear-popping speed U-99 shot to the surface.

At 03:52 a searchlight beam from Vanoc illuminated U-99 as it broke the water, and gun crews from both ships fired tracer bullets, lighting up the night sky in what Macintyre later described as a showy, but inaccurate, display. By now Kretschmer knew that U-99's engines were broken, and the steering gear mangled. He issued a final, unencrypted message to Doenitz: 'Two destroyers. Depth charges. 53,000 tons. Capture, Kretschmer.'

Next Kretschmer opened the hatch and, as U-99 began to loll on its side, sat in the shelter of the conning tower while drawing on a cigar. His men, as devoted as ducklings, lined up along the U-boat before him. Finally, Kretschmer ordered scuttling charges to be set, to ensure that no British could board the U-boat and extract useful documents and cyphers. The door to the compartment in which the charges were kept, however, was jammed shut.

Kretschmer stood and the men listened while their captain, hanging from the guard rail, apologised that he would not be able to deliver them safely home. Then he warned them that they might need to endure the freezing Atlantic water before being rescued. Finally, he sent his men below decks to retrieve their warmest clothes and await the order to abandon ship.

Kretschmer knew what it was like to abandon a U-boat. While carrying out training exercises in the Baltic two years before the war, he had been fiddling with a faulty stopper that was leaking water into the muzzle of the U-boat's gun, when he heard the angry hiss of air being released from the ballast tanks and the sound of the engines coughing to life. When Kretschmer reached the conning tower to head below deck, he found the hatch clamped tight. He stamped on it, hoping the sound might be heard below. No one answered and, after a few seconds, the U-boat began to dive. Kretschmer was lifted into the water. Grasping the periscope, he allowed the force of the rising sea to slide him up to its tip. Now, holding his breath, Kretschmer pressed his face against the eye lens to let his fellow crew members inside know they had left him behind.

Thirty-five feet below the surface, Kretschmer's lungs were burning. He let go, to return to the surface, where he struggled in his cold, waterlogged clothes to stay afloat. When his boat finally surfaced, Kretschmer was so weak he had to be lifted onto the deck.

This was the memory to which U-99's captain returned when the boat's stern jolted downwards, apparently sinking of its own accord, and threw half the crew into the sea.

Kretschmer hauled his first lieutenant, Petersen, from the hatch, while ordering him to sling a portable battery flashlamp over his shoulder in order to signal to the destroyer crew for rescue. From the lilting side of the U-boat, Kretschmer dictated the message: 'From captain to captain . . . Please pick up my men drifting towards you in the water. I am sunking [sic].'[16]

Walker, its scrambling nets lowered, approached U-99 at a suspicious crawl, unaware that Kretschmer had expended all of the U-boat's torpedoes. Some of the men hauled aboard were in the 'final stages of exhaustion'[17], as Macintyre later recalled, and needed assistance. Kassel, the petty officer who had given pineapple and coffee to the concussed Englishman Joseph Byrne the previous year, seemed to be dead, until, having been laid in the ship's warm galley, he miraculously woke. All but three of U-99's crew – the only men to serve under Kretschmer to lose their lives – were recovered.

Kretschmer, still wearing his white, brass-bound cap, had been hanging from the scrambling nets and counting his men as they climbed up. Now, with the prize pair of Zeiss binoculars presented to him by Doenitz still slung around his neck, he attempted to climb the nets. His waterlogged boots, and the drag of the water as Walker began to increase its speed, held him back and, for a moment, he thought that he might be forced to let go.

U-99's boatswain saw what was happening and scrambled down the nets to help his captain. With legs buckling, Kretschmer stood on deck to find a Colt .45 ignobly pointed at his face. He moved to throw the binoculars overboard, preferring that they be lost to the sea than go to an enemy sailor, but Peter Sturdee, a sub lieutenant aboard *Walker*, caught and passed them to Macintyre. Macintyre examined the glasses and, seeing how much better they were than his British pair, placed them around his neck, where they stayed for the remainder of the war.*

The rescued men were searched, and any documents deemed to be of interest seized. Macintyre's crew found newspaper and magazine clippings lauding the exploits of the U-boats, which one article termed 'Sea Wolves'. A sketched drawing was taken from another man. This document was of a different category to the clippings. It showed the crude outline of a convoy with a U-boat attacking from *within* the columns, a hand-drawn illustration of the tactic that had sent so many people, and hundreds of thousands of tons of food and supplies, to the ocean bed. Here, depicted in a few lines, was the secret to the U-boats' success.

Kretschmer was escorted to the Captain's day cabin, where he sank into a chair and dropped into a dreamless sleep while, outside, a sentry guarded the door.

On the morning of 21st March 1941, HMS *Walker* pulled in to Liverpool with the captain and the majority of the crew of the most notorious U-boat of the war lined up along the ship for all to see.

Kretschmer's capture had not been kept a secret. While sailing toward Liverpool, Macintyre received a signal from Admiralty asking for a positive identification of the U-boat crews that had been sunk or captured; Churchill, the signal explained, wanted to make an announcement in the House of Commons. As Macintyre moored at the Prince's Landing Stage, a dock 'usually reserved for more lordly vessels',[18] he saw Sir Percy Noble and the high-ranking members of the Western Approaches staff lined up along shore. Kretschmer, wearing his leather jacket and peaked cap, strode down

---

* Fourteen years later Macintyre returned the binoculars to Kretschmer, which now bore the conciliatory inscription, etched on a silver plate: 'Returned to Otto Kretschmer – A Gallant Foe.'

the gangway to be greeted by two armed soldiers. As the ace was escorted into an army station wagon to take him to a cell where he would be placed in solitary confinement, his watching crew, still paraded on *Walker's* deck, stood to attention and saluted.

There was no chauffeured comfort for the crew of *U-99*, who were now marched through the bomb-wrecked Liverpool streets to Lime Street station, where they were to take a train for London. News had spread and by the time they started their march of shame, spitting, jeering crowds – mainly women – lined the streets.[19] Almost everyone knew someone who had been injured or killed in Blitz or battle and, in these moments, the forty-two members of *U-99's* crew symbolised the source of every wound and indignity of the past two years. This was the collective grief of the rabble and, for the U-boatmen, it seemed at times as though the police cordons could not hold back the crowd.

Josef Kassel later said that he had been more afraid for his life while marching past these baying women than he had while steadying himself in the U-boat as it rocked with the violent energy of depth charges a few days earlier.[20] So fevered and disruptive was the demonstration that the line of traipsing men missed the train and, to their dismay, were forced to march back into Liverpool again – to Walton Gaol, where, six months earlier, a German bomb had partially demolished a wing, killing twenty-two inmates.

That same day, one of *Vanoc's* officers submitted the official report into what had happened at sea. In stark terms and with clear time stamps it laid out the key events of the night of 17th March, as well as highlighting crew members who the captains believed should be considered for official commendation.

One unassuming bullet point also mentioned the fact that *U-99's* crew had been searched and, among their possessions, an illustration of the point-blank tactics pioneered by Kretschmer had been found. The importance of the document apparently evaded those who read the report. The revelation was neither noted nor communicated to the escort commanders. The three aces were gone, but their pioneering tactic remained in play. Roberts, when he arrived in Liverpool, would have to discover it for himself.

X

The Citadel

Nine and a half months later, Roberts disembarked the train at Liverpool station in the early hours of 2nd January 1942. By day, great shafts of light would funnel through the Gothic arched windows, partitioning the steamy air. At night, however, Roberts was forced to plod, squinting, across a dark concourse, past the Nestlé chocolate machines and, beside them, the reprimanding weight-testers. He had not slept. Churchill's commission was thrilling; it finally brought Roberts in from the cold, much closer to the heart of matters than he had been before his illness. But it was also a high-risk assignment for a man for whom the question of legacy had, at just forty-one, become a preoccupation.

Roberts' task was threefold: discover the secret of how the U-boats were operating; develop effective countermeasures; and, finally, teach these new tactics to any and every captain who sailed the Atlantic. Tuberculosis may have robbed Roberts of the chance to serve at sea, but it had, in this unlikely way, provided him with an opportunity, one by which he could make his presence felt on every destroyer and corvette on the ocean.

Roberts stepped into a beleaguered city. Liverpool's buildings huddled forlornly, their roofs a thatch of splintered beams, their blown-out windows giving the appearance of hollow eyes and haunted mouths, multistorey expressions of architectural dismay. Not even the city's grand cathedral had been spared the Blitzing: one night a few months earlier a German bomb had pierced the roof of the south-east transept, bounced off an inner brick wall and exploded in mid-air to create a multicoloured downpour of stained glass.

From the beginning of the war the Luftwaffe's bombers had targeted Liverpool. But in the twelve months leading up to Roberts' arrival the bombing had intensified, in part because the Nazis suspected that the city housed a secret control bunker from which the Battle of the Atlantic was being orchestrated. Their suspicion was correct. On 7th February 1941 Western Approaches command, the headquarters from which the protection of shipping in the North- and South-western Approaches to the British Isles was directed, had moved from Plymouth to Liverpool. The city was better placed for operational control of ships using the Clyde and Mersey. By the end of the war more than ninety per cent of all the war material brought into Britain had passed through Liverpool's eleven miles of quays.

Liverpool's Harbour Board officials were, as one lieutenant put it, 'kind and remarkably tolerant', considering a naval base had been superimposed onto working docks.[1] By the time of Roberts' arrival, Liverpool was not only bomb-wrecked but also unprecedentedly busy. An average of four convoys, sometimes consisting of as many as sixty ships, arrived in the city every week. Some were damaged from brushes with U-boats, others by the extremities of the Atlantic weather. The ever-pressing need to resupply and repair ships put tremendous strain on both Liverpool's facilities and workforce. More than 20,000 men and women were involved in ship repair on Merseyside, often working twenty-four-hour shifts to mend both merchant and naval ships in an effort to get them back to sea as quickly as possible.

In the middle of the night Roberts walked across the open-air square toward the new Western Approaches HQ, a bland and nondescript eleven-storey office block known as the Exchange Buildings situated behind Liverpool's Town Hall. It was here that, in centuries past, Liverpool's merchants, nestled in the nook formed by the U-shaped complex, had carried out their business. Slave traders exchanged business cards on which the flag of their ship was drawn, a practice known as 'trading on the flags'.[2] The trading area would become unworkably muddy so was eventually paved over.

Derby House was the main building in the complex. Having been chosen as Western Approaches HQ, it had been adapted with a two-metre-thick concrete ceiling, above the military command. Roberts looked up, in the half-light, at the building that was to become his home for the remainder of the war. The west wing had already been partially demolished to build the Atlantic Hotel, work that was never completed. On the east side Derby House was pocked and blackened, having been successfully hit by German incendiaries. The entrance was fenced, sand-bagged and guarded by Marine sentries.[3] Roberts showed his papers to the armed guard and made his way down into the basement through a winding corridor and, finally, out into the grand Operations Room, the nerve centre of the Battle of the Atlantic.

Derby House was designated HMS *Eaglet* (all naval shore establishments are treated as ships, in order that their occupants abide by naval rules) and was unofficially known as 'the Citadel'. The scores of Wrens who worked there, however, nicknamed it 'the Dungeon', a reference to its warren-like corridors and rooms – more than a hundred in total, covering around 5,000 square metres – and the mood-darkening, skin-blanching dimness of the place.

The Operations Room where Roberts now stood was the exception: a cathedral of a space and the heart of the building, a place so secretive that, when the cleaners came to Derby House each morning, a curtain was drawn across the windows overlooking the room, to ensure they did not peep.[4]

It was from here that Sir Percy Noble, commander-in-chief of Western Approaches, ran a tuned operation. His mezzanine office overlooked the main plotting room, and faced a twenty-foot-high situational map of the Atlantic that stretched from the floor to the ceiling. The sea was painted dark green and land masses biscuit brown.* One account claims that the surface was magnetised.[5] Onto this map, which was cork-backed,[6] a plotter Wren standing on a wheeled, telescoping ladder would place markers to indicate the known, estimated or suspected locations of Allied convoys, German wolfpacks, escort groups and air patrols. (A duplicate plot was set up in the nearby mansion Knowsley Hall as a fall-back if Derby

---

* The Derby House plot can be seen briefly in the 1944 colour-film docudrama *Western Approaches*.

House was destroyed,[7] and while the plot at Derby House was the largest and most imposing of all, similar wall plots focused on smaller areas of the ocean could be found at coastal bases around the British Isles, from Portland to Belfast, where Christian Oldham worked.)

Seven pieces of key information were maintained at all times on the plot. Most importantly, there was the known position of all Allied ships and convoys currently in the Atlantic, and the planned routes of these convoys,* each marked in different coloured elastic, depending on their speed and ultimate destination. Each convoy was represented by a plastic clip showing its name and number, and into this clip were slotted the names of all the escort vessels on cardboard slips: yellow for destroyers, dark red for frigates and corvettes, green for trawlers and pale grey for 'sloops'. Air cover, if it existed, was indicated by a small plane token. Once every four hours the positions of the ships were moved along the stringed routes, assuming there were no U-boat attacks to upset the planned course.

Next there was the Admiralty's 'best guess' of the position of any U-boats known to be at sea. This information was often taken from coded messages intercepted by the Wrens working beneath Scarborough racecourse (a U-boat transmission would immediately be known by its telltale signal 'Dah di di di dah') and decoded by Wrens working at Bletchley Park. Once relayed to Western Approaches, it would be carried into the Operations Room by messenger Wrens and, finally, added to the plot by the Wrens plotters – life-and-death information passed along a chain of competent young women, stretched across Britain.

Initially, a U-boat was marked up as a white lozenge-shaped symbol on the plot, and when its position was confirmed, usually following a positive sighting at sea by an Allied ship, the marker was changed to a black lozenge. The position of ships and convoys at the moment of a U-boat attack was also added to the plot, along with a red ship-shaped symbol to denote the final position of any

---

* The route of a particularly sensitive convoy was only marked on the plot after the ships had departed.

vessel that was sunk. Finally, the direction and speed of the wind was shown as a white arrow, the number of 'tails' indicating its force. The positions of the ships and U-boats were rarely precise. A good fix was considered to be a location within a forty- to fifty-mile radius, and even fixes that could be up to 200 miles out were logged.

Every night Noble stood at the window of his glass-fronted office, read the sweep of the ocean on the wall opposite, and saw the dramas represented by the pins, string and tokens. At a glance he could see the thousands of men and millions of tons of shipping under his direction. From this information, he would decide how and where to deploy his fleet. Officially, Western Approaches HQ had no say over the routes that convoys took, although the Admiralty often agreed to its suggested diversions.[8] Such alterations were calculated in the Convoy Room, which was papered with gnomonic projections, sundial-like maps used for plotting great-circle paths.

'There was much conferring of staff at times of crisis,' recalled the Derby House plotter Mary Hall. 'We were given the resulting changes of route to put up on the main plot as quickly as possible.'

Finally, Noble would issue his commands via a brass speaking tube, similar to those used to communicate on ships.

'It was a strange feeling going down about half a mile into the ground,' Patricia Anne Parkyn, another plotter at Derby House, later recalled of her work. 'I loved climbing up and down the long ladders, sticking pins in hopefully the right places, being watched – like a monkey in the zoo – by countless VIPs and brass hats behind the glass wall opposite.'[9]

Wren ratings worked one of two watches, either from 08:00 to 18:00 (ten hours) or 18:00 to 08:00 (fourteen hours). The officers worked for the same length of time but changed watches an hour later than the ratings.

'During these watches we had time off for meals, and a bit of a snooze at night if we were lucky,' recalled Carlisle. Due to the long hours, a Sun Ray Treatment Room was eventually installed at Derby House to help compensate for the fifty-hour work weeks spent underground. Rather than use this, Carlisle would go out into Liverpool during her lunch break, in order that she might see some sunlight that day.

'I took sandwiches midday and went on a ferry across the Mersey and back,' she wrote. 'It was fascinating to see the ships one had been plotting, some looking a bit battered. One stormy day I was the only passenger on the top deck and the dear ferryman came out of his wheelhouse for a chat. "Real sailors' weather isn't it, miss?" I loved that.'[10]

Churchill – who had served as First Lord of the Admiralty during the First World War and the first nine months of the Second, prior to becoming prime minister – had a profound interest in naval matters. He made frequent visits to Derby House, often using them as an excuse to parade through Liverpool. On one visit Norman Robertson, chauffeur to the commander-in-chief at Derby House, was told to collect Churchill from the Adelphi Hotel and drive him to Gladstone Dock to inspect the crew of an escort ship. Robertson waited outside the hotel, his car flying the flag of St George. When Churchill emerged, he refused to walk down the steps to the car, insisting that it be swapped for an open-top vehicle to enable him to wave at the assembled crowds. A Wolseley owned by the police was found, and with Churchill finally in the car, Robertson raced to make up the lost time, aware that the sailors were waiting on the cold dockside.[11]

The prime minister's presence was felt in Derby House even when he was not there in person. A dedicated hotline housed in a soundproof booth, just outside the main plotting room, connected Western Approaches to Churchill. With a dedicated guard, the black rotary telephone featured a bright red handset and was known as MATE, or multiple access telephone equipment. It linked Derby House to Churchill's war office and nine other favoured lines and was deemed so important that it had its own back-up battery power supply. This was in addition to Derby House's emergency generator, which was powered, with a flourish of cosmic irony, by a diesel engine taken from a German U-boat captured during the First World War.

The Wrens in the Operations Room would be the first to know when things went wrong, and this knowledge would spread quickly, either through Derby House or back at the women's shared quarters in Ackerleigh House on the outskirts of Liverpool. The building, a tram ride away in Sefton Park, was named after Kathleen Ackerleigh, the first Liverpool chief Wrens officer, who died aged forty-six in a traffic accident in September 1940.

'We slept in "cabins" on double bunks, all with the Admiralty blue and white anchor covers – nice and shipshape,' recalled Carlisle of her time in Ackerleigh House. 'I was first in a huge noisy room with some odd bods indeed.'

Like Roxane Houston, the Derby House cypher Wren who mourned her friend Isabel Milne Home's death on the *Aguila*, the on-duty Wrens were deeply affected whenever the human stories behind the coloured string and pins on the plotting wall were revealed. Late one night Dorothy Carroll, an eighteen-year-old leading Wren who worked as a typist in Percy Noble's office, was called to the chief of staff's office. There, the captain informed her that thirty-four ships in a Russian convoy had been sunk.

'He was exceedingly sad and said he felt we'd lost the war,' she later recalled.[12] The officer, Captain Neville Lake, who had narrowly escaped sinking during a U-boat battle in the First World War,[13] presented Dorothy with a report of the engagement, which she was to type up. It ended with the phrase 'It's Doenitz who's done it.'

As she returned to Noble's office, 'feeling thoroughly dejected', Dorothy called in at the subterranean canteen in Derby House and bought her first packet of cigarettes.

There was little emotional respite for those on duty, even when the news was personal. One morning at around two o'clock, the Derby House plotter Patricia Anne Parkyn was handed a telegram informing her that her brother, Mytton, had been killed in action. Parkyn still had ten hours left on her shift, and there was no reprieve.

The preparations at Derby House, not only to become the directorial hub for the Battle of the Atlantic but also to fit the site for the 1,000 or so staff who would work and often sleep there, were not without controversy. During construction, Wren officers requested that the living quarters at Derby House be divided into cubicles rather than dormitories. This simple request was led by Angela Goodenough, the Wren officer responsible for insisting that as high a standard of accommodation and welfare be laid down as was compatible with necessary economy. Laughton Mathews described her as 'very determined' and as having a 'happy knack of getting her own way with male colleagues without arousing rancour'.

In the case of Derby House, which had on-site accommodation for those who needed to stay the night, however, rancour was most certainly aroused. In a March 1941 report by the chief staff officer to Percy Noble, Captain E. Bush wrote that 'the standard of living expected by the WRNS, especially the senior WRNS officers, is much too high'. Bush continued with the suggestion that a lecture be prepared for Wrens officers in which the women were made aware of 'the standard of living which naval officers cheerfully put up with both at sea and ashore in time of war'.

Captain Bush's report, for which he earned a commendation, received the full-throated support of the Civil Service. A memo marked 'secret' and attached to the front of the report described the attitude of Wrens officers in the matter as nothing short of 'deplorable' and asked that 'anything that can be done to correct such an outlook in these ladies would be much appreciated'.[14]

Angela Goodenough was having none of this. In a brisk response, she wrote: 'The remark is not understood. The large expenditure . . . was not due to the provision of a high standard of living but to the provision of the splinter-proof sleeping accommodation.' Moreover, she explained, the Wrens were never 'shown the drawings' nor 'allowed to visit the houses until the work was almost completed'. Had they been consulted, Goodenough added, she would not have been in favour of providing this kind of sleeping accommodation 'for officers and ratings who already have to spend their working hours in artificially ventilated and lighted spaces underground'.

The Civil Service responded coolly to Goodenough's note: 'The report will require further examination.' In truth, the Wrens did have slightly better living conditions than the men, with a little more cubic area per head and more space for their belongings although, as Laughton Mathews put it, 'certainly no luxury'.

'What we asked for seemed to us the minimum for a decent

living,' she wrote. When, later, a naval officer bluntly asked Laughton Mathews, 'Why should the Wrens have better conditions than the men?' she replied: 'I can't think why. But I'm not responsible for the men.'

None of this hidden drama was known to Roberts when he arrived, but he had his own pressures to contemplate. That night he was presented with a note, informing him of the whereabouts of his quarters, along with an invitation to meet Sir Percy Noble the following morning. Roberts left Derby House still not yet ready for sleep. He walked the streets, contemplating the magnitude of everything he now faced.

The next morning, Roberts returned to Derby House for his meeting with Sir Percy Noble. He needn't have felt any sense of trepidation. Derby House had become, as the war journalist Terence Robertson later put it, the place where 'all the misfits of the navy had congregated'.[15] Scores of officers who had been passed over for promotion, or who, like Roberts, had been invalided out of service by illness, had wound up there. He would be at home among the lost men who had found in war the renewed purpose that, when combined with boiler-room pressure, occasionally agitates brilliance.

Roberts met Sir Percy Noble in the commander's glass-fronted office, overlooking the Operations Room, with its industrious Wrens. The admiral was greying but still youthful, and wore his authority with, as one observer put it, 'naturalness'.[16] That day, however, just as Usborne had warned, Noble was in a hostile mood.

'I thought the Admiralty were sending me a captain,' he said, woundingly. (Later, when Noble read a letter of recommendation outlining Roberts' success at the Portsmouth tactical school, he apologised for this comment.[17]) Noble explained that, on Usborne's instruction, Roberts was to be given the entire top floor of Derby House, recently vacated by Tate & Lyle sugar company, comprising eight rooms.*

---

* Some of the surviving Wrens who worked at Derby House recall that, in addition to the top floor office, WATU also ran games in a temporary building erected in Exchange Flags Square.

Noble – fifty-two with a headful of hair and a trim waistline – was well liked and respected by his staff, whose opinions he would often seek regardless of their rank or seniority. Still, he couldn't quite mask his scepticism toward Roberts' enterprise. What, precisely, did Roberts intend to do with this school? Would it be for research, demonstrations, or something else?

Roberts explained his intention to develop a game that would enable the British to understand why the U-boats were proving so successful in sea battles and facilitate the development of counter-tactics. Finally, Roberts said, the game would become the basis for a school, where those fighting at sea could be taught the tactics. With just a few adjustments, Roberts explained, his wargame could be used for either analysis or training.

Still unsure of how play, of all things, might achieve all this, Noble gave his reluctant approval.

'Well,' Roberts recorded his new commander-in-chief saying. 'You can carry on but don't bother me with it.' Then, as if to underscore his disdain, he added: 'Perhaps you can run occasional courses for half a dozen Reserve officers?'[18] Stinging from Noble's remark, which reignited the dismay that he felt from his earlier dismissal from the navy, Roberts laboured his way upstairs to the top floor of the building.

His plan was simple. Using the floor as a giant board, just like the one he had used when teaching tactics at Portsmouth, he would design a game that approximated a wolfpack attack on a convoy in the Atlantic. One team would play as the escort commanders, the other as the U-boat captains. They would take turns to make their moves, firing torpedoes, dropping depth charges, the U-boats diving and surfacing to make their attacks, the escort ships wheeling around in great arcs as each side hunted the other.

Not knowing how long the war would last, or how the U-boat tactics might evolve as it progressed, Roberts was eager that his game could adapt to changes in circumstances. The scenarios for these games wouldn't be pulled only from Roberts' imagination. They would also be based on real battles that occurred at sea to allow participants to see why the escort commanders acted the way that they did, and whether they might have lost fewer convoy ships and sunk more U-boats had they done things differently.

This was Roberts' masterstroke. By repeatedly playing through recent action at sea and using a game to understand the situation from all angles, he would be in a strong position to see where the British commanders had misunderstood the U-boats' behaviour. The process would enable him to formulate the first universal set of defensive tactics for the navy to use against U-boats, encouraging escort ships to work together like team-mates, rather than individuals.

Before they could begin, however, Roberts needed supplies: string, chalk, great sheets of canvas, linoleum that could turn the floor itself into a game board. He also needed a willing and able staff to help him. More than anything, though, he needed information. It had been just one day since Roberts had learned the true extent of the navy's failure at sea to date, and the sheer scale of the U-boats' success. Now he needed first-hand accounts from sailors who had survived encounters with U-boats, information that could be sifted for clues as to what was going wrong.

Later that day, Roberts met the first of the officers who he had been assigned: Gerald Cousins DSC, an acting commander who, at six feet five, must have either irritated or intimidated Roberts as, in his diary, he described the man as 'fifteen years older than me and showed it' and, crueller still, 'quite dull of brain'. Then there was Lieutenant Commander Higham, a submariner who had been sunk and hauled out of the sea on a rope earlier in the war. 'This hadn't done him much good,' Roberts wrote, with a similar tartness to that which he'd directed at Cousins. In fact, Roberts added, 'he was gross'.

Faced with these incompetents, Roberts requested the transferral of an old friend, Chief Signalman Bernard Rayner, with whom he had worked at the Portsmouth Tactical School, to the nascent unit. Rayner, at least, knew how to run games. Roberts could only hope that the Wrens he was being sent would make up the considerable shortfall.

At Wrens headquarters Nancy Osborne, the forbiddingly bright, fastidious Australian administrator whom Vera Laughton Mathews had appointed the officer of the headquarters staff of the Wrens, ran her finger down the list of names in front of her.

Osborne had graduated from the University of Sydney with a first-class degree in 1921, an MA in 1924, and was the first person, male or female, to be awarded the University Medal in English.[19] She had a peculiar knack for choosing the right Wren for the right job. Since assuming the responsibility for appointing Wrens officers, she had, almost by a process of osmosis from Laughton Mathews and her formidable memory, come to learn the various attributes and skills of hundreds of young Wrens.[20]

This project, however, was a little different to the usual. Derby House, she had been told, needed Wrens officers to join a new project in Liverpool, developing a game that would reveal the secrets of the U-boat tactics. The women needed to be whip-smart – of this Osborne was certain – but what more precise qualities would equip them for this unusual task?

If the Wrens were to calculate the positions of imaginary ships and U-boats, Osborne reasoned, then they would need a keen mind for numbers. And if they were to keep pristine records of how particular imaginary attacks played out, who missed whom, and by how much, then they would also need to be good with record-keeping. Who better than Jean Laidlaw, the assiduous twenty-one-year-old former Sea Ranger and chartered accountant with whom she shared an office and who, late one night a few weeks earlier, had been the first to notice that the Wrens had passed 10,000 members?

Next Osborne picked Laura Janet Howes, who had come to England from Antigua just four years earlier. Howes, a stylish perfectionist, who was known to all as 'Bobby' after a minor film actor of the day, was a mathematical wunderkind. At school, when her teachers were off sick Howes would teach the class maths in their stead.[21] At the outbreak of war, Howes wrote to her father in Montserrat to ask if she could return home.

'Don't even think of coming home,' he replied. 'Serve your country.'

Howes, believing the Wrens to have the most handsome of the women's service uniforms, summarily signed up.

Elizabeth Drake was next. Drake was already serving at Derby House at the time as a plotter on the map facing Percy Noble's glass-fronted office,[22] a fact that would typically disqualify her from a transfer as Wrens were rarely moved from one job to another within the same shore establishment. Osborne saw from Drake's records, however, that her father Charles worked as an actuary for the Prudential Assurance company. Just as Nicholas Monsarrat had been chosen for the role of ship's surgeon based on his father's vocation, Drake was chosen to work with Roberts based on the assumption that an aptitude for mathematics, like height or temper, runs in the family. Drake, who had spent a year at finishing school in Paris, was also an expert plotter.

Finally, Osborne chose a sportswoman: Nancy Wales.* Nan, as she was known to her friends, was older than the others at twenty-seven. Born in Hull, she had moved with her family to the nearby town of Anlaby at the outbreak of war, working at her grandfather's printing works, while keeping the accounts for her father's launderette.[23] After she joined the Wrens in 1941, she had served at the shore establishment HMS *Beaver* before undergoing the familiar officer training course at Greenwich, which she passed with the highest distinction. Wales was a formidable tennis player and competed in badminton at county level. Hockey, however, was her true passion; two years later she would play for Lancashire, and then earn the unique distinction of being the only player to go on to play for their arch rivals Yorkshire, a team she captained for many years. Nobody in the Wrens, Osborne reckoned, understood team tactics quite like Nan Wales.

With her squad of officers complete, six junior Wrens, known as 'ratings', were chosen to handle the more administrative side of the game-playing. Two were secretaries, two coders and two messengers. Then she sent off the orders that would divert the course of each young woman's war and, in many cases, their life thereafter.

★　★　★

* Not all of Osborne's choices were ideal. Roberts took an instant dislike to the most senior member of the group, whose name, he wrote, he would 'prefer to forget,' and which accordingly went un-recorded in his diaries. She stayed only a short time and, following 'a social error', as Roberts put it, was relieved of her duties, to be replaced by Nancy Wales.

Following the bruising humiliation of his inaugural meeting with a dismissive Sir Percy Noble, and the dismay he'd felt at being presented with men he considered 'dull of brain' and 'gross', Roberts may have felt quite alone. Certainly, neither of the men he had been sent would last long. They were, as Roberts put it, 'vastly out of date and cantankerous'. He was not yet aware that an elite team of young women, on whose nous and support he would come to depend, had already been assembled.

The Western Approaches Tactical Unit, or WATU, had its team.

XI

Raspberry

On a freezing morning in early 1942, Janet Okell arrived at Western Approaches HQ for her first day at work in a fluster. The nineteen-year-old[1] Liverpudlian, who had lived her entire life less than ten miles from Derby House, on the banks of the River Dee in Park West, Heswall, didn't know that she was supposed to have already collected her Wren uniform.

As she passed through the rasping, gas-blocking mesh curtains into the concrete-roofed bunker, Wrens in pristine shirts and ironed skirts looked her up and down. Not only was she improperly dressed, Okell – whose curly bobbed hair made her look as school-girlish as she felt – was lost in the building's warren of cable-laden corridors. With a gathering sense of dismay, she wandered until a passing Marines corporal noticed her distress and took pity on her.

By the time Roberts arrived to collect her, Okell was in tears. She looked up into the gaunt but kindly face of her new boss, who handed her his handkerchief. She thanked him and blew her nose.

Roberts guided Okell – one of four young ratings who had been selected to support his crack team of officers in setting up the tactical school – to a heavy wooden door marked with the letters 'WATU'. Between the 'A' and the 'T', there was a circular badge, inscribed with the word 'Tactician'. At the centre of the badge was a miniature chessboard, showing a white king forlornly hemmed in by two black knights, castles and bishops, and below it the cap-italised declaration 'CHECKMATE'.

The badge had once belonged to HMS *Tactician*, a First World War destroyer that had been sold for scrap in the 1930s. The salvaged memento provided a daily reminder to every Wren and naval officer who passed through the door of the unit's ultimate purpose: to win, through a combination of superior tactics and consummate gamesmanship, the Battle of the Atlantic.

Roberts opened the door for his new Wren, and asked her to follow him past the newly refurbished offices and rooms, which included a lecture theatre that could seat fifty, into the main, expansive room at the heart of the school. All evidence of bomb damage had been scrubbed away, and the room now resembled something between a school gymnasium and, thanks to the scattered sticks of chalk and tumbles of string, a child's playroom. The floor in the centre of the room was covered in brown linoleum, painted with white gridlines and punctuated with tiny wooden models, some of which had been fashioned from wood taken from HMS *Nelson*, an armoured cruiser built in the 1870s that had been scrapped in 1910.[2]

As Okell surveyed the floor, Roberts explained that each white line was spaced ten inches apart, representing one nautical mile, while the counters represented ships and surfaced German U-boats.

'Think of it like a giant chessboard,' he said.[3]

Like *Alice Through the Looking Glass*, Okell had stepped into a board game. The map, Roberts explained, represented the Atlantic Ocean. Okell would help stage recent sea battles. The 'board' was large enough to accommodate twenty-four players at a time. In trousers and white shirts, with their sleeves rolled up, the Wrens would kneel and carefully move the pieces according to the players' orders.

Around the edges of the room, Okell noticed great sheets of white canvas. They were arranged into enclosures, like voting booths, except each one seemed to have a peephole cut into it at eye level. The average visibility from the bridge of a warship is five miles, Roberts explained. The canvas sheets were positioned in such a way that, when a player peeked through the slit, he or she could see the equivalent of a five-mile view of the tiny wooden ships on the floor. Linen side wires, which could be bent to adjust visibility, depending on the game scenario that was being played, held the apertures open.

'Like this,' said Liz Drake, a Wren officer who at just five feet two needed a six-inch stool, especially made for her, to reach the slits.[4] Drake disappeared behind the canvas and, a few seconds later, Okell saw the flap roll back and her colleague's eyes appear, blinking, in the hole. For Okell, a bridge player who had joined the Wrens from secretarial college expecting to be assigned as a typist, it was a curious scene. Roberts, with his teacherly flair, began to explain the rules of the game, recently formulated, broadly untested.

One team, positioned behind the canvas sheets at desks, played as the escort captains, he said. The other, usually captained by Roberts or his right-hand woman, Jean Laidlaw, played as the U-boats. As in the real Battle of the Atlantic, each side's objective was focused on the convoy ships: the escort ships had to protect them, while the U-boats had to attack them. Each side had a secondary objective. For the escort ships, this was to sink as many U-boats as possible, while the U-boats hoped to avoid detection and exit the battlefield unharmed.

The convoy ships, the prize in play for both sides, would automatically plod on at each turn of the game toward their destination, the battle raging around them, just as at sea. Next, Roberts explained the rules of the game. Players were given two minutes in which to submit their orders for the next 'turn', to replicate the urgency of a real battlefield. The movements of the U-boats were drawn in green[5] chalk on the floor, a colour chosen as it was impossible to make out against the floor's tint when viewed from an angle. This ensured the U-boat positions were undetectable to the players peering through the canvas screens. The escort ships' movements would then be added to the floor in white chalk, which was, in contrast to the green markings, legible to those peeking from the canvas holes. Turn by turn the pieces would move around the floor, as the escort ships dashed to the site of an explosion to drop depth charges, and the U-boats performed their feints and dodges in an effort to pick off convoy ships, while evading the escort.

Okell's role, Roberts explained, would be that of an umpire, measuring distances and marking movements in chalk to ensure that the game played out as accurately as possible. Finally, at the end of the game, the players would come together and, sitting around the board, now criss-crossed with chalk markings, Roberts

Caricature of Commander Gilbert Roberts astride his destroyer, HMS *Fearless*, shortly before his 'invaliding' from the navy. Illustrated by Captain J. E. Broome, noted cartoonist and later a graduate of WATU, c.1937.

Colin Ryder Richardson (right) with some of the thirteen children who survived the sinking of the *City of Benares*, aboard their rescue ship, HMS *Hurricane*, September 1940.

A North Atlantic convoy sails south of Newfoundland, 28th July 1942. A protective naval escort surrounds columns of vulnerable merchant ships, like sheepdogs circling a flock.

On 4th June 1941 Admiral Doenitz surveys the crew of *U-94* on their arrival at the port of St. Nazaire following a thirty-seven-day patrol in the North Atlantic. (*Bundesarchiv*)

The cavernous bunker containing the main wall plot at Derby House in Liverpool, seen here in July 1945, housed the operations room from which the Battle of the Atlantic was conducted. *(Trinity Mirror Group)*

At Derby House in September 1944 a Wren plotter marks the known positions of Allied ships, their planned routes and the Admiralty's 'best guess' of the position of any U-boats known. *(Getty Images)*

Following his 'retirement' from the Royal Navy on grounds of ill-health in 1938 Roberts struggled to find employment, eventually securing a short-lived role in the Devon Constabulary.

When Roberts' temporary home in London, Frobisher House, was hit by a 2,500lb bomb on bonfire night, 1940, he was left with a splinter.

Roberts' appointment to WATU in January 1942 presented him with a longed-for role at the heart of the war effort. Its gruelling demands affected his health, however. By January 1945, the unit's director had lost a great deal of weight.

After the war and the end of his first marriage, Roberts settled in Devon, in a house overlooking a patchwork of fields on the edge of Dartmoor, three miles from Crapstone. Here, in 1950, Roberts holds the family's new puppy, Tuppence.

Angela Goodenough (left) was responsible for Wren welfare. Here, on 12th September 1939, she consults with Vera Laughton Mathews (right), Director of the Wrens, who scandalised the driver of her service car by routinely sitting with her legs up on the back seats.

While the Luftwaffe exercised its bombing campaign on British cities, Wren dispatch riders, such as those seen here in 1941, carried naval messages on motorcycles. It was one of the most perilous roles on the home front.

Lieutenant John Lamb (left) relaxes in the wardroom of HMS *Oribi* where he first met Christian Oldham shortly after the ship docked in Belfast in May 1943. Less than two weeks later, the wardroom hosted the pair's engagement party.

On 8th August 1940 Kretschmer celebrates with the crew of *U-99* in the French port of Lorient shortly after receiving the *Ritterkreuz*, or Knight's Cross. U-boat captains qualified for the award after sinking 100,000 tonnes of enemy shipping. *(Bundesarchiv)*

The most handsome and bullish of Germany's three U-boat aces, Joachim Schepke (centre) relaxes in the sun on the 'wintergarden' of his U-boat, *U-100*. He was killed here, in March 1941, when HMS *Vanoc* rammed the U-boat in the early hours of the morning.

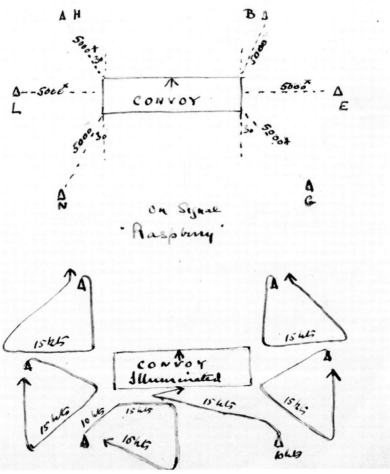

This illustration of WATU's inaugural and best-known anti-U-boat manoeuvre, 'Raspberry' (named by Jean Laidlaw as a razz to Hitler), was drawn in April 1942 by Admiral Usborne, the most senior advisor in the navy, and one of the unit's few early supporters. *(The National Archives, Kew)*

In January 1944 Jean Laidlaw stands at WATU's front door, where officers were greeted by a ship's badge, taken from the First World War destroyer HMS *Tactician*.

Naval officers peer at the game board through canvas sheets in January 1944, taking in the positions of their ships in preparation to make their next move in the game. The peepholes approximated visibility at sea.

Roberts, seen here debriefing players after a game in January 1944, was a talented communicator. He was acutely aware of the challenge of holding the interest of officers who were, typically, exhausted from the travails of the sea, and longing for a week off.

Sixty-six Wrens worked at WATU between February 1942 and July 1945. Few remained for the duration of the war. Jean Laidlaw, seen here in 1944 to the immediate right of Roberts (centre), was one of the few exceptions.

On 17th November 1942 the King and Queen visited Derby House to witness Percy Noble's handover to Max Horton as Commander-in-Chief of Western Approaches. That day Roberts (right) and the Wrens staged a demonstration of 'Raspberry' for their esteemed visitors.

From his mezzanine office Max Horton could survey the Atlantic Ocean. This vantage point enabled Horton, seen here on 21st July 1943, to alter routes, issue commands and dispatch groups of supporting warships to hotspots in need.

On 18th March 1945 a Wren checks a selection of the wooden models used to denote ships, U-boats and, in the case of the wire wool, smoke, in the wargames. According to a contemporary journalist the models were carved from wood taken from HMS *Nelson*.

Mary Poole (top left) was the first female officer to undertake WATU's course. Poole subsequently ran the torpedo attack simulator at Gladstone Dock, a sister school to WATU, the main campus where Janet Okell (top right), Bobby Howes (bottom left), and Nan Wales (bottom right) all worked.

Wren Officer Judy Du Vivier and Commander Peter Gretton on their wedding day, 29th May 1943 (left), and Elizabeth Drake and Fred Osborne on theirs, 4th November 1944. All four first met at WATU, Gretton as a student, and Du Vivier, Drake and Osborne as staff.

June Duncan, whose mother sewed stones into the hem of her daughter's coat to cheat the Wrens' minimum weight restriction, was one of WATU's longest-serving members. After the war she worked as a fashion model for magazines such as *Vogue* and *Harper's Bazaar*. *(National Museums Liverpool)*

Wrens calculate moves on the tactical floor, Derby House, January 1944. The movements of the U-boats were drawn in green chalk, which was impossible to make out against the linoleum by players peering through the peepholes thereby simulating the actual experience at sea of an invisible enemy. The escort ships' movements were drawn in white chalk which, by contrast, was clearly legible from a distance.

would reveal how everyone had fared. More details needed to be worked out, Roberts explained, and by necessity the game was a simplification of real U-boat action, but there was enough here, he said, to begin staging recent sea battles. The objective was to experience the action from the perspective of the U-boats and, from that knowledge, assess what the escort commanders might have done differently to save ships, supplies and lives.

The tour complete, Okell was told to fetch her uniform and, like every other Wren who joined WATU, report to the basement. There she would be trained as a plotter;[6] after all, the skills required to measure out distances on the giant map in Derby House's basement were precisely those required to play and direct the game. Okell left Derby House and made her way to the uniform store, situated in the nearby Liver Building[7], understanding the responsibility that she now shared.

With the rudiments of the game in place, Roberts spent a great deal of his time studying after-action reports written by naval officers who had battled U-boats and survived, in search of clues to their tactics. Being ideally situated to meet and quiz any and every naval officer passing through Western Approaches Command, Roberts did not have to rely solely on the rather staid written testimony of sailors; he could also listen to first-hand accounts by interviewing men as they returned from sea.

During the course of several interviews a chaotic picture emerged, not only of the sea battles themselves but also of the training process. Before deployment every sailor – an estimated 200,000 men by the end of the war[8] – underwent a two-week crash course in Tobermory harbour, on the Isle of Mull, under the gruelling tutelage of Sir Gilbert Stephenson (nicknamed, variously, 'Puggy', 'Monkey' and 'The Terror'). Stephenson's course was intended to build and improve efficiency among an individual ship's crew, but it did not address the effectiveness of ships working in company. Not only was there no universal set of tactics with which to fight U-boats, neither was there any training for how escort ships should work as a team. The destroyers and corvettes, it seemed to

Roberts, were broadly free to direct their response according to individual whim or notion.

Fred Osborne, Nancy Osborne's brother and first lieutenant of the corvette HMS *Gentian*, who like his sister came to Britain from Australia to join the war effort, described convoy defence as 'difficult and haphazard' in the absence of collective countermeasures.[9] 'No clear doctrine for combatting attacks on convoys had been formulated and taught,' he later wrote. As such, 'the losses were appalling'.

Roberts asked every escort captain he interviewed the same question: 'What do you do when a ship is torpedoed?' Some spoke of 'going to action stations', others about increasing their speed. When pressed, however, most shrugged in resignation. What could you do, blind in the night, explosions sounding all around, when your ASDIC operator was unable to distinguish the sound of a U-boat cleaving the water from the noise of a choppy sea, or even a shoal of fish?[10]

One man, however, had a different answer. Grizzled and terse, Captain Frederick John Walker, known as 'Johnnie' to his men, after the whisky, inspired loyalty from his crew that ran even deeper, in many cases, than their sense of duty to country. Even by 1942, after just three months captaining a ship in the Atlantic, Walker had become one of the only successful U-boat hunters in the navy.

On his first voyage as commander in December 1941, only a few weeks before Roberts and Walker met, Walker had sunk two U-boats, and led the escort ships under his command in the sinking of three more. While an Allied escort carrier and two convoy ships had been lost in this battle for convoy HG.76, it was nevertheless considered by many to be the first major victory of the war for the escort ships against the U-boats. How had it been done, Roberts asked?

Walker believed it was down to a tactic that he had developed and dubbed 'Buttercup', a nickname he used for his wife, Eileen. Before Walker docked on his return journey from the battle, he had received a message from Sir Percy Noble requesting a meeting. There he was asked to explain the secret to his success. Desperate for something on which to pin their tactical hopes, Noble and Walker's superiors seized on Buttercup. Walker was commanded to write up the manoeuvre, which was to be sent to escort commanders for immediate adoption at sea.

There was just one problem: 'Buttercup' was utterly ineffective and, unknown to Walker, Roberts had been secretly asked to expose it as such.

Captain Walker's interest in anti-U-boat tactics long pre-dated the war. In the 1920s, years before he was made a captain, Buttercup's inventor had volunteered to undergo a course at HMS *Osprey*, the school of anti-submarine warfare at Portland naval base. Never reticent to criticise instructions that he considered to be ill conceived, Walker's outspokenness earned him the respect of his contemporaries, and the misgivings of his superiors, who viewed his unmoderated candour as a character flaw.

When Walker was appointed to second-in-command of the battleship *Valiant*, he regularly clashed with his captain; a confidential Admiralty report described Walker as 'lacking powers of leadership'. Resigned to the belief that he would not make captain, Walker returned to *Osprey* as commander in 1937. In the navy there was a small window in which every officer could be promoted to the next rank of seniority. Those who failed to earn promotion within the designated time frame were known as 'passed over'. In peacetime, an officer who had been passed over could elect either to remain in the service at their existing rank till retirement age, or retire early with a modest pension and the opportunity to pursue a civilian career. Walker considered leaving the navy while he still had time to follow a new calling. As war approached, however, along with scores of other officers who had also been passed over, Walker was called upon to fill positions of importance.

Walker had long maintained that U-boats would become the principal threat to Britain's survival. In his new posting he was given an office in Dover Castle and tasked with overseeing anti-submarine defences in the Channel, specifically the laying of extensive, underwater minefields designed to frustrate any German attempt to invade England from France. For Walker, who desperately wanted a ship to command, it was a disappointing appointment.

As the months passed, Walker bombarded the Admiralty with requests to transfer to a ship. Each letter was met with another refusal. Finally, in March 1941, Walker travelled to London to meet Captain Creasy, director of anti-submarine warfare and an old friend, to make his request in person. Creasy was one of those few officers who knew the truth about Allied losses in the Atlantic, and the extent to which official statements about U-boat sinkings had been exaggerated. As such, he was keenly aware of the need for officers with experience of fighting U-boats to join the team at the newly formed Western Approaches HQ in Liverpool.

Walker may not have had this exact kind of hands-on experience, but his knowledge of tactical theory was expansive. Creasy listened to his friend's arguments about why he should be given command of an escort ship and, at the end of the meeting, offered Walker an assurance that he would request a transfer. Six months later a signal arrived at Dover from the Admiralty ordering Walker to Liverpool. He was to assume command of HMS *Stork* for duties in the Atlantic. On arrival Walker found himself among 'strangely assorted bedfellows', as his biographer put it.[11] So it was that Walker and Roberts, two of the navy's most precocious and single-minded misfits, came to meet.

The men took an instant dislike to each other. Walker, who was four years Roberts' senior and looked a good deal older, was taciturn. Roberts was effusive. Walker shunned the limelight (as a child he had performed in a ballet at the Royal Albert Hall, only to burst into tears on stage, an indignity that his elder sister claimed had contributed to his refusal to be the centre of attention[12]) while Roberts, who still felt the pain of his dismissal from the navy, was determined to fight for recognition.

'Their personalities were diametrically opposed,' wrote Fred Osborne, who would later spend eight months working alongside Roberts.[13] Then there was the rivalrous symmetry of their missions. Like Roberts, for years Walker's understanding of U-boat warfare had been purely theoretical. But after three months working out of Liverpool, Walker had the advantage of live encounters with U-boats. The 'notorious disagreements', as Fred Osborne put it, between the two men became common knowledge at Derby House and, despite repeated orders from his superiors, Walker resolutely refused to visit WATU, choosing instead to potter in his garden at home, or take his wife and child on shopping trips.[14]

Nevertheless, this first meeting between the men had been cordial and, for Roberts, useful. Before he had left for Liverpool at the beginning of January 1942, Admiral Usborne, Churchill's aide, had told Roberts that he privately doubted the efficacy of Walker's lauded 'Buttercup'. Usborne suspected that Walker's sinking of U-boats in December was not by design but 'by luck,' as he put it to Roberts, and that Buttercup had been wrongly feted for the success.[15]

When Usborne had raised his misgivings with Captain Creasy he had been told to 'mind his own business'. Irritated by this rude brush-off, Usborne asked Roberts, as one of his first tasks at WATU, to analyse the battle of HG.76, where Walker had seen such great success, in order to settle the matter one way or the other.

Oblivious to Roberts' ulterior motives, Walker outlined the tactic. On the order 'Buttercup', he explained, all of the escort ships would turn outward from the convoy. They would accelerate to full speed, while letting loose star shells – an explosive that, like a dandelion puffball, released iridescent fragments that hung in the air on a parachute for up to sixty seconds and illuminated the ocean. If a U-boat was sighted, Walker would then mount a dogged pursuit, often ordering up to six of the nine ships in his group to stay with the vessel until it was destroyed.

Walker's absolute belief in the tactic is clear in the operational instructions he wrote for the captains within his group.

'I cannot emphasise too strongly that a U-boat sighted or otherwise detected is immediately to be attacked continuously . . . until she has been destroyed, or until further orders have been received,' he stated.[16]

Coordination and cooperation, Walker explained, were key to success. He viewed the escort group as a kind of sports team, and himself, as commander, in the role of player-manager.

'This kind of warfare is not the sort that has one man as its ace protagonist,' he later said during a speech delivered at a ceremony in Liverpool to commemorate his success in the U-boat war. The mayor presiding over the ceremony had described Walker as the navy's 'number one U-boat killer', an accolade the captain imme-diately shrugged off. 'Fighting U-boats is very much like playing football, or any other sort of game,' he continued. 'You have a team of a thousand men, any one of whom can wreck the whole show if he doesn't do his job properly. Every man has his job to do. I am merely at the head of the affair.'[17]

Roberts left the meeting armed with everything he needed to restage the battle of HG.76 in the game and thereby test Buttercup's worth. Despite his misgivings about Walker's tactic, he could not deny the truth of his rival's assertion that escort ships should work not autonomously, but as a coordinated team. Regardless of Buttercup's validity, Walker's promotion of teamwork between escort ships was surely key.

Upstairs Roberts and the Wrens laid out a plot of convoy HG.76 on the floor, including tokens to represent not only Walker's 36th escort group, but also the destroyers *Blankney*, *Stanley* and *Exmoor*, and the convoy aircraft carrier HMS *Audacity*,* which had loaned their support to the convoy on its homebound journey from Gibraltar. In all, the pair arranged forty-eight ships in twelve columns.[18] Then, the two men added the tracks of the three U-boats known to have participated in the battle, U-434, U-574 and U-131.

The stage set, Roberts began to move the convoy, which spread across six white lines on the floor to represent its six-mile width, in two-minute intervals and at a simulated rate of ten knots. Each move was made in precisely the same pattern as Walker had directed the actual escort a few weeks earlier.

Blow by blow, Roberts imitated the action, as per the official reports. He replayed the moment that one of *Audacity*'s aircraft sighted a shadowing U-boat. He peeled Walker's HMS *Stork* away from the rest of the escort ships and placed the sloop in active pursuit of the U-boat, dropping a barrage of imaginary depth charges on U-131 and then, when it surfaced two 'hours' later, sinking it with a spray of gunfire. (Doenitz, who had also watched the encounter play out on his plot, albeit almost in real time,

---

* HMS *Audacity* was a German merchant ship, captured in 1941 and converted for this new purpose.

realised that *Audacity*'s scout planes had led to *U-131*'s downfall, and issued orders that in the event of sighting an aircraft carrier in any convoy, every wolfpack was to prioritise attacks on this ship above all others.[19])

Seeing the battle from a crow's-nest perspective above the board, it became clear to Roberts that this early success in the battle had been a direct result of the unusually large number of escort ships that Walker had at his disposal. This had freed him to pursue the spotted U-boat while leaving the convoy ships with adequate protection.

What was less clear to Roberts was precisely what had happened next. After successfully destroying another U-boat three days later, the first merchant ship, *Annavore*, was torpedoed and, at 11 p.m. on 21st December, so was HMS *Audacity*, whose captain had ignored Walker's orders and had taken up position on the unprotected starboard side of the convoy.

Roberts placed a tiny flag in two of the ship models, to indicate that they had been removed from the game.[20] Then, as he examined the plot, a question formed in Roberts' mind. If the U-boats were firing from outside the perimeter of the convoy, how had *Annavore*, which was in the centre of the convoy, been sunk? Might it be possible, he wondered, that the U-boat had attacked the ship from inside the columns of the convoy? There was, he reasoned, a simple way to prove his theory.

'Hold everything,' Roberts told his staff, as he rushed into his office to make a phone call.

Roberts picked up the receiver and asked the operator to put him through to the Flag Officer Submarines in London, hoping to speak to its chief of staff, an old friend, Captain Ian Macintyre.* To Roberts' astonishment, the flag officer himself, Admiral Sir Max Horton, picked up.

Horton, known by reputation to Roberts, was a man of foreboding distinction. As a young submarine commander in the First World War, Horton had become known as an unparalleled terroriser

---

* First cousin of the father of Donald 'Bulldog' Macintyre, who captured Otto Kretschmer.

of German ships, and he had sunk the first enemy ship of the Great War. On return to port, Horton would signal a successful kill by flying the Jolly Roger, a tradition that continued till the end of the Falklands War. Horton's precocious talent as a submariner propelled him up the ranks; years later his biographer would describe the admiral as 'the greatest authority on submarine warfare'.

On the phone, Roberts explained who he was and asked Horton if he might be permitted to ask a question. During the last war, Roberts asked, would you ever have crept among the ships of a convoy to fire a torpedo?

'Of course,' replied Horton. 'It is the only way of pressing home an attack.'

And out of interest, Roberts continued, what is the range of a U-boat's electric torpedo?

'Five thousand four hundred yards,' replied Horton without hesitation.

'Thank you, sir,' said Roberts, before he hung up.

'This was enough for me,' he wrote in his diary.

It was late, but Roberts asked Laidlaw and Okell if they might stay behind with him to reset the plot and run a new game on the giant board. The two women, infused with Roberts' excitement, agreed and hurriedly reset the game. This time, Roberts placed a U-boat model in the centre of the columns of the convoy and ran the events of Walker's battle in reverse. If the range of its torpedoes was around two and a half miles, it was reasonable to imagine that U-boat captains would fire from less than half that distance, in order to maximise their chances of scoring a direct hit.

Between them, Roberts and the two Wrens began to plot different scenarios that might have enabled the U-boat to sneak into the convoy without being detected. Only one checked out: the U-boat had entered the columns of the convoy from behind. And it must have done so on the surface, where it was able to travel at a faster speed than the ships. By approaching from astern, where the lookouts rarely checked, the U-boat would be able to slip inside the convoy undetected, fire at close range, then submerge in order to get away.

If this was all true, Roberts surmised that Walker's depth charge, dropped after spreading out *from* and not *into* the convoy, must have hit not the attacking U-boat, but another loitering member of the pack. If so, Usborne was correct: Buttercup's success was by fluke, not design.

Roberts and the Wrens headed to the kitchen to make coffee and a round of corned beef sandwiches. The conversation continued to centre on the battle they had left on the floor of the game room. The group discussed how if they were a U-boat captain having made a point-blank-range attack on a merchant ship, they might attempt to escape unharmed. The game had enabled the fledgling tacticians to think like U-boat captains, and from that perspective the answer suddenly seemed obvious: having made your attack, you would of course dive. Then you would sit and wait for the convoy to roll overhead.

'Eventually,' Roberts concluded, 'I would emerge, deep, from the stern of the convoy.'[21]

With the U-boat tactic abruptly unveiled, Roberts wanted to try out some potential countermeasures that might foil the plan. The four returned to the game room. Roberts assumed the role of the U-boat captain, and Laidlaw and Okell played as Walker's escort ships. The countermeasure revealed itself immediately. Rather than splay out from the convoy at speed, dropping depth charges at random, Laidlaw and Okell lined the escort ships up around the convoy. While the convoy continued on its way, each escort ship performed a triangular sweep, listening for U-boats on the ASDIC.

With a mounting sense of excitement, the team ran the procedure twice more. In both instances Roberts' U-boat was detected and sunk. It was, by now, the early hours of the morning; in all the excitement time had passed unnoticed. Roberts ordered a staff car to return the two women to Ackerleigh House.

The next morning, Roberts and the Wrens reassembled in WATU's game room and began replaying the battle, and their new counter-tactic, again and again.*

---

* Roberts' diary account differs from that of his biographer, which states that the team met with Noble the morning after their discovery. In Roberts' account, WATU takes two days to test the theory before summoning its commander-in-chief to see the results.

'I couldn't pick a hole in it anywhere,' Roberts wrote in his diary.[22] He formulated the counter-attack as a set of operational instructions and, when he felt ready, Roberts left a message with the duty officer that he would like to see Sir Percy Noble as early as possible. He had something to show him.

The next day Noble, flanked by his staff, entered the game room. The commander-in-chief warily eyed the chalk markings on the floor, and the canvas sheets decked out like ship portholes. What was all this make-believe nonsense? Undeterred, Roberts began to explain their discoveries – how the U-boats would slip between the convoy ships on the surface of the water, at night, when they were unlikely to be spotted, make their attacks, and then dive to wait until danger had passed.

The atmosphere was frosty. Noble had made no secret of his condescending scepticism towards WATU's work. Roberts detected the same tone in Noble's manner – 'snootiness', as he described it in his diary – that he had perceived during their first meeting. How could this former naval officer, with his nubs of chalk and jumbles of string, contribute anything to the battles being waged out at sea? Games, Roberts knew, were seen as frivolous things supposed to be set down in adolescence and not taken up again until retirement. They had no place in the adult world, let alone the dread theatre of war.

When Roberts explained that he had spoken to Sir Max Horton, the submarine ace, and as the escort team's counter-attack showed its effectiveness on the game floor, Noble's demeanour appeared to change. Sensing the shift in atmosphere, Roberts quickly asked Laidlaw to assume the role of the U-boat commander and Okell that of Captain Walker. Then, as the two women played out the battle, Roberts began to demonstrate WATU's findings. When Laidlaw fired a torpedo from within the convoy's columns, then dived, Roberts commanded Okell to perform the team's newly developed counter-tactic, by moving the escort ships in their triangular sweeping patterns designed to flush out the hidden U-boat. While performing the sweeps, one of Okell's escort ships picked up the Germans' position on its radar.

As the demonstration unfolded Noble and his staff seemed 'to sit forward on their chairs'. With the U-boat position revealed, Okell dropped a cascade of depth charges over its position beneath the water. There was no time for Laidlaw to manoeuvre her U-boat out of the way. Okell scored a direct hit, and the U-boat 'bubbled' to the surface. The demonstration at an end, Laidlaw rose, and Okell emerged from behind the canvas sheet, from where she had been directing the escort ships. Roberts looked at Noble, in the judgement seat.

'Congratulations,' said Noble. Then, the commander-in-chief of Western Approaches turned to one of his men and told him to take down a message, to be sent post-haste to the prime minister.

'The first investigations have shown a cardinal error in anti-U-boat tactics,' he said. 'A new, immediate and concerted counter-attack will be signalled to the fleet within twenty-four hours.'[23]

An air of friendship, Roberts noted, had arrived in the room. Noble now asked for a name for the tactic from the inventor. Roberts explained that Jean Laidlaw, who had 'done all the boring statistics', had christened it Raspberry. The manoeuvre was, she had reasoned, a razz of contempt aimed at Hitler and his U-boats.

Noble chuckled, stood and made to leave. In the doorway he paused, turned and strode up to Roberts.

'Sew on your fourth stripe,' he said. The retired commander was now a captain.

For many days thereafter, visitors came to WATU to see the game for themselves. The team would first demonstrate Walker's tactic, Buttercup, in order to reveal 'its fallacy', as Roberts put it. Having issued this two-finger salute to his celebrated rival, Roberts then oversaw the triumphant performance of his superior manoeuvre, Raspberry.

'It made me rather unpopular with Captain Walker,' he wrote.

XII

The Royal Key

No time was wasted. On Monday 2nd February 1942 the first group of naval officers arrived at the top floor of the smoke-blackened Derby House, fresh from the ocean.[1] They passed through the heavy oak door to undergo a week-long training course on 'The Game', as it came to be known. The Wrens ran the show. Some, like Okell, moved the game pieces around the floor. Others were responsible for manoeuvring U-boats, while the most personable women, like the pristinely presented Bobby Howes, guided the men through the process, often proffering gentle but incisive advice on what moves to perform and when.

For the officers playing as escort commanders behind the canvas peepholes the games were keenly intense. From his position behind the canvas sheet, the lieutenant would survey the ocean floor, then report back to his CO, who sat at a plotting table behind the screen, as though he was working in the charthouse up on his ship's bridge. As well as listening to the situation report from his lieutenant, the senior officer would receive constant new information from his assigned Wren, designed to mimic the flow of information arriving from the ship's ASDIC radar operator.

'Star shell fired here,' she would tell him. 'Explosion heard there.'

She might explain that another ship was trying to make contact on the radio, or that a destroyer had opened fire but that the splashes were not observed. From this information, the CO would have to make quick judgement calls on what to do next, based on what he understood the other escort ships to be doing. Naval officers would then write their instructions on a small square of paper known as a chit. They might choose to alter their vessel's speed or direction, fire star shells or drop a depth charge – any of the actions that were open to them in an actual sea battle. The chit was posted into a little box and duly collected by one of the young women, who passed the instruction to her fellow Wrens, who would proceed to shunt the models around the make-believe Atlantic Ocean accordingly, while kneeling on the floor and carefully marking off each instruction in pencil.

In an adjacent room Bernard Rayner and another clutch of Wrens would collect, decode, decipher and transmit signals to and from the naval officers behind the screens. These messages would be delivered to each officer, presenting an almost over-whelming amount of information on which instantaneous decisions had to be made. To mimic the chaos of battle, Roberts and the Wrens would introduce unexpected diversions to proceed-ings: a lone freighter, for example, spotted by an aircraft and reported to be blazing just over the horizon.[2] In this instance, one of the Wrens would gingerly walk across the floor and place grey cotton wool around the miniature ship to indicate billowing smoke. Another Wren, meanwhile, might suggest to her captain that he should send an escort ship to investigate and search for survivors.

The pressure of the two-minute intervals between turns mimicked the stress of action against U-boats at sea, and each officer would often be caught up in the fiction, no longer viewing the chalk lines and wooden models as game pieces, but as the real ships, wakes and explosions they represented. The game occupied an unusual position between reality and make-believe. No limbs or lives were lost here on the linoleum ocean. But neither was the game fully abstracted, in the way that Monopoly is based on, but distinct from, the property business. For the men who played WATU's game, who had often returned from sea only a few days earlier, and who were often due to sail again a few days later, the game had an unsettling quality. The choices made on the floor reflected an officer's current tactical thinking; if his ship was lost in the game, he had to cope with the knowledge that had the same situation arisen at sea, and had he acted the same way, he may well have died.

'Make your mistakes here and you won't make them at sea,' Roberts was fond of saying, a euphemistic way of pointing out the scale of risk against which the game was attempting to insure its players. For all Roberts' engaging presentation, a man who failed to drive off the U-boat or, worse, who lost his ship in the game, would leave WATU feeling sternly chastened. In this way the psychic link between Derby House and the Atlantic Ocean became fearfully strong.

'We destroy U-boats out in the oceans,' wrote one observer who sat in on a round of the game. 'But the death sentence is delivered, miles away, in the assize court, in that old building erected on the banks of the River Mersey above the old dungeon haunts of the slave-traders.'[3]

Each course, which lasted from Monday to Saturday*, and which ran weekly without interruption from the first week of February 1942 to the last week of July 1945, involved up to fifty officers at once. It consisted of four game scenarios, which each varied details such as the weather conditions, visibility, time of day and the size, speed and start point of the convoy.

Finally, when the game finished the officers would step from behind the canvas screens and, along with the Wrens, sit in a square of chairs around the room. Then, with a ten-foot wooden pole Roberts would commentate on the preceding battle, blow by blow, like a sports pundit delivering a post-match verdict. He would draw attention to moments of particular brilliance, moments of particular disaster and the turning points of each game. These summations were, for Roberts, the most enjoyable aspect of the work. He relished the opportunity to create a picture of the battle far more vivid and engaging than the reports written by officers returning from earnest action at sea.

'As we listened to him, he made the most difficult situation appear simple,' said Vice Admiral Gilbert Stephenson, of Roberts'

---

* Roberts recorded that on Sundays the team would often be called upon to give demonstrations to visiting Americans. The hours were long and gruelling and at least one of the Wrens, June Duncan, was signed off for work-related sickness.

flair. 'He appreciated the difficulty that hundreds of commanding officers had in deciding what to do when faced with any of the surprises that war at sea was constantly presenting, and he taught them how to meet these surprises till they were ready for anything.'

Although 'much lacking in physical health', Roberts 'made up for this shortcoming', as Stephenson put it, with 'enthusiasm and obsession'.[4] Men entered WATU dubious of what they were about to experience and left a week later as exhilarated converts. Roberts for his part believed that he, and especially the Wrens, had a pivotal role to play, not only in teaching tactics to men before they went to battle at sea, but also in infusing those men with self-assurance and vigour.

'It is of paramount importance . . . that the staff are always enthusiastic, in order to transmit enthusiasm and zest, and therefore also confidence to those who are at sea,' he wrote in an annual report of the unit's work.[5] Favourable word of WATU began to spread, a flicker of good news at a time when, as the First Sea Lord Sir Dudley Pound put it, the war at sea was in grave danger of being lost, and the wider war with it.*

On 18th April 1942, the Admiral of the Fleet and the most senior member of the navy, Sir Dudley Pound, wrote to Sir Percy Noble to enquire how Roberts and the Wrens were doing. A week later Noble, who had been so sceptical of Roberts and his game ideas just a few weeks earlier, sent a shimmering response.

'This unit has now been in existence for two and a half months,' he wrote, 'and is a valuable going concern.'[6]

In just ten weeks, scores of captains of escort vessels had, Noble informed Pound, taken Roberts' course. They had included two Royal Indian Navy officers, who had since returned to the Indian Ocean to implement what they had learned on their Bangor-class vessels, two Norwegian officers and one American.

'I would like it to be made a rule that as many officers as possible . . . belonging to Western Approaches ships should be

---

* 'If we lose the war at sea, we lose the war,' said Pound in his opening remarks at the thirtieth meeting of the Battle of the Atlantic Committee on 10th February 1942.

appointed to Derby House for a week's course, before joining their ships,' Noble continued.

The commander-in-chief of Western Approaches had particular praise for the ten Wrens working alongside Roberts: officers Drake, Howes, Laidlaw and Wales, and six junior ratings including Okell, who, Noble informed Pound, 'are becoming surprisingly adept at handling ships themselves for investigation, and working by general instructions for the conduct of the affairs they handle'.

Still, the combination of ministration and expertise was not always welcomed by the experienced officers on the receiving end of the Wrens' advice. Often the men would resent being told what to do, no matter how gently, by women who were barely out of school and who, in most cases, had never been to sea in peacetime, let alone during a war. During one 1942 game, Bob Whinney, who captained the destroyer HMS *Wanderer*, in which he sank three U-boats, handed his chit to one of the Wrens, Judy Du Vivier, a 'particularly clued-up girl' whom he had been assigned.

'No, sir,' she said, of Whinney's chosen move. 'I do not think that you should do that.'[7]

'Good God,' he later recalled thinking of her 'firm and polite' request. 'What on earth does this girl know about it?'

So confident and tactful was Du Vivier's tone, however, that Whinney chose to hear her out. He listened to the Wren's 'convincing' explanation in astonishment. From his perspective, a battle-worn captain was being tutored on the finer points of U-boat warfare by an inexperienced girl. For Roberts, the exchange vindicated a long-held belief: with careful design, games had the capacity to make experts of amateurs, to instil in players invaluable, potentially life-saving, battle-winning experience.

Usborne also wrote to the First Sea Lord with news of Raspberry, the night-time countermeasure against a U-boat attack from within the convoy, and Gooseberry, its daytime equivalent.[8] In the same letter, Usborne made his feelings about Walker's Buttercup clear.

'One of the first problems that C.-in-C. Western Approaches set . . . was to investigate an alternative to "Buttercup",' he wrote, before describing, in brief, Roberts' two manoeuvres, which were to replace Walker's flawed tactic.

WATU's two brand-new countermeasures, Usborne explained, were being included in the latest edition of the *Western Approaches Convoy Instructions*, a bible for escort officers that explained best practices for all manner of potential scenarios encountered while protecting the convoy ships. He further urged the need to find a way to train escort ships in their deployment as quickly as possible. One suggestion was for Roberts, the Wrens and all of their equipment to be put onto a ship and sent to Londonderry for a month, where they would be better placed to instruct captains who were working up their crews in the North Atlantic. This plan, Usborne wrote, 'would have the advantage that American Escort Groups will be able to see the Table at work and use it themselves if they wish to'. Usborne hoped that, if this were to happen, it would 'stimulate a desire for a similar instruction unit in the USA'.

Further vindication for the theory behind Raspberry came when Roberts was ordered to report to Usborne in London. There Usborne played him a recording of two German POWs who had been secretly taped while whispering in their cell while awaiting interrogation. One was a U-boat crew member, the other a tank commander who had been captured in Egypt. The U-boatman was describing an attack on an Allied convoy and used the words, in German, 'And then no man may move, or anything.'

Roberts played these words over and over again.

'What did it mean?' he wrote in his diary. It could not be that the men had to be quiet while fleeing a battle on the ocean's surface.

'Oh no!' Roberts wrote, his glee betrayed by every exclamation point. 'It was when the U-boat had fired its torpedoes, gone deep, and was coming out of the stern of the convoy, deep and quiet in order to not be heard by the British ASDIC: what a proof for Raspberry!'

Before he returned to Liverpool. Roberts met the broadcaster Richard Dimbleby, who was recording commentary for a Disney film.* Roberts and Dimbleby discussed WATU's work, and Dimbleby

---

* Richard Dimbleby's son, the broadcaster Jonathan, has no knowledge of the film, which is mentioned in Roberts' diary. 'Maybe he was discussing it as a proposal but, so far as I know, no such thing happened,' Jonathan told me.

made the masterstroke suggestion that Roberts have the Raspberry manoeuvre illustrated and made into a flick-book, so that officers undergoing training could see at a glance how it worked.

When he returned to Liverpool, Roberts commissioned the design and printing of these flick-books, which showed not only Raspberry, but all of the searches and operations designed by WATU.* These instructive booklets were routinely stolen and taken to sea by Officers undergoing the course.

(These were not the only items purloined from WATU, where a notice addressed to Course Officers had to be posted to the door. 'We have great difficulty in getting soft pencils here,' it read, 'and India-rubbers are scarcer than rubies. Please don't give them wings.'⁹)

WATU's tactics, once tested and proven in the game, were written up and added to the *Western Approaches Convoy Instructions*.

Soon enough, reports from graduates of the training school, now back at sea, began trickling back to WATU. These verified that Raspberry and the other tactical manoeuvres were working just as Roberts and the Wrens had hoped. Following the battle to defend convoy NS.122, for example, which commenced on 22nd August 1942, six months after the first training courses began, the senior escort officer said: 'Raspberry went like clockwork and whenever, during the night, the cry of "Tally-ho" was heard on the scram, I only had to check the bearings to know where a U-boat was being hunted.'¹⁰

Roberts' workload, meanwhile, had increased to an almost unbearable degree. As well as teaching, devising new scenarios for the game and testing new tactics on the plot, Roberts met incoming

---

* In his memoir Fred Osborne mentions that Raspberry and other WATU operations were illustrated by Captain John 'Jack' Broome, a former submarine captain. Broome, who became a celebrated cartoonist after the war, served as staff officer to Sir Percy Noble in Derby House, and likely illustrated the flick-book. Some years earlier, Broome had drawn an illustration of Roberts as Commander of HMS *Fearless*, so the two men knew one another. According to Broome's grandson, Andrew, the Broome estate does not possess any illustrations related to WATU's work.

escort commanders for operational debriefs and, many nights, worked in the main Operations Room at Derby House, where the markers on the map no longer represented hypothetical ships, but real vessels, crewed by real men.

Still, the work was exhilarating, especially when the first fruits of WATU's work began to be seen in summer 1942, when escort ships sank four times as many U-boats as the previous month,[11] beginning an upward trend that would continue, broadly, for the rest of the year.

The improvements in tactics were timely as they helped compensate for the fallout from an internal battle being waged between the navy and air force in London. The major source of contention between the Admiralty and the Air Ministry related to the deployment of long-range bombers. In Captain Walker's battle of HG.76 in December 1941, a lone bomber had played a decisive role in scattering a wolfpack. This led Walker to formally advise that aircraft were 'absolutely invaluable' to the protection of convoys. Following Walker's report, the Admiralty repeatedly requested an allocation of bombers to provide air support (at one point the First Sea Lord Sir Dudley Pound requested 2,000 warplanes[12]). The Air Ministry repeatedly refused.

In part, this was because Churchill had long asserted his belief that the only 'sure path' to victory lay in 'an absolutely devastating, exterminating attack by very heavy bombers . . . on the Nazi homeland'.[13] Knowing his rejection of the Admiralty's request would be supported by the prime minister, Chief of the Air Staff Sir Charles Portal wrote: 'To divert [the RAF's bombers] to an uneconomical defensive role would be unsound at any time. It would be doubly so now when we are about to launch a bombing offensive . . . which will enable us to deliver a heavy and concentrated blow against Germany.'[14]

Pound, who was at the time ill with the brain tumour that would kill him in 1943, was wearied, often falling asleep in meetings and therefore unable to effectively challenge the Air Ministry's specious assumptions and infuriating defiance. In May 1942 Pound again demanded – this time 'with all urgency' and the support of three of his most senior colleagues, admirals Forbes, Cunningham and

Tovey – an increase in the number of planes 'necessary to guard our vital sea communications'. The U-boat situation in the Atlantic was 'so grave', Pound wrote, that a stand had to be made, even if it led to 'the extreme step of resignation'.[15] Again his pleas were rejected. Despite Churchill's personal ties to the navy, and belief that the safe passage of convoys was key to Britain's survival, the prime minister was enamoured with Air Chief Marshal Sir Arthur Harris, the commander-in-chief of Bomber Command. Harris had a talent for public relations and, in modern parlance, optics. When he sent a fleet of bombers to attack Cologne on 30th May 1942, the figure of 1,000 aircraft was chosen not for any strategic benefit, but in order to capture the public imagination via newspaper headlines.

Harris had the prime minister's ear in a way that Pound did not, often sidestepping protocol to make private appeals for Bomber Command against the Admiralty. The Air Ministry's political supe-riority was made clear in the autumn of 1942 when the Admiralty's chief of operational research, Professor Patrick Blackett, a distin-guished scientist who later won the Nobel Prize for Physics, presented a comparative statistical analysis of the situation. His research showed beyond all reasonable dispute that a force of 200 long-range bombers would make a decisive contribution to the Battle of the Atlantic. Moreover, using aircraft in this way would have a far more meaningful effect on the broader war than in their current deployment, bombing German cities.

Even with meticulous statistical analysis Blackett struggled, as he later put it, 'to get the figures believed'. By January 1943, just one squadron of twelve bombers supported the escorting of convoys. As Churchill's chief of military operations later concluded, the prime minister's 'obsession for bombing Germany' resulted in 'the navy being very short of long-range bombers', which was 'the only well-founded ground for criticism of our central war direction'.[16] All of this was not lost on those who had to fight at sea. The convoy commander Peter Gretton, who became one of WATU's most distinguished students, later said that 'co-operation between the Navy and the Air Force in the field was very bad indeed, mainly due to stupid quarrels between senior officers in Whitehall.'

The bombers may have been absent, but WATU's work was aided in other ways. There was the invention and introduction of the ship-mounted high-frequency direction finder (HF/DF), a piece of equipment known to sailors by the nickname 'huff-duff'. Two ships equipped with this vessel-mounted direction-finding gear could pinpoint a U-boat location by detecting and triangulating the source of the high-frequency radio transmissions it was sending, either to other U-boats or to U-boat headquarters.* Then there was the fact that, after September 1942, the *Western Approaches Convoy Instructions*, the bible issued to all British escort officers filled with WATU-coined tactics and signals, was published for Canadian and American ships too, under the new title *Atlantic Convoy Instructions*. This book ensured escort ships from different Allied navies now used the same anti-U-boat signals where, prior to this, the British were just as bemused by the American signal 'Zombie Crack' as the Americans were by the British signal 'Pineapple'.[17]

Finally, there was the introduction of Hedgehog, a bow-mounted anti-submarine weapon that could spray a volley of mortar rounds directly ahead of the ship, toward a suspected U-boat location. The name derived from the weapon's appearance: the twenty mortar rounds were bunched together at a near-perpendicular angle, giving the appearance of a hedgehog's spikes. The projectiles were primed to explode not by fuse but on contact, and entered the war just as the U-boat captains had become adept at evading depth charges. By increasing the strength of U-boat hulls so that they could withstand the pressure at 600 feet, a U-boat captain could now listen on the hydrophones for the roar of a warship overhead, and the telltale splash of the depth charges, and immediately increase to full speed, turning sharply while diving. During the time it took for the depth charge to fall, the U-boat would have disappeared. The Hedgehog enabled the explosives to be hurled ahead, while the U-boat was still within ASDIC contact, and before it could turn and dive.[18]

In the months that followed the development of Raspberry, using information gleaned via debriefs, Roberts and the Wrens developed numerous other tactical manoeuvres to suit the expanding variety

---

* Huff-duff was initially used by coastal sites early in the war.

of wolfpack attacks. Most of these manoeuvres, which involved the escort ships performing different shapes and varieties of coordinated sweeps to find and hunt lurking U-boats, were given the memorable names of fruit and vegetables: 'Pineapple', 'Gooseberry', 'Strawberry', 'Artichoke' and a modification to the original manoeuvre, known as a 'Half-Raspberry'. These new manoeuvres provided escort ships with the tactics needed to go on the offensive, hunting U-boats before they made an attack rather than, in the case of Raspberry, after a merchant ship had been lost. Some, such as 'Umbrella', explored what to do in the event of a battle with a German surface raider – a merchant ship that had been fitted with powerful guns – rather than a U-boat.

The workload soon took a toll on Roberts. Donald Macintyre, Kretschmer's captor, recalled that Roberts was 'never well' and 'constantly in pain'.[19] The captain's weight dropped to eight stone. The rigours of overwork were compounded when, in the late autumn of 1942, Roberts and the Wrens learned that their staunch advocate Sir Percy Noble was leaving Derby House. The commander-in-chief of Western Approaches had been transferred to Washington DC to work alongside the US Navy in protecting American convoys from the U-boat threat. It was a serious blow: Noble was beloved by all at Derby House and WATU would lose a powerful ally. Their sense of dismay was heightened when they learned the name of his replacement: the imposing Max Horton, submarine ace of the First World War famed, also, for his brusque manner and quick temper.

To bid Noble goodbye and welcome Horton in his place, the king and queen arranged a visit to Derby House. On 17th November 1942, the royals arrived accompanied by Vera Laughton Mathews, director of the Wrens, on her first visit.

On arrival, Laughton Mathews asked a naval officer if her Wrens were executing their duties well.

'Well,' he replied, 'as they are doing the bulk of the work, I suppose they are.'[20]

Roberts, to his astonishment, learned that the royal party would be visiting WATU during their visit. And not only that, they had also requested a demonstration of the game. The morning of the visit the Wrens were, as Roberts later recalled, 'all of a twitter'.[21]

Despite the pressure, the Wrens performed a perfect Raspberry manoeuvre on the plot, while Roberts brought life and colour to the scene with his usual theatrical embellishments.

Afterwards, the king, who recognised Roberts from their Christmas meeting on the London Underground platform two years earlier, approached him. He asked about Roberts' health and admonished him for getting too thin.[22] Finally, King George gestured at the floor, still littered with the remnants of the game, a shanty town of play.

'This,' he said, leaning in, 'is the key to the Battle of the Atlantic.'

PART THREE

It was the job of the little ships and lonely aircraft, dreary and unpublicised, against two cunning enemies, the U-boat and the cruel sea.

Captain Gilbert Roberts

XIII

The Elephant Has Landed

John Lamb and half a dozen other British naval officers tumbled through the front doors of a well-to-do apartment block on a warm, late-spring New York evening.

Avoiding the glare of the doorman, the group jostled into the elevator and began the rattling ride to the Park Avenue building's summit. Lamb, former first lieutenant of *Vanoc*, a member of Captain Walker's crack pack of U-boat-hunting destroyers and a ship so old that it carried cutlasses,[1] had landed in Manhattan in early May 1942 while, 3,000 miles away, WATU was entering its fourth month of operation.

The twenty-five-year-old was in high spirits. After months at sea, living each day with the awful promise of violence, the past few weeks had been a blur of dances, parties and mingling with mavens of New York high society while his current ship, HMS *Glasgow*, underwent a refit in Brooklyn's shipyard.* With no firm estimate on how long the repairs might take, the sailors had thrown themselves into a city only too eager to welcome them, thank them for their service, and then take whatever money they had to spare.

Lamb's home for his stay was Barbizon Plaza, an art deco hotel on the south-west corner of 6th Avenue and 59th Street, which many decades later became the Trump Parc condominiums. Originally this fashionable building was topped with a roof of tiny glass tiles that, during the day, shimmered in the sunlight. At night they emitted a

---

* HMS *Glasgow*'s bow and stern were patched up in Singapore after the ship was hit by two torpedoes in the Mediterranean, but it soon became clear that it needed further repairs.

humming prism of light into the sky. When America's entry to the war drew the attention of German bombers, the tiles were removed to help facilitate city-wide, London-style blackouts. Despite the luxurious surroundings, Lamb's dollar allowance meant that, unable to afford to eat in the hotel restaurant, he and the other officers would buy their meals from the basement drugstore, along with the bellhops and waiting staff. It didn't matter. In the first glow of foreign adventure, when even the dullest routine is ripe with novelty and wonder, the eyes are yet to adjust to class distinctions. Besides, there was no shortage of Americans willing to dine with the British.

'Everywhere the friendliness was fantastic,' Lamb recalled in his diary. 'It was impossible to enter a bar or coffee shop and be allowed to pay for one's own refreshment.'[2]

To those Americans situated inland, the war was a distant, disinterested conflict. Not so for New Yorkers. By war's outbreak, more than 95,000 German and Austrian Jews had emigrated to America, a large proportion of whom had landed in New York City with firsthand experience of the Nazi threat to life and liberty.[3] After France fell to the Germans in the summer of 1940, the U-boats' range spanned the ocean, and as the months passed, an increasing number of American merchant ships, which had neglected to adopt the British convoy system, were lost to German torpedoes. Despite this, President Roosevelt remained reticent to enter the war. Following the attack on Pearl Harbor on 7th December 1941, when 3,500 American servicemen were killed or wounded and eighteen ships were sunk or run aground, the US declared war on Japan. Then, on 11th December 1941, Hitler declared war on the United States.

On 14th January 1942, four months before Lamb's arrival, the Battle of the Atlantic came to the New York coastline. *U-123*, captained by Reinhard Hardegen and equipped with no more than a nautical chart and a guidebook to Manhattan Island marked with its inlets and harbours, was one of the first to arrive, picking its way into the Ambrose Channel, New York's main shipping approach. Just after half past one in the morning *U-123*'s watch officer detected moving lights, around two-and-a-half miles away, to port. When the U-boat's torpedo struck the Panamanian-flagged oil tanker *Norness*, a plume of flame tore into the air, as high as a skyscraper.

All but two crew members, including one puppy, made it off the vessel before a second torpedo sent it beneath the waves. The dog's owner, Paul Georgson, managed to carry it onto a waiting lifeboat, but the sodden animal was shivering so violently that Georgson decided there was no way it could survive. 'So, I said "goodbye" to him,' he later recalled, 'then brained him on the deck.'[4]

The following day, 15th January, the U-boat drew closer still to the city, and torpedoed the British tanker *Coimbra*. The attack was near enough to shore that residents of the Hamptons called the authorities to report the swell of firelight on the horizon. Two days later a report on the front page of the *New York Times* confirmed the attack and quoted a US Navy warning that the 'U-boat menace along the East Coast' was 'increasingly serious'.[5] Over the next four months *U-123* and a clutch of other U-boats terrorised the east coast of America, operating with near impunity. The US Navy was unprepared to fend off what Doenitz had code-named Operation Drumbeat. By the time Lamb's ship pulled past the Statue of Liberty on 6th May 1942, New Yorkers felt firmly invested in what had previously been viewed as a remote, European concern.

Before their arrival in New York City, Lamb and his crew members had been busy in the South China Sea and had not had time to visit WATU and take the course. For them, Raspberry was little more than a set of written instructions on a piece of paper. Without hands-on experience of the operation, nor training on how to effectively work with other escort ships while protecting a convoy, the crew was yet to adopt the latest tactics to come out of Liverpool. Their ship, HMS *Glasgow*, bore the scars of its crew's inexperience. The opportunity, then, for an extended rest stop on a foreign continent and a break from the chaotic business of battling U-boats was a relief.

'The welcome [we] received, first from the United States Navy, then the Dockyard and finally from shore organisations and unknown citizens sustained the thrill of arrival in a legendary city,' Lamb later recalled. As the *Glasgow* underwent repairs, he and his fellow officers were free to enjoy the city, half a world away from the bombings in Liverpool and London. In the same month that the remaining US troops in the Philippines surrendered, and the

Japanese captured Burma, for Lamb and his fellow officers life almost resembled peacetime.

The benefits of the British naval presence in New York flowed in both directions. With U-boats nudging around Long Island, the sailors brought with them a reassurance. For many of the city's eligible young women, here too was an influx of young men to broaden and exoticise the dating pool. Introductions were made at the White Ensign Club, the English-Speaking Union and similar organisations, and many of the men were duly adopted by welcoming families.

Lamb received dozens of invitations to lunch, tea and dinner from families, spinsters, church members and other assorted New Yorkers. The first hostess, who invited him to tea, had laid out her silver service for his benefit. After offering Lamb a toasted teacake, she requested he make the tea as, in the presence of an Englishman, she felt 'inadequate' to the task. Lamb, having only ever made mugs of ship's thick cocoa, blagged his way through the ceremony. The young lieutenant attended his second engagement with a colleague. The pair were greeted at the door by two older women wearing silk pyjamas, who, after inviting the two Englishmen in, revealed that their husbands were serving in the Pacific and, as Lamb put it, 'gave the impression that they were ready and willing for any duty'. Lamb and his friend, he wrote, made swift excuses and 'fled'.

On another occasion Lamb started talking to a pretty young New Yorker at the White Ensign Club. Jeanette, as the woman introduced herself, invited Lamb to her parents' house for dinner, after which, she suggested, they might go dancing. Thrilled at the unexpected invitation and unburdened by the social mores that might have complicated such a night in England, Lamb agreed.

'Which one is yours?' he asked, when the pair arrived outside a tall building on smart East 69th Street. Jeanette gestured at the entire building in front of them and smiled. Lamb's date, it transpired, was Jeanette Watson, daughter of Thomas Watson, millionaire founder of the IBM corporation.

'Daddy doesn't normally allow drink in the house,' Jeanette said, as she brought Lamb a glass of sherry. 'But he thinks British naval officers have need of it.'

For the next six weeks, the Watsons welcomed Lamb into their family, introducing him to various well-to-do members of New York's social scene. Lamb considered Jeanette his girlfriend but, not knowing for how long he would be in town, or when he might be back, the pair kept their relationship social.

Some of the British engaged in more intimate relationships during their stay. According to Lamb, the captain of the Marines moved in with a woman he met at a nightclub on his first night ashore. He worked in the day, she the night, and as a result of their disharmonious working hours, Lamb recalled that the captain would often appear bleary-eyed in front of the Royal Marines guard at the colour-hoisting ceremony each morning.

For Lamb, much of that happy spring was lost in a haze of parties. He found that many of New York's butlers and bartenders were expatriate Brits and would mix him 'special' drinks, double and triple martinis, daiquiris and old-fashioneds. When Jeanette introduced her new boyfriend to friends and guests, saying, 'Now Lootenant, perhaps you would give us the British point of view . . .', Lamb would have to summon the formidable concentration of the inebriated and, in deliberate words, speak for queen and country.

A few days before Lamb visited the Park Avenue apartment block that spring, a New York bachelor friend had asked him to summon a delegation of British naval officers to come for drinks. Lamb expected just such an evening lay ahead, as he and his comrades rode the elevator up to the penthouse and knocked on the door.

As it opened, and warmth and light spilled into the corridor, Lamb was greeted with a dreamlike scene, something at once celestial and devilish. Flanking his host stood a phalanx of tall and pristine giantesses, a 'bevvy of beauties', as he later recalled.[6] He did not know it yet, but they were the Powers Girls, members of the world's first modelling agency, founded by John Robert Powers. On a deep sofa behind the women sat their chaperone, Condé Nast, editor of *Vogue*.* The two groups, separated by a universe of background and experience, greeted one another, then made faltering small talk through the evening. At last the officers bade their hosts goodnight and left the building.

'None of us made future dates,' Lamb later recalled. 'We were

---

* Nast died of a heart attack four months later.

not in the same league, we thought – certainly not financially.'

Like a dream within a dream, the curious texture of that night with the world's most notable magazine editor and his models slipped away when, long before the end of summer, Lamb received news from Brooklyn Navy Yard that his ship would not be ready for weeks. The crew could not be spared the wait and he was to set sail on the next available boat.

'All good things must end,' he wrote.[7] Lamb would have to trade the reverie of his heiress girlfriend, unrationed drinks and high-rise parties for the Atlantic Ocean, with all its exigent weather and assassins.

In November 1942, while Roberts was enjoying the afterglow of His Majesty's affirmation ('seeing stars,' as he put it[8]) on the top floor of Derby House, Admiral Max Horton, incoming commander-in-chief of Western Approaches, sidled up to the captain, the rumour of a smile on his lips.

Horton, who had advised Roberts over the telephone a few months earlier about the range of a German torpedo, was a different sort of man from the outgoing Sir Percy Noble. Noble, who had commanded cruisers earlier in his career, was easy-going, urbane and cherished by his staff, whose names he knew by heart and whom, as one staff officer put it, he managed with 'graciousness' and 'adeptness'.[9] Despite their early relationship being characterised by painful misunderstanding, Roberts later described Noble as 'a great diplomat' with 'tremendous charm.'[10]

Horton, by contrast, was squat and bullish, and had the temperament and tenacity of a great submariner. Western Approaches staff nicknamed him 'the Elephant', a reference to his blunt, charmless power. Horton addressed the women of Derby House not by name but with the rude and rankling bark 'Wren'. The smile – 'catlike', as Roberts described it – became notorious in Derby House corridors; one never quite knew whether it was going to bloom into a snarl or a purr.

According to one member of his staff, he was 'ruthless', not only in his dealings with staff, but also in his offensive-minded approach to fighting the Germans. The misery of the Holocaust had been neither fully realised nor revealed at this point in 1942, but enough was known about the Nazi treatment of the Jewish people that Horton, a Jew via his mother's side of the family, fought not just with the intellect, but with the blood. Horton developed an eccentric schedule, waking late morning to play golf all afternoon, retiring after dinner for bridge before arriving at the office around 23:30, just when the night-time battles preferred by the U-boat captains began. He typically arrived to work in worn and split pyjamas and with a tall glass of barley water in his fist, ready to direct the convoy battles on the huge plot.

There was one thing he shared with his mannerly predecessor, however: a scepticism toward this rogue group of game-players squatting in the roof of his new headquarters.

'And what duty do you think you perform on my staff?' Horton sarcastically asked Roberts after the king and queen had left the room, apparently having forgotten their phone-call, several months earlier. WATU had been training naval officers for more than nine months by this point, but apparently word of their work and success had passed by the incoming commander. Roberts bristled at the question.

'I am the director of the tactical staff,' he replied. 'If you want to know further, I suggest that you find the time to come and see what we do.'[11]

'Yes, I will,' Horton replied, curtly.

The following Monday, he appeared at WATU's front door, ready to take the course, not as an invigilator but as a student. As the week progressed the frost between the two men thawed. Just as Roberts had promised, through game-play Horton was able to both see and experience the value of the unit's work, the growing expertise of the Wrens and Roberts' own increasing confidence as ringmaster of the operation.

'It was only a game,' Horton later wrote of his conversion, 'but the lessons were driven home.' The 'ghastly mistakes' that players made on the floor would arm them with foreknowledge that would 'put them on their guard and give them confidence when they took their ships to sea on the morrow'. Roberts did well to impress Horton, who had dismissed or redeployed from Derby House a clutch of other officers he considered to be deadwood.

At the time of Horton's arrival, the Wrens, of whom there were now more than thirty at WATU, were becoming ever more knowl-edgeable. Week by week they were accruing dozens of hours' virtual combat experience, testing and perfecting anti-submarine warfare at the bleeding edge of tactical design.

'These girls became so experienced in the tactics of convoy battle that they were able to save many a salt-encrusted sea-dog from making the errors which would inevitably lead to disaster to their convoys of model ships,' wrote Donald Macintyre,[12] who had captured Kretschmer the year before and was by now a regular face at WATU, attending as both player and observer.

Through their vicarious experiences in the game the brightest and most diligent Wrens, including Laidlaw and Okell, were quietly becoming some of the most fearsome U-boat hunters in the British Empire, even if the U-boats happened to be little wooden models, and the sea a linoleum floor.

Soon after Horton's arrival, Roberts was busily working to expose what he believed was another of Captain Walker's ill-conceived tactics. This manoeuvre, which Walker had dubbed 'Alpha', involved ships performing a sweeping zigzag search in an effort to sink a so-called 'sighting' U-boat, which was suspected to be shadowing a convoy while directing a wolfpack toward its position. Roberts had tested Walker's tactic using the game and 'it didn't seem too logical'.[13] Roberts reported his misgivings to Horton.

'Well,' said Horton. 'You will do better, will you not?'

During the next few days Roberts and Laidlaw began to develop a replacement tactic, which involved exploiting the U-boat captain's natural caution by tricking him into ordering his vessel to dive to avoid an escort moving into potential spotting distance. Hearing the escort pass by and believing that he had not been seen, the submerged U-boat would then move to what it assumed was a safer location. Wargames and experience suggested this would be a slow turn designed to place the U-boat in a position parallel to the convoy while conserving its batteries. The escort ships would dash towards its predicted position, using the rumble of the convoy ships' propel-lers to mask their approach. The idea was that the U-boat, having realised that it was not under attack, would be too occupied with the wider convoy battle to notice the redirection of its adversary.

After tweaking, replaying and further tweaking the manoeuvre over and over again, the pair were happy with the tactic, which they dubbed 'Beta Search', named after the fact that U-boat transmissions always began with the Morse B (Beta), or B-bar, and Roberts invited Horton up to WATU not only to hear about their plan, but to be one of the first outsiders to experience and test its usefulness.

Before Horton arrived, Roberts summoned Janet Okell and Jean Laidlaw, and informed them, to their dismay, that they were to play as the commander-in-chief's opponent. Laidlaw would work in a side room, passing advice to Okell, who would play as the escort commander in the main room, hidden from Horton's view behind one of the canvas sheets. Roberts' decision to give a junior Wren such an important role was controversial but based on her having repeatedly demonstrated an instinctive grasp of U-boat tactics.[14] He was certain that she would be a worthy opponent to Horton. The two women huddled around the sheets of paper in Laidlaw's office, onto which the instruction for Beta Search had been written, to coordinate their plan.[15]

Peeping through the canvas porthole, Janet Okell looked even more schoolgirlish than usual, like a lookout at the classroom window poised to signal the arrival of a furious teacher to her chalk-hurling classmates. On the other side of the room, studying a fleet of tiny wooden ships on the lino-covered floor, stood fifty-nine-year-old Horton, the greatest living British submariner. Twenty-year-old Okell, by contrast, had never been in a submarine. In fact, she had never been to sea.

When Horton arrived at WATU, Roberts asked him whether he might like to play not as the Allied escort ships, but as a U-boat captain. It was a shrewd suggestion. The efficacy of Beta Search – and of WATU and its games – could be irrefutably proven if it could be shown to beat one of the most highly decorated British submariners. As much as Derby House staff had come to fear Horton, nobody doubted his extraordinary talent for submarining; time and again he had anticipated U-boats' behaviour on the real plot with ship-saving prescience.

Okell fixed the admiral with a determined stare. Her objective was straightforward: sink Horton's U-boat, its position hidden from her view, taking pot-shots at her ships. Turn by turn Okell, standing behind the canvas sheet, and supported by Laidlaw, directed her escort ships, executing a perfectly planned Beta Search. Five times Horton attempted to escape the escort ships, and five times Okell and Laidlaw destroyed his U-boat.* On the fifth sinking, Horton, who had become increasingly flustered with each loss, erupted.

'You can see, and I can't,' he roared. 'You just rigged it, didn't you?'[16]

Roberts indignantly explained that, no, the game had not been rigged. Then Horton harrumphingly asked to see who, exactly, was standing behind the canvas, laying waste to his submarines. To his disbelief, a young woman stepped out. The submarine ace had been beaten by someone who was barely out of school, who had never been on an escort ship, had never seen battle, and who, worse still, wasn't even an officer.

Finally, Roberts led the smarting Horton into the Wrens Officers' Staff Room, where Third Officer Laidlaw sat at a desk, her handwritten notes outlining Beta Search splayed out in front of her. Laidlaw and Okell shared a smile, and in that moment Horton's admiration for the Wrens surely overtook his dismay.

In the months that followed, the training establishment at Liverpool grew and grew, with WATU as its centrepiece. Such was the Wrens' effectiveness in running The Game at WATU that when it was time to expand the training facilities with new kinds of simulation, the Admiralty chose to appoint a young woman to oversee and orchestrate the work.

Mary Charlotte Poole arrived in Liverpool in the late summer of 1942, having been chosen to establish a new division within the anti-submarine school. Poole, who was born on Christmas Day, 1921, was an exceptionally bright young woman, forced by war's arrival to turn down the offer of a place at Cambridge University. She had joined the

---

* In Horton's brief telling of the anecdote, via his biographer, the pair played the game three times, not five.

Wrens aged 20 and in December 1941 was posted to the tunnels under Dover Castle to work as a signals watchkeeper. On one of Churchill's visits to the Naval Operations Room, he asked Poole if she was frightened when the German cross-channel guns shelled Dover.

'I couldn't quite believe that this man was asking me the question,' she later recalled. 'As I stood in front of him, I burst out laughing saying "Good gracious no, Sir!" I got into dreadful trouble for laughing in front of the Prime Minister, but it came from the heart. It had never entered our heads; it was part of the job. There was no fear, no nothing attached to it at all.'[17]

After completing her officer's training Poole left for Liverpool. On arrival she was shown to an enormous, empty warehouse on Gladstone Dock, a few hundred metres from Derby House. This hangar was, Poole was told, to be her new school. Captain Roberts invited Poole, who knew nothing about anti-submarine warfare and took the post simply because she thought 'it'd be lovely to be among the ships'[18] to his school, where she was to become the first woman to undertake the course, not as a helper but as a student.

Poole arrived at WATU on a Monday morning, a little later than the other students. As she walked into the main room, she was confronted with the sight of forty-nine naval officers – sub lieutenants, lieutenants, a few lieutenant commanders as well as ill or injured members of escort ships, who were made to take the course while they recuperated – sitting in chairs around the edge of the game plot, with Captain Roberts in the centre of the circle. On cue, every man politely rose to his feet.

'I didn't know where I was or what I was supposed to be doing,' Poole later recalled. 'But I did learn. It was an extraordinary way of teaching.'

The course completed, Poole learned that her offshoot school was to teach the captains of escort ships how to make evasive manoeuvres to dodge torpedoes. One of these torpedoes had been captured by the Allies and dismantled.* Through this process, the Allies figured

---

* Poole does not record the model of this captured torpedo but, considering the date of her arrival to Liverpool, it was likely to be the *Federapparat*.

out that the German torpedoes had to keep within a certain angle of approach, or lose their target. It was therefore possible to outrun a torpedo, providing the target executed a particular zigzag pattern.

To teach the men this evasive manoeuvre, Poole was given a giant simulator. A ship's bridge, almost full size, was built and installed in the warehouse at Gladstone Dock. It sat within a see-saw mechanism that allowed it to simulate the movement of the sea. Poole would run the game with a ship's captain, flag lieutenant and navigator, who were used to working together at sea.

'The [players] would all be swanning around doing nothing, then the ASDIC would pick up the torpedo,' Poole recalled. 'Then it was action stations, and all began to happen.'

Through a pair of speakers, the warning signal would sound and a pre-recorded ASDIC 'hit' would play, indicating the angle of the incoming torpedo. The crew would have to perform evasive manoeuvres using the giant apparatus. If they failed to outrun or dodge the torpedo, an obnoxiously loud banger known as a thunder-flash was let off by one of Poole's fifteen staff members.* They would also release smoke capsules to mimic the disorientating effects of a direct hit, when the alarms howled, the floor tipped and, in the most extreme cases, visibility shrank to a few feet.

'It was as real as that,' Poole later said.

Poole, like Roberts, designed a clutch of different fake battle scenarios – eight in total, which lasted forty-five minutes each – and the ship's crews would often return to replay through each variation. As with WATU, word of Poole's game spread quickly. Soon she was training the majority of escort crews that came through Liverpool, including those of aircraft carriers and, much later in February 1944, the senior officers of the giant battleship HMS *King George V*, who took three lessons in total. Unlike WATU, however, Poole's outfit was never given a formal title. To allocate a woman to such an operation was unprecedented and represented a significant victory for Laughton Mathews in her secondary campaign to loosen the tight constrictions on female opportunity. Poole was one of the many Wrens who, as Laughton Mathews later put it, 'had started

---

* No fewer than ten of Poole's staff were Wrens ratings.

in very junior positions and had developed ability and qualities of leadership of which they themselves were quite unaware'.[19] Her role was significant, her work vital and yet, without a man like Roberts at the project's centre to fight for legacy, Poole's work was forgotten.

'We were in this great big building at the end of the dock,' she later recalled, 'everyone knew where we were, but we never got a name.'

Elsewhere at the training facility, the men responsible for setting the timers on and firing depth charges were drilled till they could fire full patterns of explosives at fifteen-second intervals, building efficiency that would, at sea, often mean the difference between a hit and a miss on a U-boat. Teams responsible for operating the ASDIC sonar systems hunted imaginary U-boats on the synthetic attack teacher while, in a hut at Gladstone Dock, next to Poole's torpedo-evasion trainer, communications staff were taught how to use a new cypher machine. According to Kretschmer's captor Donald Macintyre, the 'pleasantly secluded' hut was run by a 'very glamorous Wren officer', and his younger officers made 'remarkable . . . slow progress', requiring 'a great many lessons before the intricacies of the machine were mastered'.

Liverpool became a training hive, with hundreds of individuals and teams practising and perfecting their various roles in the art of U-boat warfare, from the wet-work of hauling explosive barrels overboard, to the bird's-eye strategy taught at WATU.

Roberts was also eager to develop his talents.

'You can't put anything over unless you impress on those who are tired . . . that it is something of the highest interest,' Roberts later said. 'If you imbue them with [excitement], they will play and fight and work to the best event.'[20]

In seeking to improve his communication skills, Roberts appealed to the best-loved entertainer of the moment, Tommy Handley, a Liverpudlian turned national institution. Every Thursday at half-past eight, millions of Britons would gather around their radio sets and listen to Handley's radio show, *It's That Man Again*. *ITMA*, as it became affectionately known, provided the unique salve of comedy to the national consciousness, an oasis of absurdity in a world that had become unbearably severe. In *ITMA*, a nation so used to collective grief now had a chance to laugh together, and the programme soon broke the record for the largest radio audience show, one that has remained ever since.*

Part of the appeal lay in Handley's talent for imagining comic characters. He would exaggerate clichés and tie them off with catch-phrase ribbons. These would spread, meme-like, through the streets, factories and ships. Colonel Chinstrap, a character who lived on after Handley's death with appearances in *The Goon Show*, was an army drunk, inhaling fingers of whisky with a 'Don't mind if I do.' Mrs Mopp was a lewd charwoman (a progenitor of Mrs Slocombe from *Are You Being Served?*), forever inquiring 'Can I do you now, sir?' Signor So-So would skitter indecisively ('I go – I come back!') while Frisby Dyke had a treacle-thick Liverpool accent. Handley's triumph, for the wartime context at least, was Funf the Spy, a foreign operative who would uselessly attempt to muffle and mask his reports by speaking into a glass mostly pressed over his mouth.

It was while *ITMA* was at the height of its popularity that Handley, who had served with a kite-balloon section of the Royal Naval Air Service during the First World War, received word from Captain Roberts. Roberts wanted to know how Handley was able to capture and hold the attention of millions, and how he might employ some of the same techniques to inspire the war-weary sailors arriving at WATU's door.

Against all regulations the pair arranged to meet up. Roberts invited Handley to WATU's confidential premises on a Sunday and explained the difficulty he was finding, as a 'chairbound fellow', in capturing the attention of his exhausted students who, after multiple trips across the Atlantic, were often in desperate need of rest and relaxation. Handley gave Roberts a number of 'gimmicks' to deploy with his hands. 'He was immensely good at telling me how to talk and excite their interest', Roberts later recalled.[21] Comics transmute the angst and sorrow of their lives into comedy; they spill their guts on stage in the hope and belief that the specificity of their experience will prove, somehow, universal. Roberts was not telling

---

* A forebear of *The Goon Show*, which begat *That Was the Week That Was*, which begat *Monty Python's Flying Circus* and so on, the ghost of *ITMA* and, it follows, Handley's likeness can be seen down British comedy's family tree to today.

jokes on the radio, or in front of booze-loosened crowds, but there was a symmetry in his and Handley's roles: to pull, from the darkness of the imagination, scenarios that brought the listener to attention. Handley's advice proved effective. The Canadian officer A. F. C. Layard later described the WATU director as a 'very good lecturer, very theatrical and, of course, would like you to know that he was seventy-five per cent responsible for the recent defeat of the U-boats in the North Atlantic. He's probably right.'[22]

By the end of 1942, as many as 200 naval officers per month were playing The Game. Horton was by no means the only luminary to graduate. There was Davey 'Potato' Jones, a Welsh captain in the British Merchant Marine who had gained notoriety in 1937 for almost embroiling the Royal Navy in Spain's civil war when attempting to smuggle guns into Bilbao hidden under sacks of potatoes. There was Peter Scott, the naturalist painter who one of the WATU Wrens remembered for drawing ducks all over his navigational chart.[23] And there was a young Philip Mountbatten, future husband to Queen Elizabeth II.

The dashing Mountbatten's presence around the unit brought many of the WATU Wrens 'unending delight', as one put it.[24] He too apparently enjoyed his time there; not only did he finish the course, he also supported Roberts on the plot for a few weeks while waiting for his ship to be made ready.* So too did the journalist turned naval surgeon Nicholas Monsarrat, who had seen first-hand the devastation that U-boats could cause when uncontested, not least in the deaths of the Wrens on the SS *Aguila*. The author's time on the course made an indelible impression. In his 1951 novel *The Cruel Sea*, Monsarrat sends his fictional captain, Commander Ericson, on a 'Commanding Officers Tactical Course', clearly based on WATU. Monsarrat describes

---

* Prince Philip remained in contact with Roberts throughout his life and sent a written message of condolence to Roberts' wife upon hearing news of his death. At the time of writing this book, however, the prince wrote to say that he could no longer reliably recall specifics about his time at WATU.

in detail a 'convoy game' played out with models on the floor
of an empty room:

> 'U-boats crowded round, and their escorts had to work out
> their counter-tactics and put them into effect as they would
> do at sea. A formidable RN captain was in charge; and a large
> number of patient Wrens stood by, moving the ship models,
> bringing the latest "signals" and sometimes discreetly advising
> the next course of action. Rather unfairly they seemed to
> know all about everything.'

By late 1942 there were thirty-six Wren officers and ratings working
at WATU and, with such a large number of eligible young men
and eligible young women working together in a playful environment, there were inevitable romantic flowerings.

That year Fred Osborne – brother of Nancy the first chief officer
of the Wrens, and captain of HMS *Gentian*, a member of Donald
Macintyre's escort group – took the WATU course and caught the eye
of Liz Drake, one of the Wrens officers who had helped establish the
school. When Fred returned the following year as a teacher on an
eight-month posting, the couple became engaged to be married.
Engagements like these became a pattern, and many of the Wrens
would later attend each other's weddings, occasionally in a formal role,
as in the case of Janet Okell, who was a bridesmaid to Doris Lawford.

During his time game-playing, Peter Gretton – lieutenant
commander of the destroyer *Wolverine*, who alongside Walker and
Macintyre became one of the great U-boat hunters of the war –
became enamoured with Judy Du Vivier, the young Wren whom
Bob Whinney described as a 'particularly clued-up girl' after she
corrected one of his mistakes in the game. After his *coup de foudre*,
Gretton – later a major player in the Battle of Birds and Wolves,
the decisive confrontation of the Battle of the Atlantic – asked Du
Vivier on a date, and the pair met formally at a Liverpool restaurant
on Trafalgar Day, in late October 1942.

Promptly thereafter Du Vivier fell out with a Wren officer at
Derby House and was 'disrated' to 'ordinary Wren' after she was
minutes late to an appointment (Du Vivier believed this

disproportionate punishment was the result of romantic jealousy triggered by her relationship with Gretton[25]). To Gretton's dismay, Du Vivier was posted to the Londonderry Tactical Unit, a spin-off group that was beginning to run training courses in the mode of WATU's work. There, together with a Wren officer and two other Wrens ratings, Du Vivier helped to plot examples of convoy operations for the training of officers, just as she had learned to do from Roberts.

William Tooley-Hawkins, a handsome corvette captain who joined WATU staff in October 1943, became one of Roberts' most dearly loved colleagues (in his diary, Roberts refers to him as 'my loyal Tooley-Hawkins'). Tooley-Hawkins, who was married with a young son, fell in love with Elizabeth 'Bunch' Hackney, another of the school's Wrens, and soon and scandalously left his wife to be with her.

War, combined with the unexpected freedom it bestowed on many young women, created a boiler-room atmosphere in which relationships could thrive. Wrens, like the eligible male officers they courted, were aware of their youthful nubility, and often chose uniforms a size or two too large before taking them to Mama's tailor in the city in order to secure, as Mary Carlisle, the Wren who worked the plot at Derby House put it, a 'slinkier fit'.[26] Many of the Wrens delighted in tying the bows on their hats, on which the name of their shore establishment, HMS *Eaglet*, was printed in such a way that the 't' was masked, so it read *'Eagle'*, which they believed sounded more fashionable. Sailors were expert in tying bows, Hall explained. 'One could always find a friend in Derby House to oblige.'

The complex social negotiations between men and women who were serving in close proximity, often for the first time, was illustrated in a popular anecdote widely shared between Wrens. It involved a group of Wrens who worked with the Fleet Air Arm, and the pilot of a Fairey Swordfish biplane.

The pilot had landed his plane, fresh from action. As the group of Wrens approached, the pilot refused to disembark while ordering the Wrens to go inside. Only after the Wrens had left the scene would the pilot allow himself to be helped down by a colleague.

'My God, man,' the colleague said, 'you've been shot!'

'Thank God for that,' the pilot replied. 'I thought I'd shit myself.'[27]

At sea, Monsarrat wrote, the sailor's reputation for lascivious talk was earned ('the tone of conversation does not exactly reflect a humble worship at the shrine of womanhood', he explained).[28] Ashore, however, the writer-lieutenant maintained that all the talk of 'torpedoing' and 'other inelegant exploits' dissipated, especially when a sailor was in the position of having to talk to a woman alone, a situation that transformed the man, Monsarrat maintained, into a 'model of deference and attention'. Only when with his pack would a sailor 'lack the courage or the initiative to treat women as normal human beings.' Monsarrat also noted the sailors' 'special affection' for Wrens, who were 'looked on, not as fair game but as part of the Service, and thus to be protected and preserved from outsiders'.

Not all men were so chivalrous. The ebullient Nancy Spain, who worked as a driver before her promotion to Wren officer, wrote of an incident when two cadets pinched her bottom. In response, Spain banged their heads together so hard that they attempted to report her to the sick-berth petty officer. Nothing came of the matter, other than Spain ended the war otherwise unmolested.

Pamela Bates, a coder at Bletchley Park, remembered some of the British sailors arriving on shore 'rather short on sex', and expecting to be met with open arms and warm beds, having read that the 'Americans laid every single girl in Britain'.[29] Mary Carlisle, one of the first Wrens to arrive in Liverpool, received the advice: 'Always beware of a sailor who asks you to talk with him on a fine day, and carries his raincoat: he's up to no good.'*[30]

On shore leave, away from the horrors of the Atlantic, sailors would drink heartily. Gladstone Dock, where Mary Poole ran her ASDIC trainer, became a popular haunt for lower-deck sailors. At night, the only illumination the shaded gangway lights of the docked ships, sailors could stumble through a small door, through heavy blackout curtains and into the heat and bustle of the Flotilla club, a long wooden shed with a refreshments counter at one end, and a bar at the other. The canteen was staffed by women volunteers. Packed each night, 'the noise, the fug, the

---

* The raincoat was presumably intended to be used as an impromptu blanket, on which a couple might lie.

pilchard sandwiches and, of course, the beer' all made, as one signalman put it, 'a haven of rest where we could forget our troubles for a short time'.[31]

Spilling drunkenly from such bars after hours, some of the men would look for other, more intimate ways to forget their troubles, and in this context, more serious sexual assaults sometimes took place.

Bates recalled her and her friends having their arms grabbed on numerous occasions by a sailor who would say 'Back of the ambulance?', indicating that he had a nearby location for quick sex. Reports of rape were uncommon, yet often dealt with in ways that reflected the punitive sexual attitudes toward women at the time. One Wren recalled a young 'unsophisticated' colleague who was asked to be taken home by a sailor with whom she had danced at a party at HMS *Grasshopper* in Weymouth.[32] As the pair walked the man leaned in for a kiss, which she reciprocated. 'He then raped her,' the Wren recalled. The victim reported the assault the following morning and the sailor was charged but acquitted by the judge, who ruled that she was partly to blame, having encouraged him by allowing the kiss.

Laughton Mathews was firmly against the distribution of condoms to sailors, which despite being limited in supply and ineffective were, according to one medical Sister, 'in great demand before a dance'. Despite her progressive politics, Laughton Mathews believed that the handing out of prophylactics 'lets it be known that the lowest [standard of conduct] is expected and prepared for'.[33]

Still, whenever a Wren had 'loved unwisely', as Laughton Mathews put it with extreme delicacy, the senior Wrens officers would fight their subordinate's corner to ensure that the blame was not hoisted onto the young woman, who typically sat at the lower end of a power balance tipped by both age and rank. When one naval officer's wife phoned a Wrens superintendent to complain of a young rating who had become involved with her husband, she was surprised to be told: 'If I were the girl's father, I should horsewhip your husband.'[34]

So great was the taboo of lesbianism at the time that same-sex romance within the Wrens goes unmentioned in official policy documents. Laughton Mathews' history of the service contains no reference to lesbianism, nor does the autobiography of Wren Nancy Spain, who later became a prominent broadcaster and whose homosexuality was public knowledge. Anecdotal evidence of lesbianism within the service exists.

'There was this case of two lesbians,' recalled Norma Deering, a coder from Bletchley Park, in 2010.[35] 'Two girls were found in one bunk together, they were separated of course, one was sent somewhere else, that was terrible in those days.' If Jean Laidlaw, who lived openly with a female partner in the 1960s, recognised her sexual identity while working at WATU, she seemingly did not act upon it, either to conform to societal views about the immorality of homosexual behaviour at the time, or to avoid the risk of being caught and relocated.

Roberts, for his part, adopted a fatherly stance toward many of his Wrens.

'Many a time I heard him dressing down some senior regular service officer because one of his "little wrens" had been subjected, in his opinion, to intimidation,' said George Phillips, who wrote and delivered Roberts' eulogy.[36] As well as frequently (and seemingly innocently) taking the young women of WATU out for dinner,[37] he would often write them personal notes of encouragement.

Roberts took particular care of June Duncan, a waiflike Wren who had joined WATU in its first months. The daughter of one of Liverpool's most successful fishmongers, who supplied cruise liners with fish imported from Iceland, Duncan was one of the youngest Wrens at WATU. On holiday on the north coast of the Isle of Man at war's outbreak, when she was just fifteen years old, Duncan's parents left their daughter in Ramsey with a doctor and his family. There she studied shorthand, attended Red Cross lectures and gathered sphagnum moss on the mountains to be used in splints. She knitted hospital stockings and balaclava helmets, before returning to Liverpool, where, having caught German measles, she spent several weeks living in the family's air-raid shelter, a converted washhouse. Hoping to join the Wrens, Duncan took a secretarial course at Miss Foulkes' Secretarial College for Young Ladies, returning to school to take her School Certificate.

At seventeen, Duncan applied to join the Wrens, only to be twice rejected due to being underweight. Determined to find a way into the service, Duncan and her mother plotted to cheat the system on her third attempt. Duncan's great-uncle was a sea captain who, after a sojourn, had brought home a handful of weighty Siamese silver nuggets. Duncan's mother sewed the nuggets into the hem of the young woman's coat. At the medical, Duncan gingerly stepped on to the weighing scales, which, thanks to the hidden trinkets, tipped over the threshold.

Early in her career at WATU, Duncan spilled an armload of heavy books, known as ACIs, onto the floor. As she knelt to tidy the mess, a man appeared beside her to assist. To her astonishment, it was Philip Mountbatten, whom Duncan and the other non-officer Wrens had been instructed never to address.

'I broke all the rules by thanking him profusely, nearly dropping them again,' Duncan wrote in her diary.

Duncan was keen to serve, but her passion was in the performing arts, not the military. A nervous, sensitive child, when she was three a doctor had advised the family to send her to dancing lessons to increase her self-confidence. At first, Duncan had sat 'cringing beside my mother' as the other children 'waltzed, galloped and polka'd up and down the room'.[38] Eventually she left her mother's side to join in, and her talent for dance was revealed. Later she attended Liverpool's Shelagh Elliot Clarke School of Dance and Drama in the evenings, and when she was twelve made her professional stage debut in a musical revue at the Liverpool Empire.

Duncan's artistic temperament, combined perhaps with her catwalk looks, ostracised her from many other women at Derby House. When she was performing, men in the audience would routinely leave notes for her at the stage door asking to meet her; after the war she became a top model for high-fashion magazines, including *Harper's Bazaar* and Condé Nast's *Vogue*.

Unlike many of the women, who maintain that their lives were invigorated by their time in the Wrens, Duncan struggled. She later wrote in her diary that she 'hated every minute'. Given the warm memories Duncan recounts elsewhere in her diaries, this was perhaps something of an exaggeration. Roberts, an astute leader, encouraged her to join the WRNS Dramatic Society and

Concert Party. There, among her people, she thrived, acting and singing in local repertory theatre, culminating in the performance of a song written especially for her on the BBC radio programme *Navy Mixture*.

Roberts attended Duncan's numerous performances, often writing her encouraging notes. 'Our most sincere congratulations on a very fine performance in your show last night,' reads one typical example. 'It was absolutely grand, and we all enjoyed ourselves immensely.'

Whatever animosity Duncan felt toward the other women of WATU was not directed at her captain, whom she remained in contact with throughout the remainder of their lives, another love that outlived the war.

Love came, too, for John Lamb. Following his safe return from New York City, he was dispatched to the South Atlantic as part of Operation Torch, the Allied invasion of French North Africa in November 1942. When he returned to the North Atlantic at the end of the year, the change in climate was painfully pronounced. To compound the issue, the Atlantic Ocean was experiencing an extended period of preternaturally bad weather.[39]

Scores of corvettes were sustaining considerable damage, while the convoys were routinely forced to slow their speed, thereby increasing the amount of time it took to cross the ocean. These delays had knock-on effects: the men had less time in port to recuperate before the next escort mission. Even when Liverpool's dockyard workers were recruited for boiler-cleaning duties to save time, the crews of escort ships, who often also had to fit in a tactical course at WATU, returned to sea unrested. Tiredness at sea, as on the road, is a killer.

Lamb's ship was the new fleet destroyer HMS *Oribi*. After the first lieutenant's previous vessels, the aged *Vanoc* and the damaged *Glasgow*, the speedy *Oribi* was a new and welcome home. But even this ship, captained by the experienced and competent Commander J. E. H. McBeath, a man who was reputed to have run away to sea as a boy in South Africa and worked his way up to commissioned rank, could not fend off the violence of the Atlantic in the excep-tionally tempestuous early months of 1943.

The ship 'rarely ceased from pitching, rolling and shaking', Lamb recalled. Water constantly washed round the mess decks and cabin flats, and the upper deck was 'untenable'. During one sortie, in the far north, the *Oribi*'s rigging and guard rails iced up 'as thick as a man's arm', and 'when she rolled, she would often hover at the point of no return before deciding to right herself, decks awash and the sea sometimes even lapping the wings of the lower bridge.' It was, as Lamb later recalled, 'much worse than the enemy'.[40]

Yet the enemy was not to be discounted. The steady production of new U-boats had grown Doenitz's fleet such that wolfpacks regularly comprised more than a dozen well-coordinated vessels. In early 1943, *Oribi* fended off an attack by five U-boats losing just one merchant ship out of forty-five in the action;[41] a few weeks later, the ship helped drive off seven U-boats that were attacking the fifty-seven-ship convoy HX.233. Immediately thereafter, the weather turned, and equinoctial gales inflicted severe structural damage on the *Oribi* while steaming at high speed into heavy seas. A crack extending about one third of the way across the 'iron deck' – the toughened steel deck amidships over the engine room on which the two quadruple torpedo tubes were secured – was discovered. If left unattended, it was a category of wound that could lead to a broken back, and the end of the ship's life.

On 30th March 1943 *Oribi* detached from the escort group, returned to Londonderry and, from there, limped around the northeastern coast of Northern Ireland to Belfast.[42] Christian Oldham was in Belfast Castle, finishing a shift at the plot when a signal announced *Oribi*'s arrival.

'I paid no attention,' she said. 'It was just another ship.'

Then a call came through to the Wrennery inviting the Wrens officers to join the officers of the *Oribi* in the wardroom after sundown. Never one to refuse an invitation to a party, Oldham joined the delegation of half a dozen Wrens that made its way down to harbour, across the gangway, onto the beleaguered boat and, it would transpire, into a new future.

XIV

Nulli Secundus

Christian Oldham entered HMS *Oribi*'s wardroom to a scene of juxtapositions: the gunmetal grey of the walls, with their protruding pipes and wheels, was offset by deep leather armchairs and a raft of officers, some of whom were in black tie. John Lamb took an immediate interest in Oldham. He handed her a drink and the pair holed up in a corner of the room and talked, in increasingly conspiratorial proximity, about their wars to date, and all the excitement and cruelty they had encountered along the way.[1] Time, distance and the pressing uncertainties of war had cooled Lamb's feelings for the New Yorker Jeanette Watson. Not knowing how long they had together, he began to pursue Oldham.

Oldham, however, left the party in a state of some confusion; here was an eligible officer who was clearly interested in her; yet, for the past months, she had been missing Lennox Napier, inscrutable captain of the submarine HMS *Rorqual*.

Lamb's pressured chase was typical of young men his age at the time. Shore leave compressed the business of living into a few short days. As Monsarrat later put it, living with the unshakeable fear of death at sea meant that as soon as you docked, there was an irresistible urge 'to tell people about it before you went out on convoy again; we all thought we were going to be killed'. Romance was just another way to feel yoked, not only to the land, but also to the business of existence. Whiplash engagements were commonplace.

During the next few days and evenings, while *Oribi*'s repairs were carried out, the pair began seeing each other, and within ten days, were engaged to be married.

'No time was wasted,' Lamb wrote in his diary, a dictum to which so many young men and women cleaved during the war, where time was so short, so threatened.[2]

Oldham felt 'a bit mean' toward Napier, of whom she remained 'extremely fond', but, as she reasoned, 'these things happen'.

'I didn't feel pressured to get engaged,' she later wrote. 'It just happened.'

The other Wrens at Belfast Castle delighted in the news of their friend's engagement, a happy distraction from the rigours of the plot where, as Oldham put it, they were nightly 'plunged' into 'frightful arenas', where the battles were viewed from a distance, but 'in which we felt an intimate part'.[3]

Three of Christian's closest friends, who dubbed themselves 'the Hags' Watch', sent her fiancé a letter of reference. Stamped 'SECRET', it read:

> We have known her for five months, and find her honest, sober, kind and cheerful at all times. In fact, she has never been seen in a temper or known to be bossy. She is quite approachable in the mornings though rather dopey for the first few minutes after waking. There has been a slight tendency to madness during the past fortnight, but otherwise she is considered normal, healthy and cleanly.

Not knowing how long they had till the *Oribi* was fit to sail again and when Lamb would return to the Atlantic, the pair decided to throw a black-tie engagement party, one of end-of-the-world proportions.

In Germany, things were changing at the top, and Karl Doenitz was positioned to benefit. On 30th December 1942, a U-boat in the Arctic detected a convoy travelling from Loch Ewe in the Highlands of Scotland to Murmansk in the Soviet Union. Admiral Raeder, commander of the German navy, informed Hitler that he intended to intercept and attack the Allied ships. It was a plan of which the Führer enthusiastically approved, hoping that it might deprive the

Russian army, which was currently surrounding the German 6th Army in Stalingrad, of supplies.

But Operation Rainbow, as the scheme was code-named, was bungled when, just as two of the German heavy cruisers were about to attack, a pair of escort destroyers protecting the convoy emerged from the gloom. The admiral in charge of the operation, Oskar Kummitz, had been repeatedly warned by his superiors not to place the *Kriegsmarine*'s most valuable surface vessels in danger, and even before a single shot was fired, he immediately ordered all of his ships to retreat. To worsen matters, Kummitz's report to Berlin of his retreat was misunderstood by Raeder to be news of a conquest. When Hitler received the message, he erroneously announced to his New Year guests a great naval victory.

When the embarrassing truth emerged, Hitler summoned Raeder and subjected the grand admiral to a ninety-minute tirade, threatening to scrap the *Kriegsmarine*'s battleships and redeploy their long-range guns as coastal defences. Raeder stood and took the verbal beating, which he later described as 'vicious and impertinent'. Then he tendered his resignation. Despite the animosity between Raeder and Doenitz, whom the grand admiral considered to be both stubborn and insubordinate, Raeder recommended his rival to Hitler as his replacement.

'The only disadvantage,' he wrote in a letter laden with subtext, 'is the fact that Admiral Doenitz . . . would not be able to dedicate himself to the immediate conduct of the U-boat war to the same extent as formerly.'[4]

Raeder was correct. To cede control of the U-boat arm was unthinkable for Doenitz, whose paternal instincts toward the young men in the division he founded had been further deepened when three members of his immediate family joined the service. Doenitz's eldest son Klaus joined the staff of the 5th U-flotilla at Kiel, his younger son Peter became second watch-keeping officer in *U-954*, and his son-in-law Günther Hessler was first staff officer under Doenitz's U-boat department chief, Eberhard Godt. To abandon the U-boat arm at such a time would be, for Doenitz, to abandon his family.

Frank Birch, head of the German Naval Section at Bletchley Park, once described Doenitz's psychological ties to the U-boats, and the manner in which he directed his vessels, in terms that invoked both the sports arena and the board game: 'He places [the U-boats]; he moves them . . . his interest in the game is, therefore, a very personal one. It engenders in him the enthusiasm of a crowd at a football match.'[5]

Despite, or perhaps because of, his near-blinkered loyalty to the U-boat arm, on 30th January 1943 Hitler named Doenitz as Raeder's successor as grand admiral. He was given a massive new residence in a Berlin suburb, close to where other senior Nazis had their homes, and a permanent armed SS guard. As well as a Mercedes staff car, Doenitz had use of a private aeroplane and, unthinkably, a private train, *Auerhahn*, named after the wood grouse, complete with beds, a restaurant and conference chamber. He received a grant of 300,000 marks, around $120,000.

The extension of the fifty-one-year-old's comforts did not affect his work ethic. Nor did the expansion of his responsibilities lead Doenitz to relinquish control of the U-boats. He continued to view himself as both father and team-coach to the U-boat crews, a fact that made it inevitable that he would maintain careful control of the division. Moreover, with the Reich now on the defensive on all other fronts, Doenitz was convinced that the U-boats represented the sole path to victory.[6] Diligent control of the U-boats was, if anything, now his greatest responsibility of all. Doenitz's unshakeable belief in the primacy of the U-boats in Germany's war effort was made clear a few days later when, in his first directive issued to staff in his new role, he wrote: 'The sea war is the U-boat war. All has to be subordinated to this main goal.'[7]

Two pink gins down and even the most unseaworthy landlubber would have been unable to detect the floor's gentle dips and rises on the refurbished *Oribi*.

For the Guest Night Dinner, held in honour of the engaged first lieutenant and his third-officer Wren fiancée, the wardroom mess had the ambience, if not the furnishings, of a gala-night dinner. Aided by the relatively abundant food stocks of Northern Ireland – at least by comparison to those of Liverpool – the wardroom stewards had managed to assemble a stately menu: steak and kidney pie, plum duff pudding; the extravagance of the food was heightened by the smell of cocktails: White Ladies, gimlets, dry martinis and all the rest.

After the plates had been cleared, the port passed around and a litany of toasts delivered – to the first lieutenant and his fiancée, absent wives and girlfriends, the nearest admiral and so on – it was time, in an atmosphere of abandon, for the games to begin. Shy guests retired to the sides of the room to spectate, while Lamb and Oldham led their friends and colleagues in a match of Wardroom Polo, each player using a chair for a horse, spoons for sticks and a boiled potato for the ball.

After the whoops and laughter died down, a cry went up of the sighting of an imaginary U-boat. A volunteer was selected to play the role of a torpedo and, as the ship's gunner recited the drill, the men sombrely laid him on the long dining-room table and, when the cry of 'Fire!' went up, threw him forcefully forward. With arms nobly clutched to his sides, the human torpedo shot along the polished table, before tumbling off the far end onto a sofa. While the atmosphere in the *Oribi*'s wardroom was one of drunken celebration, the torpedo game was born of a desire to bring the reality of war into a fictional context, where it could be experienced and confronted – the elemental root of so much of human play.

While the men and women on the *Oribi* collapsed laughing and the torpedo man straightened his clothes, the final game of the night was laid out: an obstacle race, whereby every participant had to circumnavigate the wardroom without touching the deck, as if the chairs and tables were islands of wreckage in a flaming sea. The evening at an end, Oldham and the other Wrens left the ship and headed into the cool night, under a sky of buckshot stars. She did not know when she would see her fiancée again, or when they might be married, but in this brief moment, her heart was full.

In Germany, Grand Admiral Doenitz was finalising plans for what would be the greatest push of the Battle of the Atlantic to date, an offensive that he hoped would match the so-called *Die Glückliche*

Zeit, or 'happy time', of the early months of the war when the U-boats sailed and fought with near impunity.

Doenitz believed that a concentration of U-boats dispatched to the mid-Atlantic Gap, a kind of über-wolfpack far larger than any seen before, might overwhelm the convoys and decisively cut Britain's supply lines, even with recent and ongoing improvements in Allied tactics and technology. This was the quickest route to victory, a credence to which Doenitz had cleaved ever since the wargames of 1937.

With full control of both the U-boats and the wider *Kriegsmarine*, Doenitz believed he was finally in a position to realise his career-long vision of building a U-boat division of sufficient size to fully blockade Britain and throttle its supplies. The timing was opportune. America's entry to the war had exerted significant additional pressure on British shipping. Each American infantry division dispatched to Europe required 32,000 tons of shipping to cross the Atlantic.[8] This used up space that might otherwise be used for civilian food supplies, refrigerated goods, oil and raw materials. As such, more than 150,000 cubic metres of frozen food destined for Britain was left rotting in American ports.[9] The competing demands of troops, food, armaments and resources had ratcheted tension in the supply chain to an unprecedented degree.*

'We are trying with the equivalent of about one third of normal fleet to feed this country and maintain it in full war production,' wrote Lord Cherwell, Churchill's scientific adviser. 'With all the extra military demands that have emerged . . . it is not surprising that our imports . . . have suffered severely. But this cannot go on.'[10]

The Ministry of Food issued a reminder to the Cabinet that without sufficient imports of flour, meat and other key foodstuffs, Britain could survive only for between four and six months.[11] In fact, by March 1943 Britain was consuming at least 750,000 tons more goods than it was importing. The country's reserves would last for just eight weeks.

---

* This shipping tension was, arguably, the primary reason behind the decision to invade North Africa at this moment in the war, as it would require fewer resources than the Allies' original plan to invade France.

Seven hundred thousand tons of shipping had been lost to U-boats in November 1942. It was time for Doenitz to press the advantage. In his first conference with the Führer as grand admiral, Doenitz convinced Hitler that no skilled workers involved in the construction or repair of U-boats should be called up to join the army and thereby slow the rate of production.[12] The number of operational vessels was now 222, tantalisingly close to 300, the magical figure that Doenitz had settled upon via his wargames prior to the war. Only seventy-eight more were needed to pass the threshold that Doenitz believed would deliver certain victory in the Battle of the Atlantic.

To build them, Doenitz needed steel, by now a scarce resource in Germany. To this end he ceded control of naval construction to Albert Speer, minister of armaments and war production. Speer had long campaigned to assume administrative responsibility for naval construction, in order to have total control over the allocation of steel, but had been denied this power by Raeder, Doenitz's predecessor. By relinquishing control of naval construction in exchange for guarantees of U-boats and other assets, Doenitz could be certain of receiving the raw materials he needed. Finally, Doenitz would have his 300 U-boats. He would be able to destroy sufficient numbers of Allied merchant ships to remove food from British tables, fuel from British cars and heat from British homes.

'It is,' he wrote to his staff on 5th February 1943, 'a question of winning the war.'[13]

Germany's struggles on the Eastern Front, and the foreboding entry into the war of the United States, with all of its economic and industrial power, had left Hitler sleeplessly contemplating defeat. On 7th February 1943, the Führer delivered a speech in which he claimed that losing the war would mean the German people deserved to lose the struggle between the races. It was one of the first times Hitler publicly flirted with an ideology of defeat. The ascent of the optimistic Doenitz was well timed; his positivity and unflappable belief in the U-boats gave Hitler a foothold for hope. The grand admiral became not only Hitler's confidant and adviser, but, thanks to Doenitz's ambition, a source of fresh inspiration for the jaded leader.

In turn, this gave Doenitz the support he needed to ramp up U-boat production, diverting the majority of the navy's allocation of steel, which had diminished following the fall of Stalingrad, into Kiel's shipyards. Hitler's belief in Doenitz also gave the grand admiral a mandate to pursue his plan to assemble monstrous wolf-packs in the mid-Atlantic Gap.

Unknown to both Doenitz and Horton, the next few weeks would represent the climax of the Atlantic war, as the Germans made their final push for U-boat supremacy, and the Allies sought to counter them. The stage was set for a grand sea battle, the results of which would be settled before the last swifts and swallows arrived in Britain to signal summer's arrival.

On 17th April, a little more than two weeks after she arrived in Belfast for repairs, HMS *Oribi* was dispatched to the Atlantic, following reports of a U-boat attack on a convoy. Lamb and the rest of the crew were to make for the site of the attack at full speed, to provide assistance. Christian Oldham waved from the ramparts of Belfast Castle, not knowing if or when she might see her fiancé again.

'It was very distressing,' she recalled. 'But there it was. Off he went.'[14]

The *Oribi*, its emblem a young deer, its motto *Nulli secundus* ('Second to none'), entered an ocean bubbling with U-boats: 207 were currently detailed for the North Atlantic, of which an average of 111 were at sea each day. In the plotting room at Belfast Castle, the young Wren watched as the *Oribi* was added to the plot with a marker just like any other, and yet also, quite unlike them at all.

XV

The Battle of Birds and Wolves: Part I

From the top of the white and gale-whipped lighthouse on the Isle of Orsay, a twenty-four-hectare slab of grass-ruffled rock that peeks from the Hebridean sea, the keeper could just make out the ships beginning to gather. The sky was a sheet of grey. High and cold winds thrashed at the ocean which, even this close to land, heaved to form great dips and peaks, aftershocks of the storms a few miles out to sea. Most of the forty-two merchant ships that chaotically assembled during the afternoon of Wednesday 21st April 1943 were in ballast, their bellies ready to be filled with supplies of food and fuel that Britain so desperately needed when, all being well, they arrived on the North American coast in a couple of weeks' time.

Every one of the ships that formed convoy ONS.5 (Outbound to North America, Slow), or MARFLEET as it was code-named, had sailed in convoy before. Two – the American *McKeesport* and the British *Dolius* – had even survived a savaging by U-boats just a few weeks earlier. Still, experience only went so far; in this menacing weather, maintaining a tidy position in the convoy was impossible. In sight of the forsaken Scottish coastline, the boats tossed like toys in a toddler's bathtub, caught rhythmically in the brushing beam of the lighthouse.

The 'Slow' in the convoy's designation was apt; at best ONS.5 could travel at just seven and a half knots. Anyone watching the sea that day knew that, if the weather endured, there was little chance it would manage even this easy pace on the journey ahead. The convoy's chosen route would take them into some of the worst weather of the decade, through waters thick with ice. This passage, to the far north, had been chosen to minimise the risk of encountering U-boats; earlier that month three convoys had taken the same route, two of which sustained only small losses, the third making it through untouched.* The chosen course would provide the convoy with air support from nearby coastlines. Still, at the centre point of its journey, the ships would be forced to cross the notorious Gap, where, three years earlier, the *City of Benares* had been sunk and where, thanks to the deadly weather, there would be no air support to ward off attackers.

The British were unaware that ONS.5's route was already known to German intelligence, who had successfully intercepted their communications. At the height of his powers, and now, finally, with a sufficient number of U-boats to deploy his wolfpack strategy to its fullest, Grand Admiral Doenitz was poised for battle. In the days that followed, he would dispatch the greatest wolfpack ever assembled to attack a single convoy, one that would eventually consist of five times as many U-boats as escort ships. The odds against survival were great; ignorance may not have been bliss, but it at least allowed the convoy to set sail toward a battlefield from which anyone in possession of the facts would surely have fled.

Even before the ships left sight of the Isle of Orsay's lighthouse, as many as thirty-six U-boats sat between the convoy and its destination.[1] They had been placed following a 'thorough examination'[2] of recent convoy routes and organised by Doenitz into two operational patrol lines, positioned into a great arc across the Atlantic, 500 miles east of Newfoundland. As if to conceal their menace, each wolfpack was named after a bird: one *Specht* (Woodpecker), the other *Meise* (Chickadee).

The atmosphere on the convoy ships was muted and fretful. Everyone involved knew that the forthcoming journey across the Atlantic Ocean was going to be long, cold and brutal. Nobody, on either the German or British side, could have known that by the time the first ships to survive the journey spied the North American coastline, the outcome of the Battle of the Atlantic would have been settled via a long and arduous conflict: the Battle of Birds and Wolves.

★ ★ ★

---

* ON.178, ONS.3 and ONS.4.

At 14:00 on Thursday 22nd April, Commander Peter Gretton, graduate of WATU and captain of HMS *Duncan*, arrived on the scene. Gretton, leader of the convoy's bodyguards, escort group B7, came flanked by an entourage of fighting ships, the frigate *Tay* and the corvettes *Loosestrife*, *Sunflower*, *Snowflake* and *Pink*. The naval ships, sheepdogs to the merchant flock, comprised a modest force to protect a convoy of such immodest size, but the crews were as well rehearsed as any before them.

Gretton, who with captains Walker and Macintyre formed the trio of Liverpool's greatest U-boat hunters, had a reputation for being a ruthless master. He wouldn't hesitate to cut loose anyone he considered to be a weak link. 'Kindness to incompetents seldom provides a dividend,' he later wrote, 'whereas severity invariably pays.'* His assiduousness had meant the ships under his charge had spent the last few weeks training and drilling off the coast of Ireland. At WATU, Gretton had seen first-hand, via The Game, the benefit when escorts worked as a close-knit team rather than a collection of autonomous individuals. He later described Roberts' work as 'invaluable' not only thanks to the 'invention of new search schemes for finding U-boats' but also in the way the game 'helped to weld groups together'.[3] Roberts had made a number of 'very stupid officers really think', Gretton wrote, 'sometimes for the first time in their lives', and Gretton had fully absorbed the lessons he learned at WATU.

When he arrived in Londonderry, Gretton endlessly drilled his ships in the WATU-coined operations Raspberry, Half-Raspberry, Observant and Artichoke, each of which would play a key role in the coming journey.[4] These exercises had gone, as Gretton put it, 'rather better than usual'. Despite the disparity between the huge size of ONS.5 and the rather meagre contingent of ships that comprised Gretton's escort, he believed his team was fully prepared to meet the challenge posed by any waiting U-boats.

---

* One of Gretton's Commanding Officers at the time, Robert Atkinson of HMS *Pink*, became the Chief Executive of the nationalised British Shipbuilders, and lifelong friends with Gretton's son, Mike. 'Do you know Mike, I respected your father more than I liked him', the late Atkinson would tell the younger Gretton, whenever the pair met.

For many of the captains under Gretton's charge, the U-boat threat had been experienced not only through WATU's game, but in person at sea. Harold Chesterman, a powerful lieutenant with Hollywood looks, had been present two years earlier at the sinking of the SS *Aguila*, when the twenty-one Wrens and a naval nursing Sister died. Four days later Chesterman's ship HMS *Zinnia*, one of the *Aguila*'s escorts, was herself torpedoed during the same action. Her magazine exploded, and she sank in twenty seconds.

As Chesterman clung, fingers bleeding, to a slowly disintegrating smoke-float in water lumpen with bodies and wreckage, he came to the decision to give up the fight and, rather than prolong his pain, embrace the water. A few feet down, Chesterman, who was twenty-four years old, saw a vision of his young wife, Caroline, begging him to reconsider. He fought his way back up and regained purchase on his float, determined that if he was going to die, it would be by necessity, not choice.[5]

In the first light of the morning, coughing up blood and oil, he was hauled from the water by a rescuer. Sixty-eight members of *Zinnia*'s crew perished that night. Chesterman and his captain, Monsarrat's close friend Charles Cuthbertson,[*] were among just seventeen survivors – 'shrunken hostages of the sea', as Monsarrat described them.[6] The two men continued to serve together aboard HMS *Snowflake* until, when Cuthbertson was due to move on, he broke protocol by recommending that the young lieutenant assume command of his ship. Chesterman became the youngest officer to command a major war vessel, and a much-valued member of Gretton's crack team of escort ships.

Despite the adverse weather, Gretton was in high spirits, and not only thanks to a robust belief in the skill of his escorts and the experience of his captains. While attending WATU he had taken one of the game-playing Wrens, Judy Du Vivier, to dinner just before she had been sent to Londonderry. A forlorn Du Vivier bade goodbye to the striking escort commander, not knowing if she

---

[*] Lieutenant Commander Ericson, one of the principal protagonists in Monsarrat's novel *The Cruel Sea*, was based on Cuthbertson, and the sinking of HMS *Sorrel* based on that of HMS *Zinnia*.

would ever see him again. Shortly thereafter, Gretton learned that he too was to be stationed in Londonderry. Thirty years old and eager to 'get better acquainted' with this striking young woman, he wasted no time in arranging a second date.

When the pair next met on 2nd January 1943, the first time they had seen one another since their time together in Liverpool, Du Vivier explained how she had recently recovered from a bout of pneumonia. She was young and fit, she said, but the illness had been serious enough that she had been sent to a medical facility where doctors from the Royal Army Medical Corps had nursed her back to health. This brush with mortality – combined with the persistent advances toward her, as Gretton put it,[7] by male members of the British submarine service and Canadian navy stationed at Londonderry – had convinced the young, jut-jawed commander to act. Du Vivier accepted his proposal. The church was booked for the end of May. Now Gretton simply had to make it across the Atlantic Ocean twice: once to collect supplies, and then back home to deliver them in time for his appointment at the altar in five weeks. The safe and timely passage of convoy ONS.5 was, then, of both national and personal importance.

Gretton pulled alongside the convoy's commodore ship, the *Rena*, and over a loudhailer finalised plans for the coming journey with its commodore, J. Kenneth Brook, shepherd to the convoy flock. With everything in place, the commodore gave the order for the convoy ships to move into formation. By the time the forty-three merchant ships that comprised ONS.5 had left the British coastline, headed towards Greenland, the light was beginning to fail.

Gretton's destroyer was a notoriously thirsty vessel whose tanks would be empty after a fortnight at sea. In order to save fuel during the relatively safe first leg of the journey, he positioned her in the middle of the convoy behind the tanker *Argon*, one of two fuel ships ready to top up, via hoses, any ships that ran low along the way.

On the second day, Gretton attempted to refuel the *Duncan*, but the waves were too severe. The hose was plucked from its socket by the tugging force of the sea. Gretton realised that without calmer waters it would be impossible to refill from either tanker. There was no respite from the wind and waves. On 25th April 1943 the weather was so tempestuous that the ships, many of which had been knocked out of formation, were only able to progress at two knots,[8] a quarter of the speed at which they might sail in fine weather. Visibility was so poor that even at this crawl, two merchant ships collided, leaving one, the *Bornholm*, with a hole in the engine room.

The next day Gretton signalled Horton at Derby House to say that unless the weather cleared to enable his ship to refuel, he would have to separate from the convoy in order to make an impromptu stop in Greenland.[9]

'On the one hand . . . I did not want to leave my group at such a time,' Gretton wrote. 'On the other . . . I did not like the idea of running out of fuel altogether and having to be towed, possibly at a very inconvenient phase of the operation.'[10]

Meanwhile Doenitz, receiving reports of convoy sightings, added a third patrol line, *Amsel* (Blackbird), to his assembled ranks of wolves. The combined total of this force was formidable. Woodpecker contained seventeen U-boats, while Chickadee, to which Doenitz had added more units between the 22nd and 25th April, now had thirty. The new patrol, Blackbird, consisted of eleven U-boats, bringing the number of German vessels ready to intercept any crossing convoy to close to sixty.

In what would be one of the only moments of respite in the journey, the weather cleared shortly after Gretton sent his message to Derby House, and a few hours later the *Duncan* successfully refuelled.

At midday on 26th April, just as Gretton and ONS.5 entered the longitudes where the wolfpacks were assembled, the Germans made changes to the naval Enigma code settings that scrambled the messages sent between BdU, the U-boat headquarters, and the U-boats. In England, the Government Code and Cypher School, which intercepted and decoded these German messages, was abruptly blinded, unable to read the signals that, for months, had alerted ships to the whereabouts of U-boats and their plans.

Without precise information, the best that the Submarine Tracking Room in London could tell Horton, who was attempting to direct ONS.5 from his office at Derby House, was that the three U-boat groups were 'in the general area off Newfoundland'.[11] This blindness meant that nobody in the Royal Navy, least of all Gretton, knew that on 27th April, sixteen new U-boats had been instructed by BdU to assemble into a fourth wolfpack, *Gruppe Star* (Starling), east of Greenland, directly across the convoy's path.

The German war diary, written on 27th April, made clear the target of all this activity: 'The object of [Starling] is the interception of the next ONS convoy at present proceeding in the North . . . A slow south-west-bound convoy is expected there on 28 April.'[12] BdU's estimate was correct. At 09:00 on the 28th, even before Starling had properly assumed its formation, the lookout in the conning tower of *U-650* spotted a thatch of mastheads on the horizon, belonging to the ships of ONS.5.

U-650's captain, Ernst von Witzendorff, signalled the sighting to Doenitz and Godt and, as he had been taught, began trailing the convoy, writing: 'I am closing them to see what we have.' For Doenitz, the stage was set for what would surely be a successful action. At 10:43, BdU sent a message ordering all sixteen U-boats within Starling to 'attack on basis of Witzendorff's report'. One of the subsequent messages that passed between the U-boats was picked up by convoy ships *Duncan* and *Tay*, who used their ship-mounted huff-duff sets – direction-finding equipment that enabled any two boats fitted with the contraptions to identify the source of a high-frequency radio transmission, and thereby pinpoint a U-boat – to estimate the hunter's position.

Aware that the convoy was being shadowed, Gretton dispatched Chesterman's ship, *Snowflake*, to investigate, while simultaneously altering the convoy's course thirty-five degrees to starboard. *Snowflake* found nothing. The weather again closed in and the wind began to blow 'like the bells of hell', as Gretton later wrote in his report. As visibility shrank to just three miles Gretton quietly fretted that the U-boat may have been just one member of a much larger pack. Then, in the early evening, *Duncan* picked up a U-boat close on the port bow. He made chase, ordering *Tay* to make a parallel search to port. Forty minutes later *Duncan*'s bridge spotted a telltale cloud of spray, where the waves had struck a U-boat conning tower.

As *Duncan* approached, the U-boat dived. After dropping a pattern of ten depth charges, Gretton and Robert Sherwood, captain of

Tay, executed the first WATU operation of the journey, Observant, a search of the area in a square shape, each 'side' two miles long, with the U-boat's last known position at its centre.

As the weather worked against the convoy, so too it worked against the U-boats. Despite Gretton's fear that the convoy was currently surrounded by a flock of attackers, only four of Starling's U-boats had managed to rally to *U-650*. It was enough to unsettle Gretton. That evening, he listened in dismay as each member of the wolfpack made its evening report to BdU. The sound on the huff-duff was, as one report put it, like 'a chattering of magpies'. Darkness fell and with it the likelihood of an attack rose.

The air escort that ONS.5 had enjoyed from 24th April had been discontinued at midnight on the 27th, since, up until that point, there had been no Admiralty reports of U-boats in the vicinity. For now, Gretton and his handful of escort ships would face the U-boats alone.

'The night,' as Gretton wrote, 'promised to be a busy one.'[13]

In Derby House, from his eagle's-eye office Horton studied the huge map on the wall opposite, with its concentration of ships and, thanks to Gretton's reports during the past few hours, U-boats clustered south of Iceland. It was clear that ONS.5 desperately needed support. Horton scanned the plot for possible back-up, and his eye fell on HMS *Oribi*, crewed by the newly engaged John Lamb, fiancé to Christian Oldham.

Lamb's ship was a member of the newly formed support groups, a rather plain name for highly trained, quick-moving flotillas that were sent into the Atlantic with the express purpose of providing impromptu assistance wherever it was required. The support group would, essentially, loiter in the ocean, waiting to be dispatched to the nearest emergency. The *Oribi* was currently escorting the convoy SC.127, en route from Sydney to Halifax. Horton estimated that it could be spared and, if it made good time, could be with Gretton within a day or two.

The idea for these elite naval groups was devised months earlier by Sir Percy Noble, but he never had control of a sufficient number of spare ships to implement the plan. When Horton took over from

Noble, he was equally convinced that this kind of flexible, hard-punching force would be decisive in the Battle of the Atlantic. On his first day at Derby House, Horton wrote to the Admiralty to press the 'urgent need' for these support groups. His appeal was rejected: there simply weren't enough quick-footed warships available.

Horton changed tack. He reasoned that since convoys still had to cross the Gap in the middle of the Atlantic unaccompanied, why not reduce the number of ships in the escorts either side of the area by one, and form the spare ships into support groups that could operate with more flexibility inside the Gap? After all, this was the only area of the ocean where the U-boats could still act with impunity and so represented the most perilous leg of the journey for the convoys. Again, the Admiralty denied Horton's suggestion.

In March 1943, as the battle between the U-boats and the Allied escorts was in crescendo, 1,120 merchant seamen, escort sailors and passengers were killed in just four battles against U-boats. Two thirds of the 110 Allied ships lost to U-boats that month were travelling in escort. In Derby House, where the mood was bleak, Horton reasoned that the losses were not the result of failings in the tactics devised by Roberts and the Wrens, but by the simple fact that the number of escort ships protecting the convoys was no longer sufficient in the face of such devastatingly large wolfpacks.

Horton needed evidence to take to London to prove that the support groups he was petitioning for would have diminished the losses of the past month. Once again, it was the results of a wargame that substantiated his claim.

On 15th March, four weeks before ONS.5 gathered at the Isle of Orsay, the Wrens had plotted on the main wall at Derby House the progress of two real convoys, HX.229 and SC.112, each headed toward three wolfpacks totalling thirty-eight U-boats. Concurrently, one of Roberts' colleagues, Captain Neville Lake, added three fictional support groups to the wall, shadowing the real convoys.

Lake hoped to estimate what effect such reinforcements might have on the looming battle. He populated his support groups with markers to represent real warships that were currently under construction, or nearing operational capability, and used his ghost escorts to support the real convoys, fending off wolfpacks while the battle played out in almost real time on the map. As well as adhering to the current weather conditions, Lake took into account fuel consumption and the depletion of depth charges to ensure that his exercise, overlaid on the real battle, was as accurate as possible.

Although many of the Wrens forced to play out Lake's game while simultaneously trying to plot the real battle were frustrated (they described it as 'Lake's folly'[14]), the final results were clear and, for Horton, conclusive. At the end of the battle for HX.229 and SC.112, which German radio reported as *'Die grösste Geleitzugschlacht aller Zeiten'* – 'the greatest convoy battle of all time'[15] – twenty-one Allied ships lay on the ocean floor. Lake estimated that, had his fictional support groups been real, at least eight ships would have been saved.

A few days later Horton was summoned to London for a meeting with Churchill and other high-ranking members of the Anti-U-Boat Committee. Lake hurriedly wrote up his notes from the game and handed the docket to his commander-in-chief, just as Horton was leaving to board the night train from Liverpool to London.

At the meeting the following day, Churchill was in a dark mood. Oil stocks were below danger levels and, as he put it, the U-boats were once again threatening the prosecution of the war.

'What are you going to do about it?' Churchill bluntly demanded of Horton.

'Give me fifteen destroyers and we shall beat the U-boats,' Horton replied.[16]

Churchill banged his fist on the table.

'You admirals are always asking for more and more ships,' he said. 'When you get them, things get no better.'

The prime minister's outburst was forgivable; assets in any war, on any side, are always finite. The miserable task of a leader is to balance the scales in order to achieve equipoise between a rising number of needs and a diminishing allocation of resources. Choosing his moment, Horton slid Lake's wargame report across the table. Churchill glanced at it, then looked more carefully. Finally, he adjourned the meeting so that he and Admiral Harold Stark, commander of US naval forces in Europe, could study it in more detail. When Churchill reconvened the meeting, he looked up from the docket at Horton.

'You can have your fifteen destroyers,' he said.

When he returned to Liverpool, Horton told Lake that he 'had never admired the prime minister more than in that moment'. Horton later described how Lake's game achieved what two admirals had been unable to do in years of trying. Western Approaches finally had its support groups.

By the final week of March 1943, Churchill had made good on his promise: Horton had more than twenty new destroyers at his disposal, which he divided into five support groups ready to dash to wherever assistance was required.

As first lieutenant of HMS *Oribi,* John Lamb was a crew member on the third of these five elite support groups. It was an intimidating role. For the past three years, escort crews would cross the ocean hoping to avoid any and all contact with U-boats. Lamb was one of the first sailors to charge into the Atlantic with the express aim of hunting the hunters. Action was inevitable. And so it came.

Seven days after the *Oribi* left port, the ship received a signal from Horton ordering it to detach from its current escort, and make its way, at an urgent speed of twenty knots, to assist Gretton and the weather-beaten boats of ONS.5. In Belfast Castle, Christian Oldham watched her fiancé's ship break away from the safety of its convoy, and begin to make its way across the plot, toward the needle-bed of freshly pinned U-boat markers.

The atmosphere at Derby House was doubly muted. While everyone was aware of the massing of U-boats in the Atlantic, tragedy had already arrived at the bunker. Three nights earlier, on 25th April, a signal arrived, probably from ONS.5, that required an alteration to the main plot. At that moment, Patricia Lane, a young member of the Women's Auxiliary Air Force, was teetering high on the ladder used by the young women to reach the pins and string. The ladders could be slid, at speed, parallel to the map via tramline tracks at the top and bottom.

'One quickly got used to them and acquired a splendid balance, seeing how far the elastic would stretch when putting up the convoy routes,' wrote Mary Carlisle, a Wren who routinely worked the plot. (Like June Duncan, Carlisle had also cheated her way past the medical into the Wrens; while Carlisle benefited from a photographic memory, she was burdened with poor eyesight. Fearing she might fail to read the alphabet from the far wall during her eye test, Carlisle learned the position of the letters on the standardised test card in advance.[17])

Patricia Lane, however, was less experienced than the Wrens, as the WAAF only climbed the ladder once a day, at midnight, to chalk up flight schedules for the next day's convoys. When the signal came in, one of the Wrens grabbed the ladder, and pushed it eastward to the trouble spot on the plot. Patricia lost her balance, slipped and fell onto the hard floor. She was whisked out of the plotting room and taken to a nearby hospital, where she later died of her injuries. The Wren who had grasped the ladder was taken off the watch in shock, but as the threat to ONS.5 continued to build, the work had to continue. Since Patricia had died while serving at a secret headquarters, her death was unreported. As a result of the tragedy, all Wrens were made to wear a safety harness ('a positive nuisance', according to Mary Hall) while working on the main plot at Derby House.

While the majority of the action the Wrens faced was experienced at a distant remove through the micro-drama of maps and tokens, death would at times more closely touch their world. Elsie Pearsal, who had worked for an income-tax office prior to the war, joined the Wrens as a cook, for 'a change of pace.'

'I had come straight from income tax,' she said. 'I didn't know how to boil an egg.'[18]

Pearsal was sent to Blundellsands hotel in Liverpool, where she cooked for the Wrens working at Derby House. The ingredient list from which the cooks had to improvise ambitious meals was impoverished: dried tomatoes, onion and apple. The Wrens would fill great metal pans with water and stir and stir the mixture to make suet pudding.

'It took two Wrens to pour the mixture, which smelled of petrol,' she recalled.

Once cooked, the Wrens would carry the food from the hotel along the street to two Victorian houses, where those stationed in Derby House would come to eat. On one occasion Pearsal and another Wren were struggling to manoeuvre a great and cumbersome pan of vegetable soup into one of the houses. As they made it through the front door, Pearsal considered saluting the quarterdeck, then, feeling the slop of the heavy pan, decided against it. Moments later a Wren officer walked into the hallway.

'Without thinking my hand shot up,' Pearsal recalled. 'Peas and carrots went all over the thick floor mat by the entrance. I was eighteen years old.'

Pearsal and the other young Wren cooks would exercise on the beach each day. In formation, they would pass through Waterloo, on the Mersey, and from the bridge see the ships in Gladstone Dock. On the beach the Wrens would march and exercise under instruction. One morning they were turned away and told there would be no drills that day.

'We later found out that the previous night a ship had been mined and overnight bits of bodies had swept onto the beach,' she said.

Rumours of the washed-up bits of body on the beach, like the news of Patricia Lane's death in the plotting room, spread quickly through the Wrens. Each provided a reminder, in its grim and respective way, of the risks and stakes, direct and indirect, to their work.

On 29th April, four days after Patricia Lane's death, Gretton received news that his escort was to be joined by Lamb's ship the *Oribi*, and four other vessels from the third support group, currently en route from Iceland.[19]

Gretton's prediction that the previous night would be a busy one had proved correct: the *Duncan* had detected and seen off four separate U-boat advances, in a tempestuous sea where even the simple act of reloading the depth charges was a life-threatening endeavour. No ship in the convoy had been sunk or damaged. Two of the U-boats involved in the attacks, *U-386* and *U-528*, had been so severely damaged by depth charges that they had been forced to withdraw to base. Despite the success, Gretton remained nervous. The *Oribi* and its sister ship, HMS *Offa*, were still hours away, and the weather had worsened to an 'astonishing' degree, by Gretton's appraisal, 'even for the North Atlantic'.*

Frustrated at the previous night's failure, on the morning of 29th April, Kapitänleutnant Wilhelm von Mässenhausen of *U-258* slipped inside the convoy, using the technique pioneered by Kretschmer, and sat at periscope depth starboard of the convoy's fourth column. Somehow the U-boat evaded the ASDIC sweeps of the patrolling escort ships, allowing von Mässenhausen to successfully fire at the American freighter, *McKeesport*.

An alarm bell woke Gretton, sleeping after the night's work, and, at 07:30, one minute after the torpedo struck, he ordered the next WATU-coined manoeuvre of the journey: Artichoke. As one destroyer powered at maximum ASDIC speed toward the wounded ship, all others in the escort turned outward and performed a fifteen-knot sweep in line. *U-258* managed to slip away. The *McKeesport*, listing to one side, managed to maintain convoy speed for almost fifty minutes while taking water, before the order was finally given to abandon ship at 08:15. The sixty-eight men on board were picked up by the crew of the *Northern Gem*, one of the two rescue ships attached to B7 Group to pick up survivors of U-boat attacks. One man, a Swede called John Anderson, later died of exposure, the only fatality of the day.

The *Oribi* joined the escort in the early hours of 30th April, and there were no more attacks on the convoy. By mid-morning the weather had eased enough that Lamb's ship was able to refuel. It was the first time that the *Oribi* had attempted to do so at sea and, as a gale again whipped up, the inexperienced crew botched the job. 'She made such a mess of the oiler's gear that no one else could refuel that day,' Gretton wrote of a snag that was to have life-altering consequences for the commander of ONS.5's escorts. A cluster of U-boats continued to shadow the convoy but, as the storm returned once again, blown in by a force-ten gale, none of them dared surface to mount an attack, even though their targets were static and strewn.

---

* That same day, unknown to Gretton, his fiancée Judy Du Vivier was promoted to leading Wren, all memory of her apparent falling out with the unnamed officer at Derby House forgotten.

'Although the engines were turning, we were just sitting there stationary', said Howard Goldsmith, leading sick-berth attendant on Chesterman's *Snowflake*.[20]

The wretchedness of the situation is captured in Commodore Brook's logbook, where he wrote: 'Half convoy not under command, hove to and very scattered.'

As soon as Gretton had alerted Derby House of the wolfpack, the Admiralty had ordered renewed air cover to provide ONS.5 with some support. Despite the atrocious conditions, aircraft continued to make fly-bys throughout the day. Some signalled the position of icebergs, and of straggling ships. One American bomber forgot to switch off its navigation lights, an oversight that worked in the convoy's favour when the globe-like, flashing beacons caught the attention of *U-381*, which sent a frenzied signal to Doenitz reporting a sky-borne secret weapon, 'a light like a planet, that went off and on'.[21]

The combination of extreme weather and aircraft support precluded any action between the U-boats and the escort ships. Then, after an uneventful day, on 2nd May the storm eased, giving Gretton, his escorts and a Liberator from the Reykjavik squadron opportunity to round up stragglers and gather the flock back into formation. The convoy was now far enough north that ice, not waves, presented the gravest danger. *Duncan* again attempted to refuel, but the need for the tethered ships to wend around icebergs frustrated the manoeuvre.

The weather forecast for the coming days was dire. Gretton calculated that he now had only enough oil to make Newfoundland at modest speed. The exertion of action involving U-boats could empty the *Duncan*'s fuel tanks before it reached land and force the destroyer into the ignoble position of having to be towed to the North American coast, further endangering the ships it was supposed to be protecting.

After 'much heart-searching', Gretton made the decision to leave ONS.5. At 16:00, he passed command of escort group B7 to Lieutenant Commander Robert Sherwood, the highly experienced, thick-bearded and roughly spoken captain of HMS *Tay*.

'We were most depressed,' Gretton later recalled.[22] WATU had invented the tactics and Gretton had drawn up the game plan, but now Sherwood would be the one to execute it.

Duncan wasn't the only destroyer that had to leave ONS.5 due to fuel depletion that day. Three other members of the support group were similarly detached from the convoy, and Sherwood signalled Derby House to say that if weather conditions didn't improve to allow refuelling, *Offa* and *Oribi* would be the next to go. Surrounded by ice and, having entered the Greenland air gap, now sailing under skies empty of air support, Convoy ONS.5 proceeded through the night with a woefully diminished force of protectors. As the merchant ships entered the most perilous leg of the journey, just three of its former seven-strong posse of bodyguard destroyers remained.

At Derby House, recognising the convoy's vulnerability, Max Horton ordered another support group consisting of five warships to 'proceed at best speed' to reinforce the exposed convoy. It would, however, be two days before these ships could reach ONS.5's position.

Following his promotion, Doenitz had moved the U-boat head-quarters from France to the Hotel am Steinplatz in Berlin, which had been furnished for the purpose, so that he could continue to keep a close hand in directing the sea war.[23] From his position Doenitz saw that not only did he have a unique window of opportunity to strike, he also had unparalleled resources with which to execute a major attack.

Frustrated by the wolfpack's failure to halt the convoy's progress during the past week, he ordered Starling, which by now had lost some of the original U-boats, and gained a few replacements, to rendezvous with Woodpecker's seventeen vessels.

At 18:00 on 3rd May 1943, BdU signalled to the wolfpacks a stern command that made Doenitz's expectations clear: 'DO NOT HOLD BACK. SOMETHING CAN AND MUST BE ACHIEVED WITH 31 BOATS.'

As Gretton and his ship, *Duncan*, departed the scene, he could not have known that, as he later put it, the story of what happened next would be 'the most stirring of convoy history'.

XVI

The Battle of Birds and Wolves: Part II

From the moment the first reports of the impending battle for ONS.5 reached Belfast Castle, the Operations Room in which Christian Oldham worked became a hub of activity and interest. The teleprinter buzzed and rattled with the continuous flow of signals arriving from the various ships involved, including the *Oribi*. Messages passed between the Wrens at Derby House and those in Belfast Castle at frantic intervals.

'Nobody wanted to go off duty,' Oldham later wrote.[1]

The developing picture was especially distressing for the twenty-two-year-old, who could see, at a glance of the plot, the danger her fiancé faced.

'*Oribi* was obviously heading for the wolfpack,' she wrote.

In fact, *Oribi* was headed toward several wolfpacks. Due to Bletchley Park's signal-blindness, caused by the changing of the Enigma codes, the wall plots at Belfast Castle and Derby House showed only a fraction of the true number of U-boats that were currently lying in wait. Even with their partial picture, the battlefield viewed as if through a smudged window, the plot became, as Oldham later put it, 'a vivid picture of the action, with all of us taking a vicarious part in it'.

The delay between the issuing of signals from the ships at sea and their receipt at home made the progress 'even more acute'. As the tension ratcheted, time and again Oldham's friends tried, using various spurious excuses, to persuade her to leave the plotting room 'so I might not know of the dangerous drama evolving – as it were – before our very eyes'.

But Oldham would not be moved. That week, she barely visited her dorm room in Belfast Castle. Her two room-mates would endlessly tease her about the mess in which she left her bed.[2] Not this week, however.

'I could not leave the scene,' she said.

Roberts, too, watched the drama as it built on the cork plot, the horror of ship markers being swapped from white to red tokens to signal each torpedo strike. Under the title 'Chief of the Enemy', Roberts kept the night duty on the main plot at Derby House alongside Commodore Ian Macintyre and Lieutenant Colviller, chief of operations. The trio would try to anticipate what might happen next in the game at sea, and how best they might advise the players.

This work was reflected on the German side. Hoping to press their advantage, at 16:02 on 4th May the officers at BdU organised most of the U-boats of Woodpecker and Starling into a reconnaissance line, code-named *Gruppe Fink* (Finch). As these twenty-seven U-boats moved into position, several sighted *Oribi* and its sister destroyer *Offa* in the distance. At the same time, BdU directed a number of lone wolf U-boats to join Blackbird's group, to the south of ONS.5. Still the convoy plodded on. By dusk, *Tay* was picking up numerous contacts on its huff-duff: suspected U-boats on every side of the ship. *Tay*'s captain, Sherwood, ordered *Oribi* and *Offa* to make an ASDIC sweep of the area, but neither ship managed to pinpoint the location of any U-boats.

At noon on 5th May, the Allied codebreakers cracked the latest naval Enigma codes, enabling the full horrifying scale of the challenge that faced ONS.5 to emerge. The time lag between interception and decryption was such, however, that by the time Horton knew about the massed U-boats of the monster packs Finch and Blackbird, which eventually totalled forty-one vessels, the largest concentration ever focused around a single convoy[3], it was too late.

With so many U-boats assembling on the battle line, the stage had seemingly been set for an incontestable victory for Doenitz. Eager for news of a major success that he could take to Hitler, in order to justify both his recent promotion and his strategic focus on U-boat-building, Doenitz exhorted his young men:

'I AM CERTAIN THAT YOU WILL FIGHT WITH
EVERYTHING YOU'VE GOT. DON'T OVERESTIMATE
YOUR OPPONENT BUT STRIKE HIM DEAD.'[4]

U-125, captained by Ulrich Folkers, was the first to strike. His
victim was the *Lorient*, an Allied ship named after the French port
from which, ironically, its attacker had recently departed. Even
before the crew could send up its distress flares, the ship, along
with all forty-six crew members, disappeared.

Next *U-707*, commanded by Günther Gretschel, fired a fan of
torpedoes at the merchant ship *North Britain*. One struck abaft the
mast.

'The upper deck is awash,' Gretschel wrote in his war diary. 'The
vessel remains floating for a while, then suddenly stands itself up,
the bow vertical, and descends into the sea. Time for sinking: sixty-
nine seconds.'

One after another, the U-boats of Finch attacked. *U-628*, which
had been lead shadower of the convoy, torpedoed and sank the
Harbury. *U-264*, attacking from within the convoy columns, torpedoed the American cargo ship *West Maximus* and the British freighter
Harperley. All three ships went down within nineteen minutes of
one another. In response, and to prevent further casualties,
Sherwood decided that the time had come to order a manoeuvre
invented by Gilbert Roberts, named by Jean Laidlaw and drilled to
perfection by Peter Gretton: Raspberry.

The operation, which had convinced Sir Percy Noble of the
value of WATU, required various triangular search patterns to be
performed at precise sweep speeds and time durations, and was
designed to flush out any U-boats sitting within the convoy lanes.
That night, Sherwood performed a half-Raspberry, a slightly modified version of the manoeuvre that held a few escorts in place to
survey the sea for any signs of U-boats illuminated by the star shells
fired into the sky by the participating ships. The ploy worked
magnificently. Various U-boats were located, enabling a barrage of
depth charges to fend off the attackers.

During the next few hours, the 150-foot trawler *Northern Spray*
began to pluck survivors from the water: thirty-eight from *Harperley*,

fifty-one from *West Maximus*, forty-three from *Harbury* and two from *North Britain*. Under the combined weight of its grateful men, who took up every nook of space, the vessel sat low in the sea.* Still, by first light, five of ONS.5's ships had been sunk, without a single U-boat casualty. Emboldened by the night's success, and with the feverish hubris that can come with the feeling of being a member of a super-ior force, the U-boats sustained their attacks into the following day. *U-266* hit three ships, including the *Gharinda*, an old liner of the British India Fleet. Life expectancy in the freezing water was just a few minutes. Nevertheless, HMS *Tay*, leader of the escort ships in *Duncan's* absence, successfully picked up the *Gharinda's* captain, R. R. Stone, and his crew. Stone asked to be returned to his ship, which was wounded but not yet sunk, believing that she might still be salvaged.

Sherwood forcefully declined for the simple reason that, via the ship's huff-duff, he was currently tracking no fewer than seven U-boats in the vicinity. By evening, the Allies had managed to score one U-boat kill, but the tally of sunken merchant ships had grown from five to twelve, with hundreds of miles to go before the convoy reached its destination.

As dusk blackened to night on 5th May 1943, the weather stilled, and the rain turned to mist. Lamb, who was keeping the *Oribi's* last four-hour watch of the day from 20:00, was expecting mayhem. But by midnight things seemed to have quietened. In the relative calm, *Oribi's* new captain, John Ingram, who had taken command of the ship in February, issued the order of 'defence stations', so that only half of the ship's armament was manned and the remaining crew could take some much-needed rest.

To avoid the long and potentially dangerous trip along the exposed upper deck to his cabin, Lamb walked to the sickbay below the bridge, which he would often use if there was a vacant bed. He climbed beneath the sheets fully clothed, just in case.[5]

Three hours later, at 02:52, the *Oribi's* ASDIC operator reported

---

* All of those who were rescued survived the battle and *Northern Spray* arrived at St John's, Newfoundland on 8th May.

an echo from an object close by. Ingram, not knowing whether the contact was a U-boat or fellow escort, was forced, in that instant, to gamble on a course of action. He chose to attack, swinging the *Oribi* toward the contact position. Moments later, he sighted not a corvette, but a U-boat, *U-125*, 600 feet away and sliding through the mist, as ominous as a sea monster.

The *Oribi* had the perfect angle to ram.

'Ramming is a splendid method of sinking submarines,' Gretton wrote later. 'But the rammer is left in a shaky state.'[6] Still, the chance to knock a U-boat out of the battle was worth the risk, and Ingram took it. At around twenty knots, the *Oribi* bore down on the German vessel while Ingram and the skeletal crew braced for impact. They watched the U-boat's conning tower disappear behind the *Oribi*'s streaking bow, and, after a moment's pause, the ship struck *U-125* square on, a little behind the tower. Lamb was abruptly awakened by the terrible noise of tear and crunch.

'My first thought was that we had been torpedoed,' Lamb wrote in his diary. Then, as he felt the ship ride up and over something and in the fug of a rude awakening, he implausibly assumed that the ship had gone aground.

'I scrambled out of the cot,' he recalled, 'but was unable to find the deck.'

Instead, Lamb felt glass bottles underfoot. These were the medicines and sickbay utensils racked up on the side of the room, which, as the *Oribi* keeled over with the force of the collision, had momentarily become the ship's floor. By the time the alarm gongs began clanging, Lamb had successfully scaled the two flights of ladders to the bridge. There he followed the eyes of the watchkeepers and saw a U-boat's conning tower close alongside and below, to port.

The impact had knocked out the light that illuminated the *Oribi*'s wall clock in the bridge, but this was as nothing to the damage sustained by *U-125*. The submarine's tower was crumpled, its periscope warped, its flak guns bent and the hatch blown off. The U-boat was also down by the stern, although by the time order had been restored on the *Oribi*, sight of the German vessel had been lost.

'I have no doubt whatsoever that this submarine was sunk,' Ingram wrote in his report of the action.

It was a reasonable but incorrect conclusion. Battered, broken and now unfit to dive, *U-125* had managed to limp away on the surface. Ninety minutes later, at 03:31, Kapitänleutnant Folkers reported the situation to BdU: 'Have been rammed – unable to dive. Request assistance.' Six nearby U-boats responded, one after the other, to say that they were headed to provide assistance to Folkers and his dazed crew.

Before any of the U-boats could find *U-125*, at 03:54 Chesterman, survivor of the sinking of HMS *Zinnia* and now captain of HMS *Snowflake*, picked up the stricken U-boat on his ship's radar. He made toward its location. In the dense mist *Snowflake* was just a hundred yards away when the lookouts finally sighted Folkers' U-boat. Chesterman ordered the wheel to be put hard-to-starboard, hoping to ram the vessel, for what would be its second battering that night.

The U-boat evaded ramming, but *Snowflake* managed to pull alongside, so that only a few feet separated each boat, too close even for the ship's guns to depress at a sufficiently deep angle in order to take aim. The ship's port searchlight clacked on, and, in the eerie quiet, Chesterman surveyed the damaged U-boat, while slowly withdrawing in order to take a shot.

The U-boat sagged in the water, a wounded animal, bubbling from the hatch. Illuminated by *Snowflake*'s beam, some of *U-125*'s crew jumped into the water, others lined the deck hoping to be rescued and still more made for the forward deck gun. To discourage them, *Snowflake* opened up with its forty-millimetre pom-pom guns, and the remaining U-boat crew members jumped, terrified, into the sea. The muffled noise of five scuttling charges sounded out and *U-125* disappeared under the water.

Chesterman reviewed the chaotic scene. Some Germans were haphazardly paddling in a dinghy; others trod water in the freezing, misty sea. At 04:07, the captain, no doubt recalling his own time in the water nearly two years earlier, when he almost gave up hope and yielded to the sea, issued a signal to Sherwood in *Tay*.

'Shall I pick up survivors?'

Chesterman and his men waited, listening to the cries of the Germans for five minutes before Sherwood's reply arrived at last.

'Not approved to pick up survivors,' it read.

On 6th May 1946, three years later almost to the day, Doenitz stood in the wooden dock at the Nuremberg trials and was asked whether or not a sailor has a duty to attempt to rescue survivors of a sea battle in all circumstances. The question was pointed. The prosecutor believed that Doenitz had, in the latter stages of the war, ordered his U-boat crews to ignore anyone in the water*, where captains like Kretschmer had at one point rescued, fed and even nursed enemy survivors. It is, Doenitz answered carefully, a question of military possibility.

'During a war the necessity of refraining from rescue may well arise,' he said. 'For example, if your own ship is endangered thereby, it would be wrong from a military viewpoint and, besides, would not be of value for the one to be rescued; and no commander of any nation is expected to rescue if his own ship is thereby endangered.'[7]

Sherwood clearly reached the same conclusion that night, as Folkers and his surviving crew members sat in Atlantic oblivion, wondering why the British weren't coming to their aid. So it was that *Snowflake* pulled away from the scene. As the British vessel disappeared into the mist from which it had emerged, the fifty-four Germans in the water watched their hopes of survival with it depart. No other U-boat risked coming to their aid. One by one by one, the men perished.

The hours that followed were, for Lamb, a disorientating blur: a melee with corvettes and U-boats 'all mixed up' and 'momentarily illuminated' by star shells. He would hear the occasional explosion or patter of gunfire in the mist while, in the background, 'like

---

* The prosecutor was correct. During a later trial, in October 1945, Kapitänleutnant Heinz Eck of *U-852* confirmed that U-boat command had issued a directive stating: 'No attempt of any kind should be made at rescuing members of ships sunk, and this includes picking up persons in the water and putting them in lifeboats, righting capsized lifeboats and handing over food and water... Be harsh, having in mind that the enemy takes no regard of women and children in his bombing attacks of German cities.' Eck and three U-boatmen, who were accused of firing on survivors in the water, were convicted and, the following month, executed by firing squad.

theme music in a nightmare film', he heard the ever-present hypnotic 'ping, ping, ping' of the *Oribi*'s ASDIC, which against all odds had survived the impact with *U-125*.

Major damage had, however, been caused to the ship's bow, and one of its propellers was broken.[8] *Oribi*'s forepeak and lower central store were flooded, but the ship remained watertight and, manoeuvring with care, able to resume station. By first light, the score card looked quite different to twelve hours before. In the final tally, one U-boat had been lost for every 2.6 merchant ships.[9] Doenitz ordered the remnants of the wolfpacks to retreat. He later stated that he 'regarded this convoy battle as a defeat'. This was an understatement. The Battle of Birds and Wolves would come to be known by the Germans as *Die Katastrophe am ONS.5*.

Its work complete, HMS *Oribi* detached from the convoy, and at a steady speed of twelve knots headed for St John's, Newfoundland, and safety. At the plot in Belfast Castle, Oldham read the message that her fiancé's ship was en route to the North American coastline, and collapsed with relief.[10]

That day a cypher message was sent from the Admiralty to HMS *Tay* via the wireless operators at Derby House. It read: 'My compliments to you on your unceasing fight against the U-boats. Please pass to Commander of Convoy my admiration for steadfastness of his ships.'[11] Then on 9th May, the *Oribi*, along with all of the other escort ships involved in the battle, received a congratulatory message from Churchill, who was in Washington DC at the time. It read, with unadorned straightforwardness, 'My compliments to you on your fight against the U-boats.'

Sixty hours later Lamb and his fellow shipmates pulled into St John's, a 'peaceful paradise' after the last few days of torment, a 'drawn out, exhausting and rather confusing affair'.[12] At 13:00 on 12th May, as the main body of ONS.5 approached Halifax, Commodore Brook issued his final report of the journey: 'Approaching Pilot Station. Convoy completed.'

The *Oribi*'s bow was reinforced by concrete in dry dock, and then the ship proceeded south to Boston for permanent repairs. Lieutenant

Lamb did not record whether he met up with his former girlfriend Jeanette Watson during his stay on the east coast, to explain the change in his circumstances. Of the matter he only wrote, simply: 'My return to the States . . . could have been taken as untimely and careless but for the understanding of my erstwhile New York girlfriend and the tolerance and relief of my Wren fiancé who had been fighting the great battle vicariously from her Atlantic plot.'

Lamb was safe, for now, but it would be months before he saw Oldham again, who cut out and kept, for the rest of her life, a clipping from the *Daily Express* describing the events of the battle. The article, based on the information available at the time and headlined 'War's Biggest U-battle: Navy beats off 25', concluded with the assessment that this was 'probably the greatest U-boat battle of the war'.[13]

Otherwise, relatively little was made of the Battle of Birds and Wolves. On 11th May, toward the end of the nine o'clock news the BBC newsreader Stuart Hibberd reported the sinking of five German submarines in the Atlantic the preceding Thursday.

'Others were probably sunk or heavily damaged,' he added. 'Two were rammed.'[14]

The story was picked up by only a handful of newspapers and, when writing the official history of Royal Navy operations during the war, Captain Stephen Roskill made only a glancing reference to the battle. Both Doenitz and Horton, meanwhile, recognised the decisive quality of what had happened. Both men separately suggested that the battle for ONS.5 was a pivotal moment in the war against the U-boats. Horton first commended the escort ships for 'a classic embodying [of] nearly every method and form of tactics current at the time.' Then he added, 'It may well be that the heavy casualties inflicted on the enemy have gravely affected his morale and will prove to have been a turning point in the Battle of the Atlantic.'[15]

Rodger Winn, who ran the U-boat tracking room in London, concurred, writing that the battle was the 'most decisive' of all convoy engagements, and represented 'the extreme and . . . last example of coordinated pack attacks'.*

---

* Winn's assessment was only made public in 1975, after it was released by the Public Record Office.

In a 1959 review of Doenitz's memoir for the *Sunday Times*, Roskill, apparently emboldened by Doenitz's appraisal, wrote: 'The seven-day battle fought against thirty U-boats is marked only by latitude and longitude and has no name by which it will be remembered: but it was, in its own way, as decisive as Quiberon Bay or the Nile.'

His ship refuelled and in dock at St John's, a continent away from his beckoning appointment at the altar, Peter Gretton learned of what had happened after he left the battle for ONS.5 with dismay.

'I shall never cease to regret that I did not risk the weather and stay with them till the end,' he later wrote.[16] In Gretton's estimation, he had missed 'the golden moment of a lifetime'.[17] Despite recognising that his choice to break away and pass command to the able Sherwood was 'entirely correct' and 'based on common sense', the decision 'haunted' Gretton.

Over the next few days, the *Duncan* was resupplied and brutally modified. After experiencing pronounced rolling in the journey with ONS.5, Gretton ordered all unnecessary weight removed from the upper decks, including thick layers of accumulated paint, which were chipped from the bodywork. When *Duncan* departed St John's the jetty was a jumble of discarded lockers, cables and piping.

On 11th May, Gretton left for Liverpool. After exchanging official documents with the convoy's commodore, Gretton passed a private note urging him to keep the merchantmen in line so that the convoy SC.130 might make it to port on schedule, for 25th May, four days before his wedding. The commodore, J. Forsythe, replied pledging his best efforts. Besides, Forsythe added, he too had an engagement to keep for that same day: a golf match.[18]

On 14th May, as Gretton crossed the Atlantic, Doenitz met Hitler at the Führer's Wolfschanze, or 'Wolf's Lair' in Poland, to discuss the future of the wolfpacks. Not wanting to suggest that his U-boat captains were losing to superior tactics, Doenitz attempted to pin the Allied victory on their technological advancements. 'The enemy's new location devices are, for the first time, making U-boat warfare impossible and causing heavy losses – fifteen to seventeen boats a month,' Doenitz ventured when the conversation turned to the ocean front.

'These losses are too high,' Hitler interjected. 'It can't go on.'

Still Doenitz persisted in his belief that the tide might again be turned, issuing a message the following day to all U-boats promising 'better weapons for this hard struggle of yours'. Even if the arrival of such weapons – which included, Doenitz believed, technology to somehow render the Allied huff-duff sets impotent, was imminent (and it was not), it would have been too late for one young U-boat officer.

Four days later, on 19th May, Gretton and his convoy were at the midway point of their return journey across the Atlantic when they were joined by a sloop and three frigates from Horton's first support group. Shortly thereafter, HMS *Jed*, which had been a participant in the battle for ONS.5, spotted *U-954*. Together with the cutter *Sennen*, the two ships executed the WATU-coined manoeuvre Observant. *Sennen* dropped a pattern of ten depth charges, at least one of which punctured the hull of *U-954*, whose crew included Lieutenant Peter Doenitz, the grand admiral's youngest son. There were no survivors.

On learning the news of his son's death, Doenitz reportedly showed little emotion. His wife was less accepting; in 1945 she searched lists of prisoners of war held in Canada and North America, hoping against hope that her son had somehow been rescued. Peter's death only strengthened Doenitz's resolve.* The following day, when U-boat HQ supplied him with details of another eastbound British convoy, Doenitz sent survivors of the battle in which his son had died to intercept them, alongside fresh U-boats.

'If there is anyone who thinks that fighting convoys is no longer possible,' he wrote, in a message broadcast to the U-boat commanders involved, 'he is a weakling, and no real U-boat commander.'

---

* As a senior officer, Doenitz had special dispensation to withdraw a son from the front, in order to ensure that, according to Nazi ideology, the best of German blood would survive the war to enrich the race. Following Peter's death, Doenitz sent his elder son, Klaus, to train as a naval doctor. On 13th May 1944, during a holiday visit to Cherbourg, France, Klaus was invited to accompany friends on a reconnaissance sortie on a torpedo boat along the English coast. At 00:30, the boat came under fire from a French destroyer. The vessel was hit twice and began to sink. According to survivor reports, Klaus, who was an epileptic, had a fit in the water and drowned.

Gretton, meanwhile, made Liverpool in time. He and the former WATU Wren Du Vivier were married on 29th May 1943 at St Mary's, Cadogan Square by the RC naval chaplain at Derry. The pair spent the weekend at the Savoy hotel ('comfortable, and there were no air raids'[19]), visiting the theatre before travelling by boat to Donegal for a three-day honeymoon. On the fourth day, Gretton returned to the Atlantic.[20]

On 30th June 1943 in the Guildhall, London, the prime minister announced to the assembled crowd of dignitaries the turnaround in the Battle of the Atlantic. 'Everyone has heard of the Battle in Tunisia when 350,000 Germans or Italians were made captive or slain,' he said.

> There was another, a no less notable battle which was fought in May in the Atlantic against U-boats. For obvious reasons, much less has been said about that . . . In May the German Admiralty made extreme exertions to prevent the movement to Great Britain of the enormous convoys of food and materials . . . which we must bring in safely and punctually if our war-making capacity is to be maintained. Long lines of U-boats were spread to intercept these convoys and packs of fifteen or twenty U-boats were then concentrated in each attack . . . The fighting took place mainly around the convoys, but also over a wide expanse of ocean. It ended in the total defeat of the U-boat attack. More than thirty U-boats were certainly destroyed in the month of May, floundering in many cases with their crews in the dark depths of the sea.

Then, grasping his lapels for dramatic effect, Churchill continued.

> Staggered by these deadly losses the U-boats have recoiled to lick their wounds and mourn their dead. Now as a result of the May victory and massacre of U-boats, we have had in June the best month we have ever known in the whole forty-six of the war.

As Churchill took a moment to clear his throat, the cheers and applause rattled around the hall.[21]

Two months later, in July 1943, the tonnage of Allied ships launched, principally from American shipyards, finally overtook the figures of tonnage sunk. Doenitz, whose stated aim had always been to sink more ships than the enemy could build ('a continual bloodletting which must cause even the strongest body to bleed to death',[22] as he described it), and who avidly studied the monthly statistics kept by his staff,[23] had lost. The combination of WATU-developed tactics, the newly minted support groups and the closing of the air gap combined to make May 1943 the month in which the U-boats lost the Battle of the Atlantic, the war within a war.

That month, which the Germans subsequently dubbed 'Black May', Doenitz lost forty-one U-boats. It was a decisive tally on this, the impersonal scoresheet of war. The grand admiral of the German navy, who never lost his first love for U-boats or the young men who crewed them, ordered the withdrawal of wolfpacks from the Atlantic battlefield. It was, he urged, merely a temporary and 'partial' change of operations area. Four months later the US admiral Ernest King downgraded the U-boats to the category of 'problem' rather than 'menace'.[24]

The so-called tonnage war was finished, and with it, in most ways that mattered, the Battle of the Atlantic.

XVII

Honours

Christian Oldham watched as, once again, the same row of well-to-do Marylebone houses wheeled past the car window. It was the day of her wedding and next to her in the back seat of the chauffeured Rolls Royce sat her father, wearing a grave expression.

'Are you quite sure?' he said.[1]

It was the third time that the admiral and his daughter had circumnavigated the tree-muffled Manchester Square, just north of Oxford Street in central London.

'If you have any doubts at all,' he continued, 'don't do it.'

After limping into St John's after the Battle of Birds and Wolves, HMS *Oribi* underwent repairs and, a few weeks later, returned to sea. The U-boats may have retreated, but for twenty-three-year-old Oldham, the worrying threat they represented had been replaced by a generalised anxiety of often having no clue where in the world her fiancé had got to. Other than the remote possibility that HMS *Oribi* would drift again onto the wall plot at Belfast Castle, Oldham's best hope for locating Lamb was to check the pink list, which kept an imperfect, often out-of-date record of the whereabouts of every vessel in the British fleet.

Letters went some way to salving the lovelorn, anxiety-pressed heart, and the pair wrote weekly ('all the usual idiotic things' young lovers say to one another, she later recalled). But there was no telling how long a letter might take to wend its way through the labyrinthine naval mail system before it landed, miraculously, on the mat of its moving target. By the time a response arrived, weeks had passed.

All of this made planning for a wedding difficult. Still, Oldham's mother had taken a bold decision. Working from the estimated date of the *Oribi*'s next boiler clean, she had booked a church for a Wednesday in December. She had also bought her daughter, for £6, a white, velvet, second-hand wedding dress from an advertisement posted in *Country Gentleman's Association Magazine*.

After waving him off from the ramparts of Belfast Castle in May, Oldham had reunited with Lamb just once, a few days before today, the day of their wedding. The reunion had been much longed for, but Lamb's excitement was tempered by the intimidating presence of his future mother-in-law, who had accompanied her daughter to size up the young lieutenant. Lamb was, Oldham later recalled, 'much daunted by the whole thing', and in his rush to get the encounter over with as quickly as possible, failed to make a glowing impression. After perilous months at sea, ramming U-boats and enduring the raillery of his fellow sailors, Lamb could be forgiven for failing to adapt to such a delicate social situation. As Oldham later put it, the meeting 'was not a great success'.

Still, it had done nothing to dampen the young Wren officer's determination. In the back seat of the wedding car, she checked the knot of the cord that gathered the waist of her simple dress.

'I have no doubts,' she replied, after a moment, to her father's question.

The car pulled toward Spanish Place and, just before two o'clock in the afternoon of 15th December 1943, Oldham walked in silver slippers through the doors of St James's Church. The congregation included the officers of HMS *Oribi*. They grinned at their lieutenant as he stood at the altar. As she continued up the aisle, Oldham's feelings for the submariner Lennox Napier were gone. In the months since Oldham's engagement, Napier had begun to date her friend, Eve Lindsay, whom he would eventually marry. No animosity passed between the women, then or now.

When she reached the altar, Oldham turned to face the man whom, for a week in May, she had fretfully watched cross the Atlantic Ocean. Seeing the nest of U-boats Lamb's ship faced, she had been unsure if they would meet again. Yet here they were, about to have a wartime wedding which, in the aftermath of that great battle, felt somehow closer to peace than ever before.

At the reception at Dartmouth House in Mayfair, the guests were met with the sight of a towering Christmas cake, baked by Searcys of Sloane Street. Rationing was still an imposition, but the effects of the victory over the U-boats could already be seen on dinner tables across the country. The percentage of imports lost to sinkings had now fallen to less than one per cent, and the Ministry of Food had built up stocks of more than six million tons of food.[2] Thanks in no small part to the *Oribi's* efforts, food was, once again, flowing freely into Britain and, that day, the bride, groom and their guests benefitted.*

Less than a mile away, in the Operations Room at the Admiralty, the wall chart showing the number of convoy ship sinkings, week by week, painted a reassuring picture. Once, at the most desperate point of the Battle of the Atlantic, the graph had nudged the red line that marked the level at which Britain would starve. Now there was a generous buffer between the current losses and the threshold of disaster.

'The Battle of the Atlantic has taken a definite turn in our favour,' wrote Admiral Sir Max Horton in a message dispatched to all Allied units under his command, including the staff at WATU, two weeks after the conclusion of the Battle of Birds and Wolves. 'The returns show an ever-increasing toll of U-boats and decreasing losses of merchant ships in convoy . . . The tide of battle has been checked, if not turned.' The success was, Horton continued, the outcome of 'hard work', 'training' and 'efficiency', much of which was down to the efforts of the men and women of WATU.

Now is the time, Horton urged, 'to strike and strike hard'.[3]

There would be little opportunity for the escort ships to act

---

* The British government was also accountable for ensuring its colonial subjects had food during wartime, a responsibility in which it often failed. In Bengal, for example, between two and three million Indians died of preventable famine in 1943 after the British government prioritised distribution of food supplies to the military, civil servants and other 'priority classes'. This tragic fact must temper any sense of national pride at this moment of overcoming wartime hunger on the home front that same year.

upon Horton's command. U-boats had become scarce. While this caused some frustration and boredom for captains like Gretton, Macintyre and Walker*, for the merchant ships and the British people who, finally, saw their supplies of food, vegetables, heating oil and fuel increase, it was life-changing.

In the seventeen weeks that followed 17th May 1943, the Allies sailed sixty-two east- and westbound convoys along the North Atlantic routes without losing a single ship to a U-boat. More than 12 million tons of food and supplies arrived unimpeded into Britain from eastbound convoys. Seizing the opportunity, senior officers at the Admiralty increased the size of convoys, which in June 1943 averaged sixty-two merchant ships, compared to just forty-three the previous month.[4]

Two secondary factors contributed to the change in U-boat fortunes. In America on 1st May, while the Battle of Birds and Wolves was still being fought, US Navy commander-in-chief Admiral Ernest King created a strategic group in his Washington HQ specifically to combat the German U-boats. By the end of the month the US 10th Fleet, as this new group was known, was coordinating with Derby House in training US escorts, while simultaneously gathering its own intelligence to aid the US Navy's war against the U-boats.

Then in late May the Allies also confirmed that BdU had cracked the British naval cypher, and had been intercepting communications with convoys at sea for months. This had enabled Doenitz and his men to intelligently guide the wolfpacks toward convoys. Realising the exposure, the US and British navies switched to a newer code, known as Naval Cypher No. 5 – once again blinding Doenitz and the U-boats.

On 21st September 1943, Prime Minister Churchill addressed the House of Commons to perform a victory lap.

---

* Walker, the oldest of the three men, suffered a stroke, attributed to exhaustion, on 7th July 1944, and died two days later. Despite the issues with some of his tactical operations, Walker sank more U-boats during the Battle of the Atlantic than any other British or Allied commander. More than a thousand people attended his funeral at Liverpool cathedral, including his rival, Captain Roberts, who never publicly spoke or wrote of their professional clashes.

I have repeatedly stated in this House that our greatest danger in this war . . . is the U-boat attack upon our sea communications and upon Allied shipping all over the world . . . The great victory which was won by our North Atlantic convoys and their escorts in May was followed by a magnificent diminution in sinkings . . . For the four months which ended on 18th September, no merchant vessel was sunk by enemy action in the North Atlantic . . . During the first fortnight in this September no Allied ships were sunk by U-boat action in any part of the world. This is altogether unprecedented in the whole history of the U-boat struggle, either in this war or in the last.

'The high percentage of killings has certainly affected the morale of the U-boat crews, and many of the most experienced U-boat captains have been drowned or are now prisoners,' Churchill continued. 'The House will also realise that we have taken full advantage of the lull in the U-boat attack to bring the largest possible convoys, and that we have replenished the reserves in these islands of all essential commodities, especially fuel oil, which is almost at its highest level since the outbreak of the war.'[5]

Members of the Cabinet and of Parliament on both sides of the House stood and erupted in a prolonged display of cheering and applause.

And a few weeks after Churchill's pronouncement, feeling grateful and well-fed, John and Christian Lamb's guests watched as the newlyweds climbed into a squat green Austin Seven, and drove away to their honeymoon.

In the dying days of 1943, Jean Laidlaw was poring over papers in one of WATU's top-floor offices when Captain Roberts appeared at the glass window of her door. There had been many staff changes at WATU in the previous few months. A Norwegian lieutenant, Per Lure, had joined the team to become controller of one of the five games that were played simultaneously each week (this appointment eventually led to the creation of a table dedicated entirely to

Norwegian naval officers, around a hundred of whom passed through the school before the end of the war).[6]

Liz Drake, one of WATU's founding officers, had joined Roberts' staff on 15th March 1942. The year that followed had been eventful for the twenty-one-year-old. After earning a promotion to second officer on 19th April 1943, Drake had met and fallen in love with the Australian officer Fred Osborne, brother of Nancy Osborne, the senior Wren who had hand-picked the women of WATU. Then Drake's father, her only living parent, had died. She fell ill and took some time off her duties. When she returned, Fred had left WATU's staff to return to sea, and Drake was told to prepare to leave WATU for a new appointment in Belfast, as duty staff officer.[7]

Drake wasn't the only founding member of WATU to be moved on: a few weeks earlier the glamorous Bobby Howes had left for Gibraltar, where she was to work as chief plotting officer.[8] The skills that the women had learned while working on the game had made them some of the most highly valued Wrens in the service, ideal individuals for Laughton Mathews to dispatch to new roles of senior responsibility as they arose.

For every Wren who left, two took her place. Howes was replaced by Pauline Preston, who was made a third officer in May 1943 and later married Lieutenant Ivan Ewart, a lieutenant RNNR torpedo boat captain. Elizabeth 'Bunch' Hackney, who later married another of WATU's staff members, William Tooley-Hawkins, joined alongside Margaret Richards, Mary Dakin and Doris Lawford, a graduate of King's College London whose sister also worked at Derby House as a signal officer, and whose father had come out of retirement to work as an escort commander with Arctic convoys.

Janet Okell had recently been promoted to leading Wren, while June Duncan continued to cope with the rigours of war by spending her evenings rehearsing for and starring in local plays. The ever-faithful Laidlaw, however, remained unmoved from her position as Roberts' right-hand woman. She would stay, as he put it, 'my No. 1 for the whole war'[9] – the 'invalided' captain and the young lesbian, running the show.

Despite frequent staff changes, business at WATU was exception-ally brisk, with more officers taking the six-day course than ever before. In order to prevent his courses from becoming 'tired and stale', as Roberts put it, he and Laidlaw constantly freshened the game scenarios, often adapting story and tactics to reflect develop-ments in the war at sea. In one game, officers had to counter-attack Japanese heavy submarines; in another, German torpedo boats. Fears that the course might become routine or rote gave Roberts 'constant anxiety', he wrote.

As Roberts opened the office door, a letter in his hand, Laidlaw smiled expectantly. He slid the paper across the desk and she imme-diately saw that it was an official document. Laidlaw read the contents in delight. In recognition of his work at WATU, Roberts was to be made an 'Additional' Commander of the Most Excellent Order of the British Empire in the New Year's Honours List. For a man who, just a few years earlier, had been rejected by the navy and, through illness, disqualified from service, it was a healing recompense. Roberts, Laidlaw and the other Wrens had fought tenaciously, not only against the U-boat threat, but also against the scepticism of those who doubted the usefulness of game-playing in wartime.

For Laidlaw and the other staff of WATU this had, at times, made him a challenging man to work for.

'Roberts had the difficulties of personality that very sick people often have,' wrote Fred Osborne, who worked at WATU throughout 1943. 'He was difficult to serve under, very jealous of the position and reputation of the school, and he did not brook disagreement.'[10] Audrey Pitt, a Wren who worked at Derby House from 1942 through to the end of the war was fond of saying: 'If you can cope with Gilbert Roberts, you can cope with anyone.'[11] George Phillips peppered his eulogy for Roberts, under whom he served, with unflinching descriptions such as 'stubborn and forceful', 'tough and aggressive' and known to 'bring frustration upon his staff by his steamroller tactics.'[12] Nevertheless, 'we respected and loved him', Phillips added.

If Roberts fought for the position and reputation of the school, he did so not only for his own glory, but also that of the Wrens with whom he worked – even if he occasionally had to be reminded to share the recognition. Roberts had arrived at Laidlaw's door at the urging of his wife Alice, who had suggested that he ask the woman who had been so instrumental to WATU's success to accompany him to the Palace for the ceremony. Alice and Roberts' relationship was entering its final months (a marriage of which not only did Roberts write nothing in his diaries, but which he also actively sought to conceal following his divorce), but he nevertheless heeded his wife's advice.*

'Will you come?' he asked Laidlaw.

Age, rank, but most of all gender meant that Laidlaw would never be recognised in such a way; if she felt a throb of envy, she kept it to herself. On 15th February 1944 she and a Wrens rating accompanied Roberts to Buckingham Palace† to applaud their captain as he received an award that they would have to share, like so much of the substance of this war, from a distance. 'I took them', Roberts wrote, 'as an honour to themselves, for without them, what could have been done?'

As soon as Roberts' name was made public, there was interest in and speculation about what precisely this unknown and retired captain had done to earn such a prestigious honour at such a crucial moment in the war. From the unit's formation through to this moment, WATU's work had been kept secret, not least because of its situation in Derby House, a place whose location needed to be concealed. With the U-boats in retreat, however, the decision was made to make Roberts' and the Wrens' work public, not only through the Honours List, but also in the press.

In early January 1944, the journalist A. J. Whinnie arrived at WATU to watch a group of officers play the game, see the Wrens at work and to interview Roberts, who was still devising new tactics to

---

* The precise timing of the breakdown of Roberts' marriage is unclear; it is, decorously, not referenced in his papers. A contemporary newspaper report mentions that he invited Laidlaw and another Wren to accompany him to the Palace at his wife's urging; eighteen months later, Roberts left WATU and moved into a new house, alone.

† The Central Chancery of the Orders of Knighthood records that Roberts was presented with his insignia at an investiture ceremony at Buckingham Palace, by King George VI. It holds no record of the name of the second Wren who accompanied Roberts and Laidlaw to the ceremony.

confound the latest German invention, an acoustic torpedo called the *Zaunkönig* ('Wren')* that could redirect itself toward the supersonic sound made by a ship's propellers in the water.

Whinnie, who wrote up the story of what he saw for numerous publications, was accompanied by the photographer Reuben Saidman, often employed by the *Daily Herald*. The Wrens were used to having official photographers from the Admiralty around, documenting their work.† On one occasion Laidlaw had even been made to pose in front of the WATU badge on the unit's front door. In the shot, she smiles serenely while staring at the chessboard on the badge, as if enjoying the afterglow of victory. These photographs were not intended for the public eye, but for record-keeping.

Saidman, by contrast, was a newspaperman whose father and three brothers were also professional photographers. Saidman's dramatic pictures appeared not only in the *Daily Herald*, but also alongside a sparkling article in the glossy and, at the time, widely popular *Illustrated* magazine, under the headline 'Behind the Atlantic Battle: A school where they devise new tactics to beat the U-boats'.

'Go to sea with Britain's anti-submarine groups,' Whinnie wrote in his *Illustrated* article, 'and you will hear references to "the game" and "two-minute moves". They are referring to the Western Approaches Tactical school.'

And with that, knowledge of WATU's work spread from the decks and hulls of the Allied warships to the dining rooms and sofas of British homes. WATU was no longer, as one newspaper article put it, 'Hush-Hush'.[13] For a moment, albeit fleeting, WATU was, as one Wren, put it, 'famous'.[14]

---

* Roberts claimed that after September 1943, no escort vessel was sunk by a 'Wren' after the introduction of his evasive tactic, 'Step Aside'. For a full description of the tactic, refer to Paul Strong's 2017 paper, 'Wargaming the Atlantic War'.

† A trove of these images, most of which were inexpertly taken, at least compared to Reuben Saidman's beautifully framed shots, can be found in the Imperial War Museum archives.

XVIII

The Gun in the Night

On 23rd May 1945, the day when Roberts' cabin was broken into, the captain arrived in the town of Flensburg as the first delegation of British interrogators sent to U-boat headquarters following Germany's surrender. He and his group, which included ONS.5's Commander Peter Gretton, came in peace. Yet, Heinz Walkerling, the former U-boatman assigned to serve Roberts during his stay, had good reason to despise the British. Two years earlier in early March 1943, while taking part in a wolfpack attack on an eastbound convoy in the North Atlantic Walkerling had witnessed the sinking of his compatriots on *U-444*. Thanks to WATU's work, hundreds of U-boatmen, some of whom would have been personally known to the German, had been killed in action.

If Roberts had any reservations about being assigned a U-boat officer for an assistant, he did not raise it. He saw nothing of concern in Walkerling's demeanour and described him in his official report as 'a pleasant but rather ineffective weakling'.[1] If anything, the German seemed keen to please, helping Roberts track down potential interviewees from whom to extract information to take back to England.

Roberts was eager to interview German naval officers who had served either at BdU or as U-boat commanders in order to verify his deductions and suppositions. But there were few candidates left in Flensberg.

'Many had been killed, some were prisoners of war in Russian hands and others were already dispersed or disbanded,' Roberts wrote in his report.[2] 'BdU was unable to state their whereabouts.'[3]

Compounding this confusion was the fact that on 8th May, German naval personnel had been forbidden from sending messages to one another. Nobody seemed to quite know where anybody else was. There was, however, one high-value prisoner aboard the *Patria*, the ship which Roberts had boarded soon after landing in Germany. Walkerling led Roberts to the cabin of Rear Admiral Godt, Doenitz's chief of staff and the man responsible for the organisation and operation of all U-boats. Roberts and Walkerling found the German officer 'violently incensed' and in a 'shocking temper'.[4] In pristine English, Godt explained that British soldiers had forced their way into his HQ and torn the plot from the wall. Then, Godt claimed, the men had broken into his private cabin to steal various items, including a silver frame in which he kept a photograph of his daughter.

His dismay at the British troops' unmannerly behaviour had been further compounded when Godt was kept on a parade ground among a crowd of officers and ratings for no less than five hours, awaiting a search by British intelligence. Also, Godt added mournfully, he hadn't had any lunch.

Roberts could see he was unlikely to extract any useful information unless he was able to calm Doenitz's chief of staff. Besides, he could see for himself the mess that the soldiers had made of Godt's room and was now 'just as angry' as the German officer. Roberts requested to see the nearest brigade commander. A major general arrived, and Roberts demanded the silver photo frame be found and returned. Without it, Roberts said, I 'would have no cooperation with the Germans and my mission would be useless.'

Not realising that he was being rather forcefully addressed by a retired naval captain, the more senior officer agreed to locate and return the trinket, which duly arrived at Roberts' room. With Godt appeased, the two men sat down in Roberts' cabin for the interview. Roberts placed a tape recorder on the bench beside him, so that his interviewee would think they knew when they were on- and off-record. But a member of Roberts' delegation, Commander Harry Taylor Gherardi, set up a second tape recorder, disguised as a suitcase, under Roberts' bunk. Gherardi was a former FBI agent from Rhode Island, the grandson of the first Italian-American admiral in the United States Navy, Bancroft Gherardi. At the start of the war, he joined the United States Navy Reserves and, due to his experience as an intelligence agent, was sent to Britain to inter-view U-boat captains.[5] His secret suitcase recording device recorded any and all conversation, so that nothing would be lost. Nothing would be, in other words, 'off-record'.[6]

Roberts found Godt to be 'a good subject for interrogation', not least because within a few minutes he had confirmed what Roberts and Laidlaw had deduced via the game: that following Kretschmer's pioneering manoeuvres, U-boat crews were specifically trained to penetrate the columns of a convoy, fire at the merchant ships from point-blank range, and then perform a dive to evade detection.

With the thrill of having his theory confirmed by the highest-ranking officer in the German U-boat wing beneath Doenitz, a cascade of questions fell from Roberts. Did the Germans, he asked next, use a game like the one at WATU to develop or refine tactics? Godt replied that they did not, but that a year earlier he had seen the edition of *Illustrated* magazine in which Roberts and the Wrens of WATU had been profiled.

'He admitted the value of such an establishment,' Roberts wrote in his report, 'but he did not consider adapting it to his needs as it was "too late in the war".'

Unprompted, Godt went on to 'marvel' at the use of Wrens in such duty. He explained that women were used a great deal in the German navy. This much was probably already known to Roberts as four weeks earlier, on 22nd April 1945, no fewer than 500 German 'Wrens' had surrendered ('sullenly, but without resistance', as one newspaper report put it[7]) to the 7th Armoured Division, or 'Desert Rats' as they were better known, at a North Sea naval station in Buxtehude. Godt explained, however, that women would never be employed in the German navy for such important work as that carried out by WATU. In fact, Godt added, women 'did not even assist in the working of the Atlantic plot'.

Finally, Roberts asked whether Godt knew of any of the tactical operations that WATU had developed, and which had proven so effective in changing the fortunes of the Allied ships. Godt replied that of course he realised that there were concerted tactical movements, and also probably several choices for selection, if a U-boat was found before or after a torpedoing. The name of just one of these manoeuvres was known to the Germans, he said.

'Which one?' asked Roberts.

'Operation Raspberry.'[8]

The satisfaction of knowing that news of WATU's creation had reached the highest ranks of the German navy surely contributed to the deep sleep into which Roberts fell, a few hours before his cabin door opened.

The chaos at Flensburg was reflected in the French port of Lorient with its vast and concrete-shielded U-boat bunkers. In recent weeks Lorient had become a siege city populated by monstrous rats and tenacious U-boatmen. On the eve of Germany's final surrender, it was now the last stalwart of Doenitz's grand and now failed U-boat scheme.

Most German garrisons in France had surrendered following the liberation of Paris in August 1944. Lorient, which, other than the unscathed fortresses of its U-boat bunkers Kéroman I–IV, had been reduced to a city of rubble, was a rare pocket of German resistance: 26,000 German soldiers had taken up residence in a city whose streets had not heard the laughter of children playing for more than two years.

In early 1943, just prior to the Battle of Birds and Wolves, Churchill had conceded that after a sustained bombing campaign, the U-boat bunkers were apparently indestructible.* Instead he had ordered the annihilation of the city, hoping that, by ruining Lorient's infrastructure, the men stationed in the U-boat bases might, in turn, starve. On the night of 15th January 1943, 200 bombers dropped incendiary bombs on the French port. During the next week, 353 civilians were killed and more than 800 structures damaged or destroyed: approximately ninety per cent of the buildings within the city walls. Telephone and gas lines were broken. One half of the post office

---

* A 2,000lb Armour bomb, the largest used by the R.A.F., dropped from a height of 20,000 feet, would penetrate eight feet of concrete roof.

was cleaved away, the building left showing an indignity of beams through its gaping roof.

Citizens were officially evacuated on 3rd February, and between 50,000 and 60,000 inhabitants were evacuated to surrounding towns and villages, so that 'only workers employed by the Germans', those who were 'indispensable for providing fresh supplies, food and public health', remained. If Kiel, with its churning U-boat factories, was the mechanical heart of Doenitz's U-boat scheme, Lorient was the front line of operations, and the city paid a heavy price for its unlikely promotion to a position of utmost importance in the Atlantic war. According to the city's official figures, between 25th September 1940 and 8th May 1945, it sustained 370 aerial bombings.

Led by the fifty-seven-year-old General Wilhelm Fahrmbacher, the Germans resisted Allied attempts to liberate the port, which continued to serve as a place for U-boat crews to recuperate and replenish supplies. Fahrmbacher sustained his soldiers' morale with a daily supply of bread made from flour mixed with sawdust, a fact hidden from most of the troops. In order to eke out supplies, Fahrmbacher had the local railway track pulled up and the sleepers removed to be sawed up to help make dough.

In just two years Lorient had gone from a place of champagne and plenty for the Germans to a city of poverty. Coffee was brewed not from coffee beans, but from ground acorns or, sometimes, from thinly sliced and baked carrots. For the French citizens, leather shoes had not been sold in the city since 7th November 1940, when France had been directed to send all its leather to Germany. Now those same impositions had come to the occupiers. Unlike the French, they may not have had to make clothes from the scavenged parachutes of downed American pilots, but many soldiers had only their fraying uniforms to wear.

In the first week of May 1945, Fahrmbacher summoned his quartermaster.

'How many railroad sleepers have we left?' he asked.

When the quartermaster hesitated, the general knew that the situation was grave. Finally, the quartermaster replied: 'One.'

That afternoon, knowing that his thousands of men could no

longer hold out on bread made from a single railway sleeper, Fahrmbacher sent a message to Doenitz.

'Wish to sign off with my steadfast and unbeaten men,' it read. 'We remember our sorely tried homeland. Long live Germany.'

The last of the French U-boat ports, from which the Battle of the Atlantic had been so hard-fought, had fallen. If Fahrmbacher's men felt relief at the news, it was surely nothing to that experienced by the U-boatmen at sea who, four days earlier, had received a final message from the founder and leader of their beleaguered division:

My U-boatmen,
    Six years of U-boat war lie behind us. You have fought like lions . . . A continuation of our fight is no longer possible . . . Undefeated and spotless you lay down your arms after a heroic battle without equal. We remember in deep respect our fallen comrades, who had sealed with death their loyalty to Führer and Fatherland. ·

After their commander's recent edicts to go on fighting, the order to surrender their boats came as a tremendous surprise to Doenitz's U-boat captains. Many wondered whether the enemy had taken control of the cypher system and sent a faked message.[9] For those who believed the order, relief, seemingly, was followed by confusion about precisely what to do next. Adalbert Schnee, the U-boat officer who served under Otto Kretschmer before sinking the Wren's ship, SS *Aguila*, made a dummy attack on a convoy – the last of the war. He approached within the columns of ships, as per his former captain's tactic, then escaped undetected, before heading to Norway.

Some U-boats made for neutral harbours. Two crossed the Atlantic, for a final time, and made for Argentina, while five left for Japanese waters. Many waited for the code word *Regenbogen* ('Rainbow') – the signal to scuttle their vessels. It never came.

Heinz Walkerling stood in the dark of Roberts' cabin, the Luger heavy in his hand. In this moment, the German had both the means and the motive to kill the British captain. But Walkerling had not come to assassinate his new master. He padded across to the polished table in the sitting room adjoining Roberts' bedroom, placed the weapon down and retreated to his own cabin, clicking the door behind him.

Walkerling later explained that he wanted to ensure Roberts had the means to protect himself during his stay aboard the German liner. After all, not everyone could be guaranteed to be as respectful of rank as a U-boat officer. If his actions happened to demonstrate to Roberts the danger in which he had placed himself by stubbornly refusing a weapon, then so be it.

'I don't know where he got it, or how it eluded the search parties,' Roberts later wrote, of the moment he saw the gun lying on the table. Yet still the stubborn captain would not be moved to arm himself. The next morning, after quizzing Walkerling about what he'd done, Roberts passed the weapon to another member of his party, a corvette captain who was 'a bit of an Autolycus', as Roberts put it in his diary, comparing the commander to the burglar of Greek myth.

The gun disposed of, Roberts spent the next day on the U-boat plot with Vice Admiral Godt, with whom he was now on 'excellent terms'.[10] On the plot, Roberts met some of the men who, like the Wrens at Derby House and Belfast Castle, had maintained the live position of ships and U-boats on the maps. When introduced, the men appeared to blanch. Their fear was soon explained. As Roberts began his tour of the facility, he visited the U-boat Operations Room. There, enlarged and tacked to a wall, he saw his own photograph, cut out from the *Illustrated* magazine article. There was a handwritten caption beneath the image: 'This is your enemy, Captain Roberts, director of Anti-U-boat Tactics.'*

After a moment, one of the men took the photo and handed it to Roberts.

---

* Mention of the inscription appears only in *Captain Gilbert Roberts R.N. and the Anti-U-Boat School,* a 1979 biography by Mark Williams, a writer Roberts later accused of being prone to 'glib exaggeration'. In turn, Williams' book does not mention that Roberts made the effort to sign the photo, a detail exclusive to his unpublished diaries.

'I autographed it,' Roberts recorded. 'I already had a copy.'

Godt agreed to pass to Roberts three valuable documents: his staff's U-boat daily position summary, patrol orders and the weekly intelligence summaries charting Allied convoys. While Roberts read over these documents, he dispatched the former FBI agent Gherardi to make a list of last known positions of every operational U-boat. This would allow the Allies to cross-reference their estimated list of U-boat sinkings against the facts.

'I found it astonishing,' Roberts wrote, of the exercise, 'how very accurate the assessment had been by our own Anti-Submarine Committee at Admiralty.'

Godt took the opportunity to vent at Roberts his frustrations with the belatedness of the expansion of the U-boat arm, and the regretful crewing of submarines by barely trained Luftwaffe officers, rather than sailors, after the Blitz.*

Roberts, knowing the answer but wanting to hear it from Godt himself, finally asked whether the tactic pioneered by Kretschmer – of a U-boat slinking into the middle of a convoy, attacking merchant ships, then, in the ensuing chaos, diving to wait, engines silenced, till danger had passed – was an official instruction.

'Yes,' Godt replied. 'You take her to the bottom. There you sit, undisturbed, to eat and rest.'

It had been a long day and Godt was tired. He had, it seemed, enjoyed the opportunity to discuss the U-boat war with his erstwhile enemy. Before he retired Godt turned to Roberts and asked if he might shake his hand. Roberts nodded, and the pair reconciled.

During the next few days Roberts continued his rounds of interviews, speaking at length to numerous U-boat captains, including Doenitz's son-in-law, Commander Hessler. ('A humourless head-nodder and heel-clicker,' as Roberts described him, with typical flair. 'Not my type.') Hessler confirmed what Godt had told him, that 'every U-boat captain desired to get inside the columns of the merchant ships because they were safe there from being attacked'.[11]

---

* Luftwaffe officers who transferred to the U-boat arm were subject to just three weeks' training at sea after which, Godt sneeringly told Roberts, they 'thought they knew it all'.

One evening, Roberts returned to his suite and found it filled, this time not with loaded pistols but with bottles of champagne. It was a gift from Godt, Walkerling explained, who had taken them from Doenitz's private store, as 'he wouldn't need them again'. Roberts and his team each took two bottles of Bisquit Dubouché to take home, leaving 'several bottles for immediate use'.

Their work at U-boat headquarters was finished. But prior to returning to England, Roberts and Gherardi travelled to Kiel, where many of the U-boats were built and launched. A few weeks earlier, on 20th April 1945, the port had been razed in a concerted bombing raid, and the party arrived to find the harbour filled with the corpses of ships. The *Admiral Sheer* lay with her keel rudely stuck in the air. The *Hipper* and *Emden* lay wearily on their sides, the first having been struck by three consecutive bombs while in dry dock.[12] Roberts recalled seeing the dockyard filled with U-boat bodies, 'smashed and scuttled', fragments of Doenitz's ruined dream poking from the water.[13]

Vera Laughton Mathews, the founder of the Wrens, visited the port around the same time, and described the streets as 'nothing but piles of bricks and debris, among which thousands of bodies must still be buried'.[14] She wrote of seeing 'pale ghosts emerging from the ground' to flit among the ruins. The air was 'heavy with corruption', she wrote. 'I sympathised with the young officer who remarked, "I should hate to be bitten by a mosquito here."'

Laughton Mathews recalled being fed and entertained 'royally', sitting among *objets d'art* looted from France and drinking bottles of 'obviously stolen' wine.

'It was difficult to retain a sense of proportion and to know what was right,' she wrote, of her feelings of moral nausea at being looked after in proximity to 'starving' Germans.

'It is not at all a pleasant feeling to be a conqueror,' she concluded, the first of war's lessons, seemingly, to be forgotten in peacetime.

For Roberts there was a certain professional fascination to his visit to Kiel. He and the American were taken aboard *U-3008*, a brand-new Type XXI U-boat that had been commissioned just a few months earlier. While one of the U-boat's hydroplanes was broken, meaning that it could not dive, Roberts and Gherardi took her briefly to sea. It was his first trip on a U-boat, and Roberts was able to feel the conditions of life on one of the vessels which, for the past three and a half years, he had hunted via The Game. In his official report, Roberts noted his surprise at the apparent comfort of the crew's quarters on this new class of U-boat, as well as the presence of a gramophone player and a stack of records.

Before Roberts returned to England he spoke with a U-boat captain who, it transpired, had witnessed the destruction of HMS *Hood*.[15] Of all the interviews he undertook, this was the most fraught with emotion; Roberts' friend Bernard Stubbs, the former BBC reporter with whom he had shared that Christmas night on the London Underground platform, in the unexpected presence of the king, had died in the sinking of the *Hood*. Roberts asked his questions quickly, then left.

While the interrogators continued their work, Roberts bade goodbye to Gherardi and took a car to the aerodrome. There he 'thumbed a Dakota' which was headed to England carrying a senior member of the Nazi Party who was due to be interrogated.

Roberts and the German official spoke intermittently during the flight. After landing at Hendon, the captain hitched a lift to Speke, Liverpool in a Canadian aircraft headed to Iceland. The result of the mission?

'Nothing,' Roberts wrote, victoriously. 'I learned absolutely nothing.'[16]

The Sisterhood of the Linoleum

The crew of U-249 stood on the deck of the boat that had been their home for the past five weeks at sea[1], their hands raised in surrender, their backs turned from the English shoreline. The men were weary, their uniforms crusted and frowsy. On receiving Doenitz's final message to his U-boats, U-249's captain, thirty-three-year-old Uwe Kock, had, on 9th May, surfaced and raised a flag in surrender to an overheard plane. Kock and his crew had been escorted to Weymouth Bay in Dorset, on the south coast of England, by this Liberator aircraft of the Fleet Air Wing of the US Navy. When they arrived in harbour the following day, the men lined up on the deck to await further instruction.

While they stood in submission, breathing the fresh air of peace, the crew members heard the sound of a launch approaching from the harbour behind. A few of the Germans shared an apprehensive glance. Unable to contain his curiosity, one young man threw a glance over his shoulder, then immediately looked forward again, his eyes widened in disbelief.[2]

The German nudged the man beside him, who in turn looked back. Presently, each crew member turned to see what was happening. There, a few metres away, was a boat filled not with the kind of stern-faced naval heavies they'd expected, but with a clutch of Wrens, most of whom were in their teens, led by none other than Nancy Osborne.

Hearing news of the incoming U-boat, Portland's senior naval officer, Admiral R. J. R. Scott, asked Osborne, the woman who had sent Christian Oldham on her course as plotter, and hand-picked

WATU's staff, to accompany him on his barge.* Together, he said, they would accept the Germans' surrender. He asked Osborne to bring with her a few other Wrens, including a petty officer, a visual signaller and three Wrens ratings, saying that he thought it would be 'very good' for the Germans to see the Wrens crew.[3]

The scene of the young Germans stealing elated glances at the women would remain bright in Osborne's memory for the remainder of her life. Years later, she recalled: '[Their] surprise and delight . . . had to be seen to be believed.'

Wrens were intimately involved in the long and arduous administrative work that was involved in ending a world war. Young women were dispatched to Berlin, Hamburg, Kiel and Minden, and a number of Wrens interpreters were also posted to work alongside the German-manned mine-sweeping operations in the Baltic Sea. Wrens officers worked not only as secretaries and PAs, but also as signal and duty officers responsible for finding and cataloguing any naval war material, much of which had been hidden, that was discovered. Wrens helped to organise the scuttling of ships loaded with poison gas shells,[4] the repatriation of German soldiers from Norway and the identification and reclamation of Allied ships that had been commandeered by the Germans.

Once collected, the German naval papers were sent to France to be translated and evaluated for relevance in the Nuremberg trials. This work was carried out by a unit that included Wrens, special-duties linguists who had been part of the first contingent of servicewomen sent to France after D-Day.[5] There they had holed up in an old farmhouse in Courseulles-sur-Mer. Evelyn Glazier was a member of the unit, tasked with reading through an estimated 50,000 German files. She was responsible for identifying evidence that was later used in the trials of twenty-two Nazis at Nuremberg. She also translated documents that included Hitler's recorded testimony.[6] Among these stacks of evidence one of Glazier's colleagues found the identity of U-30, the U-boat that sank the Athenia on the first day

---

* Vera Laughton Mathews briefly mentions this incident in her autobiography Blue Tapestry (p. 245). She identifies the admiral as Sir Carlisle Swabey, contradicting the contemporaneous newspaper report, used here as the source.

of the war, when 117 civilian passengers and crew were killed in an act that was condemned as a war crime. So efficient was their work that an American commander wrote to Vera Laughton Mathews to ask whether Glazier and one of her Wrens colleagues might be spared to work as translators at Nuremberg as part of the US delegation, a request to which Laughton Mathews consented.*

Following Germany's surrender, not all of the 63,000 Wrens still in active service were needed.[7] As the summer drew on, many Wrens began the business of demobbing to return, ostensibly, to the civilian lives that had been placed on indefinite hold up to six years earlier. Most of the women found, however, that those lives no longer existed.

'You'd left all your friends, the atmosphere was different, and people weren't so keen to help each other anymore,' said one Wren of the sorrowful transition. 'There was no counselling and it was so difficult to settle back in to civilian life . . . it was an anticlimax. We were just left to get on with life as best we could.'[8]

War, in its way, imposes a certain form on the formlessness of life; it binds people with a common purpose, a project into which each person lends their particular strengths, be it fighting in the trenches or mending uniforms. When war ends there is, seemingly, a first flush of relief, a joyous moment in which to celebrate the birth of this new, longed-for peace, seen in every VE Day photograph, with its smiles and streamers. Then more complicated feelings arrive, ones that cannot be so easily captured on film. These feelings have to do with the death of a shared resolve, one that for six painful, perilous years, transcended generations, class and gender.

'Whether they can put it into words or not, this was the tremendous gain: the sense of having taken part in something of enormous importance, of having justified their existence,' wrote Vera Laughton Mathews of war's unexpected gift. Peace had come, but at the cost of purpose. This was the unmentionable loss of the Second World

---

* Stephanie Higham, née Pigott, who worked as Max Horton's Assistant Duty Staff Officer from September 1944 onwards, was also sent to Germany as an interpreter Wren at the end of the war. She attended the Nuremburg trials each morning, then rode, sailed or skiied in the afternoons before the evening parties began.

War, the death that could not be mourned. After all, the purpose of the war was to bring about precisely such an ending. Nevertheless, across jobless Britain, a vacuum was keenly felt.

'The end of the war was a blow in lots of ways,' said Peggy Hill, a Wren based at Swansea naval base. 'Everybody felt the same. It was the end of a completely different way of living, like coming back to earth again. The missing went on for years.'[9]

None felt 'the missing' more keenly than the women who, via war's arrival, had been given an unprecedented opportunity to occupy spaces and roles that had been closed off to them. They had entered the war as one thing and exited as quite another.

'The Wrens have carried out duties once thought to be completely outside the scope of womenkind,' wrote one journalist for the *Western Morning News* in October 1945.[10] 'They have kept secrets, so vital, that at times the fate of the nation depended upon them. They have been positioned to watch great dramas of combat mirrored on huge maps which told Britain's peril from the U-boats.'

For the Wrens, the arrival of peace meant somehow relinquishing a new-found identity. As she handed in her uniform, one young woman was seen to pat her sea boots and mutter: 'Cheerio, old pals.' Wrens seemed, in war's crucible, to have been profoundly shaped and unified by their chosen service. When she died in 2015, at the age of 93, Mary Poole, the Wren officer who ran the torpedo simulator in Liverpool, still kept her Wren headdress on her bedside, next to a photograph taken in 1943 of her in uniform.[11] For many of these young women, their time in the Wrens was both formative and definitive.

'I am going home to my husband, himself just released, and that is a great thing,' said one Wren on the day of her demobbing. 'But I would not have missed this wonderful experience, this great sisterhood, for anything.'

When they arrived home, however, many of the young women found it difficult to reintegrate with former contemporaries.

'They didn't know what my life had been,' said Claire James, a plotter who became a leading Wren. 'I'd led a totally different life to anybody at home. I'd gone through things people at home hadn't. I found it very difficult, settling back.'[12]

WATU, its identity now public knowledge, earned its own mention in the news reports.

'This team spirit was reflected in another sphere, for at the Officers' Tactical School at one of the great ports Sir Max Horton schemed and planned to beat the U-boats,' read one. 'In that school they constantly played a "game" which took place on the floor. It was a game that, played properly, saved countless lives. In this great work the Wrens cooperated to a remarkable degree, plotting and recording with skill, speed, and precision, which won the admiration of all who were privileged to see them at work.'[13]

The fresh opportunities that the country had, for a moment, afforded women in war were widely rescinded. Many firms, together with the teaching profession and the Civil Service, operated a marriage bar after the war, leading some women to slip off their wedding rings in order not to have to vacate their positions.[14] When the men returned, the women were expected to meekly retreat to their former roles, as homemakers and keepers. This was in addition to the challenge of finding peacetime jobs to which the young women's new-found skills might transfer. Having given many young women a profession that was, at least in the case of the plotters, particular to a now vanished moment, many Wrens were left without a vocation.

'The things I learned were completely useless after the war,' said Christian Lamb, who, after a stint at the plot in Falmouth, where the *Oribi* was undergoing repairs (again, she was looked after by Nancy Osborne, who gave her the appointment so that she could be close to her new husband), gave birth to her and John's daughter, Felicity. 'I really had no qualifications.'

This was, seemingly, less true for the women of WATU, who, through game-playing, had acquired numerous transferable skills. Laidlaw returned to London to continue her career as one of the country's first female chartered accountants, eventually retiring as chief accountant for the firm of solicitors Baker & Mackenzie. Her time in the service inspired lifelong loyalty to the Wrens; she advised the organisation on financial matters throughout her life, and left money to the Association of Wrens when she died.[15] 'This was more than wartime,' her nephew Bill Laidlaw said. 'This was something to do with her identity and who she was.'

Janet Okell, who lived in the Liverpool area until her death in 2005, became office manager for the manufacturing company Heap & Partners. According to her niece, Okell was 'very fond of the girls', no doubt employing many of the managerial techniques she witnessed, first as a Wrens rating and then later as a leading Wren.*

After the war Nan Wales, who never married and, like Laidlaw, was described by her family as 'a very private person',[16] returned to her home of Hull, but remained in the Wrens. She became first officer of the Hull shore establishment HMS *Gaeatea*, continuing to play hockey at county level, and eventually teaching sport in a high school, thereby keeping her hand in game-playing for years.

June Duncan was told that she was 'too thin' and lacked 'the physical strength' to pursue her dream to become a professional actor after the war.[17] Instead she turned to modelling, gracing the catwalks of London, Paris and Rome, and the pages of glossy fashion magazines such as *Vogue* ('It was a hell of a life, but damned hard work').[18] Later, she became the assistant editor of *Harper's Bazaar* magazine and, after she retired and moved to Devon, returned to her first love as theatre critic for a local newspaper. Ostensibly Duncan's work at WATU had nothing to do with her chosen career, but in interviews she would often credit Roberts for his belief and support in her.

'He was a very hard task master,' she once said, 'but a brilliant man. The way he worked out tactical games was astonishing. I feel proud to have been a member of a team which did so much to help win the Battle of the Atlantic.'[19]

Many of the relationships forged in WATU endured. Fred Osborne and Liz Drake were married on 4th November 1944, and, at the end of the summer of 1946, sailed to Australia, where Fred became a government minister in the Liberal Party. William Tooley-Hawkins and Elizabeth Hackney, who attended the Slade School of Fine Art in London before joining WATU, married in 1947 and became publicans, running the Traveller's Rest in Reading, and later

---

* In his diaries Roberts claims that Okell, along with Doris Lawford, was made an officer at the end of the war. There is no evidence to corroborate this claim. Neither Okell nor Lawford's names feature in the Navy lists for July or October 1945, nor January or April 1946. It was, perhaps, wishful thinking on Roberts' part.

the Red Lion in Brixham, Devon. Peter Gretton and Judy Du Vivier remained married for the rest of their lives, as he rose up the ranks in the Royal Navy to become a vice admiral.

For Laughton Mathews, who had devoted her life to the ennoblement and promotion of women, victory altered her guiding question.

'How to encourage the virtues of war, the heroism and sacrifice, kindness, endurance and fidelity,' she now wondered, 'absent of its horrors?'[20]

For Laughton Mathews those horrors were not second-hand knowledge. She had known grief in her role as leader of the Wrens, of course, particularly following the deaths of the young women killed on the SS *Aguila*. And when visiting a London establishment ostensibly for the training of Polish Wrens rescued from the concentration camps, she had seen the 'suffering and degradation . . . written in their grey shrinking faces'. But it was only when she travelled to Nuremberg, in part to see the work of her crack interpreter Wrens, that she understood the outlandish kind of evil that had been perpetrated by the Nazis.

There Laughton Mathews visited a room known as the 'Chamber of Horrors', a funfair moniker for a place displaying a panoply of harrowing artefacts: soap made from human fat, lampshades made from tattooed human skin and photographs of the piles of children's shoes stacked outside the gas chambers. After she returned home, Laughton Mathews wrote that she did not sleep for a week. One photograph in particular kept her awake. It showed a group of young Jewish girls, running in a circle while armed German soldiers looked on as they decided, she imagined, on whether the children's fate should be 'the crematorium or the brothel'.

In the nights that followed, Laughton Mathews wept every night for those girls, knowing that they were likely dead, but hoping that, in some mysterious way, her grief might retroactively ease the girls' suffering in the moment the photograph was taken, the kind of magical thinking required to contemplate the unconscionable.

'I was filled, too,' Laughton Mathews wrote two years later, 'by a helpless agony that men should have the power to inflict such humiliation on women.'

This is what she had always been fighting for, ever since being spat on by passers-by while standing in the gutter selling copies of the *Suffragette*: an alternate 'conception of womanhood', one that existed not only counter to that promoted by Nazism, but also, in a quieter but no less meaningful way, promoted at home, in the workplace and in society at large.

On 8th June 1946, 200 Wrens took part in the London Victory Parade. The four-mile long procession, which included representatives from all of the armed forces and more than 500 vehicles from the Royal Navy, the Royal Air Force, British civilian services and the British Army, was led by Wrens dispatch riders on their motorbikes. The procession marched at a leisurely pace. Fire engines trundled. Scottish and Irish pipers piped. Laughton Mathews, accompanied by the two other directors of the Wrens, Dame Leslie Whately and Lady Welsh, sat in the Royal Stand behind Queen Elizabeth, King George VI, Clement Attlee and Winston Churchill awaiting sight of the main Wrens contingent.

First came the sailors. Then the Marines. Now a small contingent from the naval nursing service. Finally, in white caps, the Wrens. As they passed the king and queen the women turned their faces in well-drilled unison. The sound of the bands, the cheering, the applause, muffled to silence in Laughton Mathews' ears. While everyone else saw the pristine uniforms and mechanical precision of the marching, Laughton Mathews saw the women in sweat-soaked boilersuits and ripped overalls, their faces smudged with engine oil. She saw her Wrens in bell-bottom trousers, tearing fleet-footed up ladders to deliver urgent messages, while sailors leaned over the handrails. She saw her Wrens in leather-strapped tin helmets, leaning into lingering corners atop motorbikes, the sound of bomb-fall crackling in their eardrums.

And she saw her Wrens in a Liverpool attic, on bended knee, watchfully pushing wooden ships across the linoleum floor, hundreds of miles from the terrors of the Atlantic, yet close enough that they could feel the salt water crusting on their fingertips.

Postscript

Between the first week of February 1942 and the last of July 1945, when WATU officially closed, close to 5,000 naval officers played the wargame run by Captain Roberts and the Wrens, during more than 130 courses.[1] In addition to the thousands of British naval officers who completed the course, Roberts and the Wrens trained delegates from the United States, Canada, Australia, New Zealand, India, Malaya, South Africa, Denmark, Belgium, the Netherlands, Norway, Poland and France (and four university professors).[2]

Many graduates of the game credited the battles they waged on the linoleum floor as being instrumental in their subsequent victories during encounters with U-boats at sea. Similar tactical units sprang up across the British Empire – from Belfast to Bombay, Sierra Leone to Halifax – some of which were also staffed by young Wrens who, by playing the game time and again, also became experts in anti-submarine warfare. By 1945, a total of sixty-six Wrens had completed the course in order to become staff at WATU or its sister units.[3]

Two-thousand-six-hundred-and-three merchant ships and 175 of the convoys' escorting naval vessels were sunk in the Battle of the Atlantic, the longest continuous military campaign in the Second World War. More than 30,000 merchant seamen, and more than 6,000 Royal Navy sailors died in the Atlantic during the war, many following attacks by U-boats.[4] It was an astonishing loss of life, tempered by the work of the men and women of WATU, and the sailors who deployed their tactics at sea.

For his ingenuity in developing and teaching these tactics, Roberts earned awards around the world, including the King Commander's

Order of St Olav of Norway, the Commander's Order of Polonia Restituta of Poland and the Officer's Order of the Legion of Honour of France. On 8th June 1945 Roberts received a letter from A.V. Alexander, First Lord of the Admiralty. It read: 'There is no doubt that the Tactical Schools and Courses which you organised were of great value, and it must be a source of satisfaction to you and your staff at the success achieved against the varying methods of enemy attack. I shall always feel indebted to you.'[5]

Not one of the Wrens involved was to receive public recognition for her contribution. At war's end, Sir Max Horton wrote in his report of Roberts: 'This officer and his school of tactics have played a far-reaching and significant part in the Battle of the Atlantic. I lose his services with the deepest regret.'

The commander-in-chief of Western Approaches, who had been defeated in the game by two of WATU's Wrens, then sent the following personal signal, directed to all who had served in the unit, an incandescent tribute to their quiet, momentous achievement:

'On the closing down of WATU I wish to express my gratitude and high appreciation of the magnificent work of Captain Roberts and his staff, which contributed in no small measure to the final defeat of Germany.'[6]

Epilogue

When I was a child, my brother and I played a variation of Battleship on the floor of my grandparents' house in Devon. Theirs was an elaborate, quasi-luxurious version of the game, stored in a leather trunk in the corner of a mildew-scented dining room, along with a tatty copy of Monopoly and a war-era toy farm (the plastic pig minus a trotter or two, the red tractor with its acne'd paint).

It was certainly a grander proposition than the one my brother and I played at home, which used grey plastic tokens to represent the ships and brightly coloured pegs to mark torpedo strikes. Theirs was played out on a crinkled map spread across the floor. We'd take turns to throw the dice and manoeuvre our ships into position. Then, at the press of a button on a destroyer, a small plastic disc would tear along the glossy board like a miniature hockey puck. Each ship had a hole in the base of the plastic, where hull met map. If your aim was true, the disc would slot snugly into this hole. Through some toymaker's magic, a direct hit would cause the top of the model to spring into the air, like a cap rocketing from the top of a dropped bottle of lemonade. It didn't always work; sometimes the disc would lodge halfway into the hole, causing the double irritation of failing to set off the exploding mechanism and blocking further attacks. But when everything went to plan, the effect was thrilling.

My brother and I would play, in our short shorts, until we tired of it and ran outdoors. It kept our attention for long enough to occupy chunks of time from the grand expanse of those early summer holidays. I didn't stop to consider why, of all games, my grandparents owned *this* one.

My grandfather, Dynely Parkin, didn't speak much about the war. His role, like that of all the other merchant sailors who sailed from Liverpool to America and back again, was to ferry vital food and fuel supplies across the Atlantic. It was essential work but did not fit the image of heroism promoted by the post-war books and films.

Three years younger than Wren Janet Okell, my grandfather was not quite fourteen years old at the outbreak of the Second World War. That month he was stationed in Kent on the training ship HMS *Worcester*, which was narrowly missed by numerous bombs dropped by German planes. At seventeen years old, on 11th June 1943 he joined his first ship, the *Empire Castle*, a 7,000-ton refrigerated cargo liner that, six months earlier, had been launched for the first time within sight of Christian Lamb's position at Belfast Castle.

On its maiden voyage, a few months before my grandfather joined her crew, *Empire Castle* sailed out of Liverpool to New York as a member of convoy UC.001.[1] Seven days into the journey, the convoy of thirty-three ships was spotted by a wolfpack, *Gruppe Rochen* ('Skate', after the fish), which sank three ships and damaged four the following day. The *Empire Castle* survived its inaugural encounter with a U-boat pack and returned safely to England. By the time my grandfather boarded it, the ship was still unscathed by the ravages of the Atlantic Ocean, both man-made and natural.

Five days after my grandfather joined the crew, *Empire Castle* set sail in convoy ON.189, bound for New York. The journey across the Atlantic plotted a similar route to that which convoy ONS.5 had taken directly into the Battle of Birds and Wolves, just four weeks earlier.

To weigh down the empty ship on its outbound route, the *Empire Castle*'s hold was filled with ballast, the rubble of bombed Glasgow houses, due to be emptied on arrival in New York and switched with food and other supplies for the onward journey. (The rubble was then used to build jetties in the city's docks, a patch of Scotland forever embedded in Manhattan's waterfront.)

'We steamed at the speed of the slowest ship along a prearranged course, sailing as far north as was practical to keep out of the way of any lurking U-boats,' my grandfather wrote of his inaugural voyage.[2] The enormous challenge of coordinating manoeuvres between more than fifty ships was clear even to a seventeen-year-old.

'We sometimes had to zigzag: a monumental task,' he wrote.

Thanks, in major part, to the decisive victory in the battle for ONS.5 the previous month, my grandfather sailed into the miracle of a clear ocean. On 1st July he and the Scottish rubble arrived in New York untouched.

Survival in a time of war is more often the result of dull serendipity, not wit or tactics. It is the fuse that fails to detonate the oil bomb embedded in the pavement outside your front door; it is the letter announcing that you are to sail to Gibraltar, as part of a doomed contingent of Wrens; it is the angle at which the destroyer strikes your U-boat's conning tower, where you stand.

My grandfather joined the crew of *Empire Castle* nineteen days after Doenitz ordered his U-boats to retreat. It is a matter of providential timing that he made safe passage to America on his maiden voyage, and was not counted among the 30,248 merchant seamen who lost their lives during the war.[3] He and, it follows, I, owe our lives to the Royal Naval escorts that deployed WATU's tactics with such precision and accuracy.

In his house in Devon, close to where Captain Roberts began his post-war life, my grandfather would sometimes watch as, like the Wrens, my brother and I pushed our toy ships across the griefless cardboard ocean.

On a damp spring night in 2018, I drove into the British Defence Academy in Shrivenham outside Oxford. Here, at a rambling military complex set behind a series of tall, barbed-wire fences and tilting CCTV cameras, soldiers young and old come to study the art, science and technology of warfare. Somewhere near the middle of the grounds, behind a hedge and beneath a thicket of trees, I found a chilly cabin, buzzing with fluorescent strip lights, where a group of bearded academics and clean-shaven retired officers hunched around a table.

They mumbled and joked, munching on crisps, noting but barely acknowledging my arrival, in that wary way groups of older, hobbyist men often do. Earlier that day, the British prime minister at the time, Theresa May, had expelled twelve Russian diplomats from Britain in retaliation for a nerve-agent attack carried out, in broad daylight, on two Russian nationals who fell unconscious on a bench in the centre of the town of Salisbury. The government believed beyond all reasonable doubt that the poison used in the attack, Novichok, was produced at a Russian laboratory. The poisoning had to be the work of Russian agents, therefore the diplomats had to go.

The men in the cabin were assembled not to discuss the Russian case, or the equanimity of Britain's response, but to play a wargame based on the day's events. Each man assumed the role of an interested nation. Russia picked at his nails in the seat next to Ukraine, who eyed Greece on the left, who furtively checked out the United States in the seat opposite who was looking rather smug about the powerful role he'd been given.

A large laminated map was spread across the table in front of the men, and around this were scores of coloured cards and counters representing assets ranging from battleships to social media accounts, that could be used by players in the game.

From chess to Space Invaders, war has always been a central theme in play. Professional wargames, such as the one that I had come to watch that night, are something else: a playful means by which governments and militaries might peer into the future by winding the clock forward on current events. How might the Americans respond to a Russian nerve-agent attack on British soil? Would Russia accept culpability or protest its innocence when accused? Games like these provide military officers and diplomats with the opportunity to consider an issue from a foreign perspective.

Just as Captain Roberts discovered in the Second World War, wargames have their sceptics, and fade in and out of fashion across the decades. As one analyst put it to me, wargames tend to be in greater demand in times of chaos. Even when there is an appetite among military commanders to test out their plans and strategies, doing so within the context of a game can be risky. 'The commander and his planning staff often get to see their plan methodically destroyed,' Paul Strong, a wargame designer and analyst from the Defence Science and Technology Laboratory (DSTL), told me. 'No one enjoys that experience, even if skilled commanders recognise the value of their operational concept being tested to destruction.'

At a time of international uncertainty, wargames are unusually popular and widespread. In 2017 the Kremlin created a wide-scale wargame in which the Russians engaged in a conflict with a fictional country, Veishnoriya.[4] The designers of this game made fake social media accounts for the country. ('Foreign Office of one of the most invaded lands in history, make you plan visit scenic Veishnoriya today!' reads the Twitter bio of one such account.[5]) As one *New York Times* headline put it, 'Russia's War Games With Fake Enemies Cause Real Alarm'.[6]

Outside of the realm of professional sport, with its strato-spheric salaries and legitimising sheen of advertising, games are usually viewed as childish diversions. But in the military and in government, games are seen differently. Playing games is how theories grand and small are tested and refined, and through which vital, potentially life-saving experience is gained in an affordable and secretive manner. Wargames, for example, were used by the British government to simulate potential public protests to President Trump's visit to London in July 2018, and to imagine the potential effects on social stability of a second referendum on the Brexit vote*.

Wargames have the power not only to shape policy, but also to introduce entirely novel ideas. During the Cold War, US Army officers decided that in a world where nuclear war could be started (and ended) with the press of a button, it might be sensible for the president to be able to call the Kremlin without having to wend through diplomatic channels. This resulted in the installation of a hotline between the White House and the Russian president's office, often represented in films as a red telephone.

The fictional stories wargames propose must be both believable

---

* According to a report in *The Times*, civil servants 'role-played' as leading figures in the Brexit drama, such as Jacob Rees-Mogg and Boris Johnson.

and relevant. The Institute for Creative Technologies at the University of Southern California often puts the US military in touch with Hollywood writers, while NATO runs a writers' room, much like that which you might find on a hit television show, employing no fewer than fifteen writers.*

Wargames also incidentally feature in my family history. My grandfather's younger brother Anthony, who was nine years old when war broke out, later became a major in the British Army. When he died, I found a document stamped 'Top Secret' among his papers. The rules and scenario of a wargame from the 1970s involving the British Army and a fictional European country, just like Veishnoriya, were printed inside. The game's Cold War scenario included pages and pages of arcane backstory. Like the Wrens before him, he had never mentioned it to his family.

I had come to Shrivenham to learn more about wargames in the military today. The British Army would not allow me to watch a 'real' example, as the subject matter is often classified, but I had been permitted to sit in on a variation designed for practice play, and to speak with its designer, one of a few modern-day designers who work in Britain today, following in Captain Roberts' tradition.

Like my late great-uncle, Tom Mouat is a former army major. Following retirement, Major Tom briefly set up a private detective agency, before being re-recruited into the military to become, essentially, Her Majesty's commander-in-chief of board games. He speaks with the clear, easy voice of someone who understands and is comfortable with his position in the hierarchy in which he operates. Experts like Major Tom, who run these games in various countries around the world, have exclusive access to rooms that most people never have the chance to enter. They are privileged to witness how history-changing decisions are made, and what role, alongside argument and logic, fallible human traits of personality, hubris and tact play in war rooms.

That night in Shrivenham, Major Tom stood at one end of the table, crunching a pair of dice in one hand. He set out the game's

---

* The Joint Warfare Center.

premise – the nerve-agent attack, the foreign ministries' retaliation, Russia's public displays of indignation and protestation. Then, one by one, each of the players proposed a 'move' in the interests of the nation they represented, provocatively moving troops from here to there, offering aid to neighbours, usually with an ulterior motive in mind. The other players would then discuss the proposed move and its likelihood of success. Then Major Tom would crystallise all of the discussion into a number that the player must roll on his pair of perfectly balanced casino dice in order for the proposed action to prove successful. Hinging the success and failure on a dice roll might seem to undermine the role of diplomacy in the game, but Major Tom is unequivocal in his belief that only by introducing this element of chance can the game properly simulate the capriciousness of reality.

'Some people might say: "If you're using dice then it's nothing more than a game of chance",' he said. 'But if you think that, then you don't understand risk. And if you don't understand risk, then perhaps you really ought to be in another job.'

During the course of two hours, I watched as six consecutive turns were played out. America moved one of his aircraft carriers into the Baltic Sea. Britain expelled yet more diplomats. Russia held indignant press conferences in which he claimed to have been vindictively demonised. Greece tried to make profitable alliances with anyone who'd take a meeting. Between turns, the players would mingle, in character, around the room, making deals in grubby corners, often while munching on handfuls of salt and vinegar crisps. These men were the latest characters in a long, clandestine tradition of wargamers, reaching back to Roberts and the Wrens, and beyond.

Information regarding the existence of WATU has been in the public domain since 1944, but Roberts, the Wrens and their unit never gained much attention.

In the spring of 1948, Admiral Sir Martin Dunbar Nasmith, the first commander-in-chief of Western Approaches, asked Roberts to design and install an exhibit to be displayed at the National

Maritime Museum in Greenwich.[7] The exhibit, which took a year
to make at a cost of £14,000*, showed, behind glass, a bird's-eye
view of a miniaturised sea battle using tiny models of convoy and
escort ships, in battle with U-boats. The model was as large as three
billiard tables placed side by side and surrounded by tiered seats
where visitors could sit and listen to Roberts' recorded commentary,
in which he explained some of the tactics he had devised.†

In a letter dated 24th July 1948, the director of the museum
described the exhibit as 'an invaluable piece of contemporary
evidence which will show how a Convoy was organized, and how
the perils which it had to meet . . . were dealt with and defeated
in the Battle of the Atlantic'.[8]

WATU's specific role in the campaign, however, earned only a
brief mention in the biographies of the major naval players. Those
determined captains at sea and the anxious admirals at home were
all granted special dispensation to tell their stories soon after the
war; everyone else involved, including the Wrens, was forbidden
from talking or writing about their work for fifty years.‡

Sensing the whitewashing of his and the Wrens' role in the war,
in the 1970s Roberts, who was by now in poor health, agreed to
grant a historian, Mark Williams, a series of interviews and access
to his personal papers. Williams wrote a biography of Roberts
under the stuffily grandiose title 'In Service to the Crown', but the
manuscript was rejected by its intended publisher, W. H. Allen, in
1975. It took four years for Williams to find a new publisher, who

---

* Paid for by the Shipping Companies of Britain.

† 'It is most unusual to find people who speak a script without it sounding read,'
wrote H. Lynton Fletcher, who recorded Roberts' commentary, in a 1959 letter
congratulating him on the exhibit. 'Even more difficult to get a virile, objective
interpretation. I do congratulate you.' In a magnanimous gesture, Roberts
included his former rival Captain Walker's support group EG2 on the model.

‡ While pondering how much scholastic work remains to be carried out on the
Battle of the Atlantic, the Canadian historian Marc Milner noted in the afterword
of his 2003 book *Battle of the Atlantic*: 'American and British literature on the
Atlantic . . . has been moribund for decades.' Moreover, he argued, 'the development
of tactics and doctrines within Western Approaches command [have] never been
looked at by modern scholars'.

released the book under the reworked title *Captain Gilbert Roberts R.N. and the Anti-U-Boat School.*

Roberts was 'disappointed'[9] with the book, and his relationship with Williams, whom he believed to have stolen and sold one of his prized photographs, soured prior to publication. The author, Roberts wrote in his diary, 'doesn't know the meaning of the word "truth",' and was prone to 'glib exaggeration'.[10] In relation to the biography, at least, this was its own exaggeration. The author, Williams, misspells the names of some of the Wrens who are glancingly referenced, including both Janet Okell (who becomes 'O'kell') and Nancy Wales (who becomes 'Wailes'), but these are straightforward factual errors rather than malicious fabrications. And while some of the anecdotes contained in the book deviate from Roberts' own telling of the same stories in his diaries, the book provided a valuable first account of, among other things, WATU's largely forgotten role in the war.

After the war's end, on 15th August 1945 Roberts packed his belongings into a box and left Liverpool for good. As with his former rival Captain Walker, who had died in 1944 from exhaustion, the effort of war had left Roberts wearied and sick. Since its founding in January 1942, WATU had remained open every day of every week.

'Like the classic London music hall "The Windmill",' Roberts wrote, 'we never closed.'

Gravely underweight, Roberts was admitted to hospital to recuperate from the cost of his ceaseless effort. When he was released by the doctors, he headed south to begin a new life in Devon.[11] His marriage had fallen apart and, with the Allied victory, the role he had filled with such determination for the previous three and a half years had gone too. There wasn't much need for wargame designers in late 1945.

One day, while out walking, he started chatting over the fence with a little girl, Susan, who lived a few doors down the road with her mother, Jean. Roberts and Jean soon began a relationship and, to abide by the social expectations of the time, married quietly on 23rd August 1947.* They moved to a new town where they could

---

* Susan was thirty-six-years old before her mother revealed to her the date of the secretive wedding, a measure of the debilitating shame associated with many second marriages at the time.

pretend that they were each other's first loves, and that Susan was their only child. Roberts built a house for the three of them and their dogs, Sailor and Tuppence. Perhaps to compensate for the loss of his career at sea, like the admiral in *Mary Poppins* who converts the roof of his town house to look like a boat's deck, Roberts designed the house in the style of a ship's cabin.

'Like the American pioneers who created rich farms from desolate plains of the Mid-West,' a local newspaper report read, 'a former naval captain has turned a derelict wood and two fields on the Moor . . . into a prosperous produce farm . . . with a drawing-room reminiscent of a sea-captain's cabin.'[12]

Still, while Roberts had experienced an extraordinary turnaround in his career, from the abandonment he had felt following his diagnosis through to the exhilaration of receiving his CBE from the king, he continued to feel underappreciated. On 8th May 1951, Roberts received an unexpected letter from the Admiralty offering him a modest award of £200 from the Herbert Lott Naval Trust Fund for 'most valuable contributions to anti-submarine tactical development'. In the margin of the letter Roberts wrote, sarcastically, 'Just a little late.'*

The greatest blow to Roberts' self-esteem came, however, two decades later when on 4th January 1965 he received a letter informing him that he was to receive a knighthood. It was a gesture that vindicated Roberts' work and promised to erase, finally, the scar he still bore from his dismissal from the navy so many years earlier. The following day the phone rang. The letter, the caller explained, had been sent in error; the invitation was retracted.

'Why didn't they just let him have it anyway?' his daughter Susan asked me (in a later conversation she speculated that the honour may have been rescinded because her father was divorced and estranged from his first family). This final betrayal precipitated

---

* Roberts' indignation was compounded by the fact that the award had initially been granted to an Admiralty staff officer. When a friend mentioned what had happened, Roberts produced evidence that the officer in question 'had nothing whatsoever' to do with WATU. Only then was the financial award redirected. 'In such ways does the Navy regard its retired,' he wrote in his diary.

a decline in Roberts' health. It was a cruelty, she said, from which her father never recovered. Through the souring of his biography project, the navy's parsimonious recompense and the lost knighthood, Roberts died on 22nd January 1986 feeling that his role in the war, and that of the Wrens who served alongside him, had never been fully recognised.

Throughout his life, Roberts had fought relentlessly for WATU's legacy. He saved it all, every memory, every clipping, all stored in a brown leather trunk stamped with his name, a one-man campaign for posterity and a trove without which the writing of this book would not have been possible. But it was a losing battle. WATU's story was but a thread in the larger forgotten tapestry of the Battle of the Atlantic, a campaign that all but vanished from the public eye. What hope would Roberts and the Wrens have, when the entire sea war was overlooked? As Paul Strong, whose 2016 article 'Wrens of the Western Approaches Tactical Unit' first reignited interest in the unit's history, put it to me, 'even when the campaign was remembered, the heroic work of the escort commanders and merchantmen was easier to visualise than the patient efforts of WATU'.

When writing the screenplay for Nicholas Monsarrat's novel *The Cruel Sea*, the studio cut the wargaming scene that was based on WATU. The image of a group of men and women standing around a board game surely did not chime with the public's expectation of what it looked like to fight a war. Besides, games are childish things, are they not? Nobody takes them seriously.

While Roberts may have felt dismay at the speed and totality at which his contribution was forgotten, it was nothing compared to the disappearance of the women's role. Not one of the Wrens of WATU received any individual accolade for her contribution. The only recognition came on 8th May 1945, when the Board of Admiralty sent a general message of thanks to the Wrens at all stations at home and abroad. It read: 'The loyalty, zeal and efficiency with which the officers and ratings of the Women's Royal Naval Service have shared the burdens and upheld the traditions of the Naval Service through more than five and a half years of war have earned the gratitude of the Royal Navy.'

It was a tribute that placed the women's role as both subservient to and separate from that of the men. For the vast majority of young women, this was the only formal acknowledgement of the role they had played during the war.

In the 1940s, the Royal Navy was still reckoning with the idea of women performing the duties of its men; it was not ready to record their heroic stories of doing so. In the years that followed, scores of books recounting the exploits of key men in the drama – Admiral Sir Max Horton, Sir Peter Gretton, Donald Macintyre, Otto Kretschmer – were published. In some cases, the biographers sought permission from the navy to memorialise sensitive material from the war in this way, an exemption from the rule by which other officers and sailors, including the Wrens, had to abide.

Some of the surviving Wrens told me that they never spoke to their husbands about what they had done in the war. And so their stories were mostly lost, resulting in an agonising lacuna of detail about the role of these women in war. None of the families of the WATU Wrens I spoke to knew anything about the specific work their relatives had performed during the war.

Outside of WATU's doors, a few notable voices broke the silence. Vera Laughton Mathews, as the second founder of the Wrens, wrote a vivid memoir in 1948. Nancy Spain, who had been a sporadically successful freelance journalist at war's outbreak, wrote one of the only contemporaneous accounts of life at war as a Wren. *Thank You, Nelson*, a riotous short book, published in 1942, is filled with the kind of grubby, tactile detail of what it is to live among sailors that is absent from the stately, sterilised memoirs of the admirals. The majority of other books written by Wrens about their work in the Second World War, however, appeared fifty-odd years later, toward the end of their lives, a position of remove at which names, dates and the sequence of events can become unreliable. The authors often appear to share details between their books, no doubt to compensate for time's smudging effect on memory.

Undoubtedly many Wrens simply believed that their stories weren't worth memorialising, or that perhaps they weren't theirs to tell. While, personally, their experiences had usually been life-transforming (and, in the case of WATU especially, had shown the power of unlikely partnerships, and the good that can come from citizens intent on sharing their unique gifts), some simultaneously viewed their work as routine.

'An awful lot of people don't know what the women did during the war,' said Carol Duffus, a Wren who helped run The Game at WATU's satellite school based in Canada. '[But] I felt that I was able to do something useful . . . There are an awful lot of other women who did useful things and they will never probably be recognised. I'd like to have people know that they were important.'[13]

In some cases, the memories of Wrens who made the effort to record their experiences were outright discarded. After the death of her partner Beryl in the 1970s, Jean Laidlaw, Captain Roberts' right-hand woman, lived alone, in the same London house in Maida Vale into which she had moved with her parents as a teenager. While clearing the house after her death in August 2008, Laidlaw's nephew found a sheaf of papers. His aunt, he discovered, had typed up her memoirs from the war. It is a document that surely held tremendous value in offering a perspective of one of the WATU Wrens. Not appreciating the document's historical value, Laidlaw's nephew told me that he either sent the memoir to the Association of Wrens or, more likely, binned it. Neither the Association of Wrens nor the National Museum of the Royal Navy have any record of receiving the memoir.

Among the core WATU team, only June Duncan's memories survived. She kept a diary and ensured her family knew about its existence, an act no doubt inspired by her proximity to the world of journalism (she was, for a time, an assistant editor at *Harper's Bazaar*[14]). Less than a paragraph, however, was dedicated to her time at Derby House.

Liz Drake, the last surviving of the WATU Wrens, who died during the writing of this book, captured her life story in just three pages. Of her time at WATU Drake recorded no more than her date of arrival at Derby House in 1942 and the date of her departure two years later, in January 1944.

All that happened in the intervening months was omitted, a maddening stretch of empty space that says so much.

Acknowledgements

Thank you to the families of the men and women of WATU who contributed their memories, photographs and documents for the research of this book, and without whom this story could not have been told in this way.

Thanks to John Lunt and Bill Laidlaw, cousin and nephew of Jean Laidlaw; Mike Gretton and Anne Cowan, son and daughter of Sir Peter Gretton and Judy Du Vivier; Janet Reynolds, daughter of Laura Janet 'Bobby' Howes; Margaret Swanson and Janet Hinings, stepdaughter and niece of Janet Okell; Tony Bridger, nephew of Nancy Wales; Susan Armstrong, daughter of Doris Lawford; Trish Browne, daughter of Pauline Preston; Rodger Tooley-Hawkins, son of William Tooley-Hawkins and stepson of Elizabeth Hackney; Michael Osborne and Penny Smith, son and daughter of Fred Osborne and Elizabeth Drake, and nephew and niece of Nancy Osborne; Jez Robinson, grandson of Mary Horsfall. Thanks to Christian Lamb (née Oldham), her carer Dr Lauraine Vivian, her elder son Simon Lamb and her daughter, Lady Rollo. Thanks to Sarah and Patrick Watson, daughter and son-in-law of Colin Ryder Richardson.

Special thanks to Susan Osman, daughter of Captain Gilbert Roberts.

Thank you to the other living Wrens who shared their memories, in particular, Rosemary Smith, leader of the Manchester Wrens; Patricia Davies, and Elsie Pearsal, the Derby House cook.

Thank you to Julie Crocke, senior archivist at the Royal Archives; Isabel Hernandez, archivist at Kensington Central Library; Brigadier Archie Miller-Bakewell, Private Secretary to HRH the Duke of Edinburgh; Pauline Rushton, senior curator, Art Galleries and

Sudley House, National Museums Liverpool; Celia Saywell, representative of the Association of Wrens and Women of the Royal Naval Services; and Emma Stringfellow, curator of the Western Approaches museum.

Special thanks to Laura Berry for her invaluable research support mapping the genealogies of various Wrens and naval officers, and in locating their living relatives. Thanks to Holly Neilsen for her research support regarding military boardgames.

Thank you to Paul Strong and Sally Davies of the Defence Science and Technology Laboratory whose initial research revitalised interest in the unit, and who kindly agreed to work as consultant readers on this book. Special thanks to Sally for sharing relevant research findings, particularly regarding the origins of WATU's badge, and for helping to identify Wrens from unit photographs.

Thank you to Rex Brynen, Brian McCue and Peter Perla for providing valuable background on wargames in the Second World War.

Thanks to Alex Barron of the New Yorker Radio Hour who commissioned me to report on wargaming both contemporary and historical, and to Major Tom Mouat who, during the making of that programme, first told me about 'Raspberry'. Thanks to Tom Bissell, who first suggested that I write this book, and to my father, Paul Parkin, for reading early drafts.

Special thanks to my editors Juliet Brooke and Vanessa Mobley, my copyeditor David Milner, and to Jane Finigan of Lutyens & Rubinstein.

My deep gratitude to Christian Donlan, Tom Fenwick, Darren Garrett, Ed Hawkins, Vicky Jones, Will Porter and Keith Stuart for their encouragement throughout the writing of this book. Finally, unending thanks to Nicky Parkin for her unending support.

A Note on Sources

A Game of Birds and Wolves is a work of historical narrative non-fiction. Neither the dialogue nor events described in this book have been fabricated or elaborated, but are taken from diaries, memoirs, first-hand interviews and secondary historical sources according to the best recollections of the various players and protagonists. Where I found minor discrepancies in dialogue between sources, I have used the version closest to the date of the event described.

Archival and Unpublished Sources

Associated Press Archive, AP
Bodleian Library, John Johnson Collection
British Film Institute National Archive, BFI
Derby House 'Area Combined HQ' blueprints
Duncan, June, unpublished diaries, courtesy of Liverpool Museum
General Register Office, Southport, GRO
Gretton Family Papers, private collection of Michael Gretton
Hall, (née Carlisle) Mary, unpublished memoir, courtesy of Second
    World War Experience Centre
Horsfall, Mary Charlotte, eulogy, courtesy of Jez Robinson
Imperial War Museum, IWM
Kensington and Chelsea Local Authority Archives, KCLA
Laidlaw, Jean, Last Will and Testament
Lamb, John, *Last Tales of a Dog-Watch*, unpublished memoir
Naval History.net, NHN

Osborne, Nancy, unpublished memoir

Osborne, Fred, *Looking Astern After 50 Years*, self-published memoir, Sydney, 1995

Parkin, Dynley, unpublished memoir

Roberts Family Papers, private collection of Susan Osman

Roberts, Gilbert, *Life and Letters of Gilbert Howland Roberts*, unpublished diaries

The National Archives, Kew, Surrey, TNA

U-boat Archive.net, UBA

Wales, Nancy, eulogy, courtesy of Bridger Anthony

Wartime Memories Project, WMP

Western Approaches Museum, Liverpool, WAM

WW2 People's War Archive, BBC

Yale Law School, Lillian Goldman Law Library, YLS

Select Bibliography

Baker, R., *The Terror of Tobermory*, Birlinn, Edinburgh, 1999

Blair, C., *Hitler's U-boat War 1939–1942*, Cassell, London, 2000

Boog, H.,W. Rahn, R. Stumpf & B. Wegner (eds.), *Germany and the Second World War, Volume 6: The Global War*, Oxford University Press, Oxford, 2001

Buchheim, L-G., *Das Boot*, Cassell, London, 1999

Buchheim, L-G., *U-boat War*, William Collins Sons & Co., London, 1978

Chalmers, W. S., *Max Horton and the Western Approaches*, Hodder & Stoughton, London, 1954

Churchill, W., *The Second World War, Volume II: Their Finest Hour*, Houghton Mifflin Harcourt, London, 1949

Churchill, W., *The Second World War, Volume III: The Grand Alliance*, Houghton Mifflin Harcourt, London, 1950

Churchill, W., *Winston Churchill: My Early Life*, T. Butterworth, London, 1930

Clerk, J., *An Essay on Naval Tactics, Systematic and Historical*, Alan Black, Edinburgh, 1804

Collingham, L., *The Taste of War: World War II and the Battle for Food*, Penguin, London, 2011

Costello, J., & T. Hughes, *Battle of the Atlantic*, HarperCollins, London, 1977

Curry, J., *The Fred Jane Naval War Game* (1906), Lulu.com, 2008

Davidson, R., & M. A. Eastwood, *Human Nutrition and Dietetics*, Churchill Livingstone, London, 1986

Dimbleby, J., *The Battle of the Atlantic*, Penguin, London, 2015

Doenitz, K., *Memoirs: Ten Years and Twenty Days*, Greenhill Books, London, 2012

Elliot, P., *Allied Escort Ships of World War II*, Naval Institute Press, Annapolis, Maryland, 1977

Gannon, M., *Black May*, Dell, New York, 1998

Garfield, S., *Private Battles: Our Intimate Diaries: How the War Almost Defeated Us*, Ebury Press, London, 2007

Gentile, G., *Track of the Gray Wolf: U-boat Warfare on the US Eastern Seaboard, 1942–4*, Avon Books, New York, 1989

Gretton, P., *Convoy Escort Commander*, Corgi Books, London, 1971

Hammond, R. J., *Food and Agriculture in Britain 1939–45: Aspects of Wartime Control*, Stanford University Press, Stanford, 1954

Herzog, L., *60 Jahre deutscher U-boote: 1906–1966*, J. F. Lehmanns Verlag, Munich, 1968

Houston, R., *Changing Course*, Grub Street, London, 2005

Kelley, D. M., *22 Cells in Nuremberg*, McFadden, New York, 1961

Kennedy, J., *The Business of War*, Hutchinson, London, 1957

Lamb, C., *I Only Joined for the Hat*, Bene Factum, London, 2007

Laughton Mathews, V., *Blue Tapestry*, Hollis & Carter, London, 1948

Layard, A. F. C., *Commanding Canadians: The Second World War Diaries of A. F. C. Layard*, University of British Columbia Press, Vancouver, 2006

Le Berd, J., *Lorient sous l'occupation*, Editions Ouest-France, Rennes, 1986

Leroux, R., *Le Morbihan en Guerre 1939–1945*, Joseph Floch, Mayenne, 1979

Lund, P. & H. Ludlam, *Nightmare Convoy: The Story of the Lost Wrens*, W. Foulsham, Slough, 1987

Macintyre, D., *U-boat Killer*, Seeley, London, 1976

Mason, U., *Britannia's Daughters*, Leo Cooper, 1992

Middlebrook, M., *Convoy: The Battle for Convoys SC 122 and HX 229*, Allen Lane, 1976

Milner, M., *The Battle of the Atlantic*, The History Press, Stroud, 2011

Monsarrat, N., *Life is a Four-Letter Word – Book Two: Breaking Out*, Pan, London, 1972

Monsarrat, N., *Monsarrat at Sea*, Cassell, London, 1975

Nagorski, T., *Miracles on the Water*, Robinson, London, 2007

Neitzel, S., & H. Welzer, *Soldaten – On Fighting, Killing and Dying: The Secret Second World War Tapes of German POWs*, Simon & Schuster, London, 2012

Nicholson, N., *What Did You Do in the War, Mummy?*, Pimlico, London, 1995

Noakes, L., *Women in the British Army: War and the Gentle Sex*, Routledge, London, 2006

Offley, E., *Turning the Tide*, Basic Books, New York, 2011

Overy, R., *Why the Allies Won*, Pimlico, London, 2006

Padfield, P., *Dönitz: The Last Führer*, Gollancz, London, 1984

Padfield, P., *War Beneath the Sea*, John Murray, London, 1995

Paton, M., *The Best of Women*, The Women's Press, London, 2000

Perla, P., *The Art of Wargaming*, United States Naval Institute, Maryland, 1990

Prien, G., *Fortunes of War: U-boat Commander*, Tempus, London, 2000

Reynolds, D., *Rich Relations: The American Occupation of Britain, 1942–1945*, HarperCollins, London, 1995

Roberts, H., *The WRNS in Wartime*, I. B. Taurus, London, 2018

Robertson, T., *The Golden Horseshoe*, Evans Brothers, London, 1955

Robertson, T., *Walker R.N.*, Evans Brothers, London, 1956

Salewski, M., *Die deutsche Seekriegsleitung: 1935–1945*, Bernard & Graefe, Frankfurt, 1970

Schaeffer, H., *U-boat 977*, William Kimber, London, 1953

Seth, R., *The Fiercest Battle*, Hutchinson, London, 1961

Smith, K., *Conflict over Convoys: Anglo-American Logistics Diplomacy in the Second World War*, Cambridge University Press, Cambridge, 2002

Spain, N., *Thank You, Nelson*, Hutchinson, London, 1942

Stanley, J., *Women and the Royal Navy*, I. B. Tauris, London, 2017

Storey, M., (ed.), *Battle of the Atlantic: An Anthology of Personal Memories*, Picton Press, Liverpool, 1993

Strong, P., *Wargaming the Atlantic War*, Paper for MORS Wargaming Special Meeting, 2017

Suhren, T., *Ace of Aces*, Chatham, London, 2006

Thomas, L., & C. Howard Bailey, *WRNS in Camera*, Sutton, Stroud, 2002

Watt, F., *In All Aspects Ready*, Prentice-Hall, Ontario, 1985

Wells, H. G., *Little Wars*, Frank Palmer, London, 1913

Whinney, R., *The U-boat Peril*, Arrow Books, London, 1989

Williams, A., *Battle of the Atlantic*, BBC Books, London, 2002

Williams, M., *Captain Gilbert Roberts R. N. and the Anti-U-Boat School*, Cassell, London, 1979

Williamson, G., *World War II German Women's Auxiliary Services*, Osprey, Oxford, 2003

Wilt, A. F., *Food for War*, Oxford University Press, Oxford, 2001

Notes

I
Last Man Standing

1 'Life and Letters of Gilbert Howland Roberts', unpublished diaries, pp. 147ff.
2 'Behind the Atlantic Battle', *Illustrated* magazine, 26th February 1944.
3 Padfield, *Dönitz: The Last Führer*, p. 478.
4 'Heinz Walkerling,' UBA.
5 'Life and Letters of Gilbert Howland Roberts', unpublished diaries, pp. 147ff.

II
As You Wave Me Goodbye

1 'Colin Ryder Richardson: Oral History', January 2000, IWM, 20805.
2 Ibid.
3 'SS *Volendam*,' UBA.
4 As quoted in Dimbleby, *The Battle of the Atlantic*, p. 93.
5 Hermann Lawatsch, *U-530*, as quoted in Middelebrook, *Convoy*, p. 60.
6 *Battle of the Atlantic*, footage filmed by Karl Heinz Geiger, Oracle Home Entertainment (2003).
7 Robertson, *Walker R.N.*, as quoted in BBC's *People's War*.
8 Offley, *Turning the Tide*, p. xxiv.
9 Kurt Neide, *U-415*, as quoted in Middlebrook, p. 57.
10 Suhren, *Ace of Aces*, p. 89.
11 'Rolf Hilse: Oral History', April 2004, IWM, 26952.

III

They Will Come

1 Christian Lamb to author, various interviews May to July 2018.
2 Recounted by Samuel Palmer for WMP.
3 Collingham, *The Taste of War: World War II and the Battle for Food*, ch. 'The Battle for Food'.
4 Wilt, *Food for War*, p. 224.
5 Hammond, *Food and Agriculture in Britain 1939–45: Aspects of Wartime Control*, p. 231.
6 Robertson, *Walker R.N.*, p. 9.
7 Nagorski, *Miracles on the Water*, p. 62.
8 Ibid., p. 65.
9 Suhren, *Ace of Aces*, p. 85.
10 Padfield, *Dönitz: The Last Führer*, p. 203.
11 Nagorski, *Miracles on the Water*, p. 79.
12 Memorial to J. H. Wallace, Ullapool, Old Telford Church.
13 'Conscription: The Second World War,' parliament.uk.
14 Mason, *Britannia's Daughters*, p. 44.
15 Middlebrook, *Convoy*, p. 204.
16 Neitzel & Welzer, *Soldaten – On Fighting, Killing and Dying: The Secret Second World War Tapes of German POWs*, p.121.
17 'Rolf Hilse: Oral History', April 2004, IWM, 26952.
18 Interview with Rolf Hilse, *International Express* (Australia), 10th February 2004, p. 24.
19 Gannon, *Black May*, p. 166.
20 Monsarrat, *Life is a Four-Letter Word*, p. 19.
21 Nagorski, *Miracles on the Water*, p. 123.
22 Ibid., p. 129.

IV

Wolves

1 Padfield, *Dönitz: The Last Führer*, p. 25.
2 Ibid., p. 79.
3 'Walter Forstmann,' UBA.
4 Kelley, *22 Cells in Nuremberg*, p. 106.

5 'Hindenburgriese', Karl Doenitz (unpublished), p. 9.

6 Doenitz, *Ten Years and Twenty Days*, p. 4.

7 Ibid.

8 Doenitz, *Die Verwendung von U-booten im Rahmen des Flottenverbandes.*

9 Nagorski, *Miracles on the Water*, p. 129.

10 Ibid., p. 130.

11 Ibid., p. 131.

12 Ibid., p. 107.

13 'Bericht uber FdU Kreigspiel', 13th April 1939 (PG33390).

14 Herzog, *60 Jahre deutscher U-boote: 1906–1966*, pp. 170–2.

15 As recounted in Padfield, *Dönitz: The Last Führer*, p. 204.

16 'Aufschlusselung neuer U-bootstonnage und neuer U-bootstypen', Carls, 6th May 1938.

17 Prien, *Fortunes of War: U-boat Commander*, p. 93.

18 Padfield, *Dönitz: The Last Führer*, p. 256.

19 'Memorandum for Submarine Commanders' (translated), TNA, ADM 223/331.

20 Robertson, *The Golden Horseshoe*, p. 55.

21 Padfield, *Dönitz: The Last Führer*, p. 181.

V

Pineapples and Champagne

1 Middlebrook, *Convoy*, p. 69.

2 Suhren, *Ace of Aces*, p. 65.

3 'SS Firby,' UBA.

4 Middlebrook, *Convoy*, p. 5.

5 'Truth, Reality and Publicity', Admiral J. H. Godfrey, TNA, ADM 223/320.

6 Ibid., p. 2.

7 Buchheim, *U-boat War*, ch.1: 'Occupation: The Atlantic Bases'.

8 Padfield, *Dönitz: The Last Führer*, p. 246.

9 Le Berd, *Lorient sous l'occupation*, p. 21.

10 Leroux, *Le Morbihan en Guerre 1939–1945*, p. 22.

11 'Orders for U-Boats in Harbour at Lorient', 1940–1, TNA, ADM 223/343.

12 Leroux, *Le Morbihan en Guerre 1939–1945*, pp. 89, 97–8.

13 *Taking Control: Women of Lorient, France Direct their Lives Despite the German Occupation (June 1940–May 1945)*, Victoria Le Corre (2002), p. 77.

VI
Never at Sea

1 Unpublished account of life of Nancy Osborne (1990).
2 Fletcher, *The Wrens: A History of the Women's Royal Naval Service*, p. 14.
3 John Lunt to author, August 2018.
4 Thomas & Bailey, *WRNS in Camera*, p. 101.
5 Unpublished account of life of Nancy Osborne.
6 Middlebrook, *Convoy*, p. 73.
7 Peggy Hill, as quoted in Nicholson, *What Did You Do in the War, Mummy?*, p. 130.
8 Laughton Mathews, *Blue Tapestry*, p. 148.
9 Private papers of Miss Janet Sheila Bentram Swete-Evans, IWM, 14994.
10 Stanley, *Women and the Royal Navy*, p. 99.
11 'Women of the Royal Naval Services Uniform Policies', courtesy of WAM.
12 'Capt. Edward H. Molyneux, 79; Dominated Fashions for Years', *New York Times*, 23rd March 1974.
13 Elliot, *Allied Escort Ships of World War II*, p. 171.
14 Osborne, *Looking Astern After 50 Years*, p. 11.
15 Monsarrat, *Monsarrat at Sea*, p. 5.
16 Monsarrat, *Life is a Four-Letter Word*, p. 31.
17 Lund & Ludlam, *Nightmare Convoy: The Story of the Lost Wrens*, p. 36.
18 Monsarrat, *Monsarrat at Sea*, p. 6.
19 Doenitz, *Ten Years and Twenty Days*, p. 428.
20 'Adalbert Schnee,' UBA.
21 Buchheim, *Das Boot*, p. 21.
22 Suhren, *Ace of Aces*, p. 89.
23 Churchill Address to House of Commons, 9th September 1941, Hansard.
24 Davidson & Eastwood, *Human Nutrition and Dietetics*, p. 67.
25 Prime Minister to Minister of Information, 14th April 1941, *The Second World War, Volume III: The Grand Alliance*, Churchill, p. 128.

VII
Roberts

1 'Record of Bomb Incidents 1940–41', KCLA, Incident Number 16, 'Opposite Number 59'.

2 Ibid., Incident Number 20, 'Opposite Number 9'.

3 'Life and Letters of Gilbert Howland Roberts', unpublished diaries, p. 123.

4 Ibid., p. 67.

5 'Life and Letters of Gilbert Howland Roberts', unpublished diaries, *unidentified newspaper clipping*.

6 'Life and Letters of Gilbert Howland Roberts', unpublished diaries, p. 70.

7 Ibid.

8 'Life and Letters of Gilbert Howland Roberts', unpublished diaries, *unidentified newspaper clipping*.

9 Wells, *Little Wars*, p. 97.

10 Perla, *The Art of Wargaming*, p. 19.

11 'An essay on Naval Tactics, Systematic and Historical', Clerk.

12 Perla, *The Art of Wargaming*, p. 40.

13 Churchill, *Winston Churchill: My Early Life*, p. 3.

14 Email to author from Kelly Wade, Associate Manager, Global Communications, Hasbro, Inc.

15 Bodleian Library, John Johnson Collection, Indoor Games Box Nine.

16 Curry, *The Fred Jane Naval Wargame* (1906), p. 7.

17 *The World at War: Wolfpack: U-Boats in the Atlantic (1939–1944)*, BBC2, originally broadcast 9th January 1974.

18 'Life and Letters of Gilbert Howland Roberts', unpublished diaries, p. 106.

19 Atlantic Trade Protection', TNA, ADM 1/9466.

20 'Life and Letters of Gilbert Howland Roberts', unpublished diaries, p. 105.

21 Ibid., p. 115.

VIII
Oak Leaves and Christmas Trees

1 'Very Secret' Report, SRN 178, TNA, WO 208/4141.

2 Williamson, *World War II German Women's Auxiliary Services*, p. 11.

3 Laughton Mathews, *Blue Tapestry*, p. 77.

4 Noakes, *Women in the British Army: War and the Gentle Sex*, pp. 116–17.

5 *Dictionary of Labour Biography*, Volume 13, p. 155.

6 Record of Bomb Incidents 1940–41, KCLA.

7 Lamb, *I Only Joined for the Hat*, p. 5.

8 Ibid., p. 34.

9 Macintyre, *U-boat Killer*, p. 28.

10 *Christmas Under Fire*, propaganda film, BFI.

11 'Life and Letters of Gilbert Howland Roberts', unpublished diaries, p. 124.

12 'British food control', *Army News*, 14th May 1942.

13 'Fighting fit: how dietitians tested if Britain would be starved into defeat', Laura Dawes, *Guardian*, 24th September 2013.

14 'British and Foreign Merchant Shipping Losses 1941–42', TNA, MFQ 586/7/372.

15 DA/SW subcommittee minutes, TNA, ADM 1/1219.

16 *Private Battles: Our Intimate Diaries: How the War Almost Defeated Us*, p. 56.

17 Macintyre, *U-boat Killer*, p. 30.

18 Overy, *Why the Allies Won*, p. 31.

19 Smith, *Conflict over Convoys: Anglo-American Logistics Diplomacy in the Second World War*, pp. 45–6.

20 'Life and Letters of Gilbert Howland Roberts', unpublished diaries, p. 131.

21 Ibid.

IX

The Aces and the Note

1 Prien, *Fortunes of War: U-boat Commander*, p. 92.

2 Ibid., p. 80.

3 Appendix III, 'U.99 Interrogation of Survivors', April 1941, UBA.

4 Doenitz, *Ten Years and Twenty Days*, p. 174.

5 Robertson, *The Golden Horseshoe*, p.127.

6 Ibid., p. 114.

7 Ibid.

8 Ibid.

9 Prien, *Fortunes of War: U-boat Commander*, p. 128.

10 Macintyre, *U-boat Killer*, p. 28.

11 Ibid., p. 32.

12 http://vandwdestroyerassociation.org.uk/HMS_Walker/index.html

13 Blair, *Hitler's U-boat War 1939–1942*, p. 256.

14 Macintyre, *U-boat Killer*, p. 35.

15 'Vanoc's report of proceedings dated 19/3/41', TNA, ADM 1/11065.

16 Macintyre, *U-boat Killer*, p. 39.

17 Ibid., p. 49.

18 Ibid., p. 54.

19 Robertson, *The Golden Horseshoe*, p. 156.

20 Storey (ed.), *Battle of the Atlantic: An Anthology of Personal Memories*, p. 11.

X

The Citadel

1 Lamb, 'Last Tales of a Dog-Watch', p. 35.

2 Historic England.org, 'Exchange Buildings'.

3 Betty Sinclair as quoted in *Battle of the Atlantic: An Anthology of Personal Memories*, p. 109.

4 Ibid., p. 103.

5 Watt, *In All Aspects Ready*, p. 164.

6 Emma Stringfellow, Western Approaches museum curator, to author, October 2018.

7 Unpublished memoirs of Mary Hall, courtesy of WAM.

8 Middlebrook, *Convoy*, p. 48.

9 'Patricia Anne Parkyn', WW2 People's War Archive, BBC.

10 Unpublished memoirs of Mary Hall, courtesy of WAM.

11 Norman Robertson as quoted in *Battle of the Atlantic: An Anthology of Personal Memories*, p. 107.

12 'Dorothy Oldfield', WW2 People's War Archive, BBC.

13 Private Papers of Captain H. N. Lake, IWM, 16731.

14 'Liverpool Combined Area HQ: completion and enquiries into cost of conversions at Derby House and WRNS accommodation,' TNA, ADM 1/11581.

15 Robertson, *Walker R.N.*, p. 31.

16 Watt, *In All Aspects Ready,* p. 165.

17 'Life and Letters of Gilbert Howland Roberts', unpublished diaries, p. 131.

18 Williams, *Captain Gilbert Roberts R.N. and the Anti-U-Boat School*, p. 86.

19 Unpublished account of life of Nancy Osborne, p. 1.

20 Ibid., p. 2.

21 Monica Janet Sandford to author, 2018.

22 Osborne, *Looking Astern After 50 Years*, p. 18.

23 'Life and Letters of Gilbert Howland Roberts', unpublished diaries, p. 132.

XI
Raspberry

1 Janet Okell DOB: '30th August 1922', GRO, vol. 8a, p. 586.

2 'U-boats Killed on Office Floor', *Liverpool Daily Post*, 28th January 1944.

3 'Life and Letters of Gilbert Howland Roberts', unpublished diaries, p. 132.

4 Michael Osborne to author, January 2019.

5 'Behind the Atlantic Battle', *Illustrated* magazine, 26th February 1944.

6 'Life and Letters of Gilbert Howland Roberts', unpublished diaries, p. 132.

7 Unpublished memoirs of Mary Hall, courtesy of WAM.

8 Baker, *The Terror of Tobermory*, p. 155.

9 Osborne, *Looking Astern After 50 Years*, p. 16.

10 Heitmann, *Atlantic War Conference*, chapter 27.

11 Robertson, *Walker R.N.*, p. 55.

12 Ibid.

13 Osborne, *Looking Astern After 50 Years*, p. 19.

14 Robertson, *Walker R.N.*, p. 138.

15 'Life and Letters of Gilbert Howland Roberts', unpublished diaries, p. 131.

16 Robertson, *Walker R.N.*, p. 33.

17 Ibid., p. 157.

18 'Life and Letters of Gilbert Howland Roberts', unpublished diaries, p. 133.

19 Williams, *Battle of the Atlantic*, p. 158.

20 'Life and Letters of Gilbert Howland Roberts', unpublished diaries, p. 133.

21 Ibid.

22 Ibid.

23 Ibid.

XII
The Royal Key

1 'Life and Letters of Gilbert Howland Roberts', unpublished diaries, p. 132.

2 'Behind the Atlantic Battle', *Illustrated* magazine, 26th February 1944.

3 Ibid.

4 Introduction to Less-Knowles Lecture, Trinity College, Cambridge, 1951, Vice Admiral Sir Gilbert Stephenson.

5 'Western Approaches Tactical Unit: Annual Report', 1944, TNA, ADM 1/17557.

6 'Correspondence with Commanders-in-Chief, Dominions' Navies and Allied Admirals', TNA, ADM 205/22A.

7 Whinney, *The U-boat Peril*, p. 119.

8 Ibid.

9 'Scarcer than rubies', *Liverpool Daily Post*, 28th January 1944.

10 Milner, *The Battle of the Atlantic*, p. 128.

11 Records held at WAM.

12 'Air Requirements for the Successful Prosecution of the War At Sea', TNA, AIR 19/9/243.

13 'Memorandum to Minister of Aircraft Production', 8th July 1940, as quoted in Churchill, *Their Finest Hour*, p. 567.

14 Air Staff Paper, cited in Brodhurst, *Churchill's Anchor*, p. 266.

15 Ibid., p. 269.

16 Kennedy, *The Business of War*, pp. 246–7.

17 Milner, *The Battle of the Atlantic*, pp. 125–6.

18 'The Battles of the Atlantic', Royal United Services Institution, lecture delivered by Gilbert Roberts, 12th February 1947. Journal 92.566, 202–15, DOI: 10.1080/03071844709433989.

19 Macintyre, *U-boat Killer*, p. 122.

20 Association of Wrens, *Battle of the Atlantic: Official Publication*, 2013.

21 Williams, *Captain Gilbert Roberts R.N. and the Anti-U-Boat School*, p. 117.

22 'Life and Letters of Gilbert Howland Roberts', unpublished diaries, p. 137.

XIII
The Elephant Has Landed

1 Lamb. *Last Tales of a Dog-Watch*, p. 35.

2 Ibid.

3 United States Holocaust Memorial Museum.

4 Gentile, *Track of the Gray Wolf: U-boat Warfare on the US Eastern Seaboard, 1942–4*, p. 12.

5 'New U-boat Victim Confirmed by Navy', *New York Times*, 17th January 1942.

6 Lamb, *Last Tales of a Dog-Watch*, p. 60.

7 Ibid.

8 'Life and Letters of Gilbert Howland Roberts', unpublished diaries, p. 137.

9 Chalmers, *Max Horton and the Western Approaches*, p. 150.

10 'Gilbert Roberts: Oral History', IWM, 2766.

11 Ibid.

12 Macintyre, *U-boat Killer*, p. 121.

13 Ibid., p. 135.

14 Paul Strong, 'Wargaming the Atlantic War,' Paper for MORS Wargaming Special Meeting (2017), p. 12.

15 'Life and Letters of Gilbert Howland Roberts', unpublished diaries, p. 136.

16 Ibid., p. 135.

17 Eulogy for Mary Charlotte Horsfall, courtesy of Jez Robinson.

18 'Mary Charlotte Horsfall: Oral History', IWM, 24920.

19 Laughton Mathews *Blue Tapestry*, p. 272.

20 'Gilbert Roberts: Oral History', IWM, 2766.

21 Ibid.

22 Layard, *Commanding Canadians: The Second World War Diaries of A. F. C. Layard*, pp. 33–5.

23 Unpublished diaries of June Duncan, pp. 8–9.

24 Ibid.

25 Mike Gretton to author, October 2018.

26 Unpublished memoirs of Mary Hall.

27 Elsie Pearsal to author, August 2018.

28 Monsarrat, *East Coast Corvette*.

29 Roberts, *The WRNS in Wartime*, p. 189.

30 Unpublished memoirs of Mary Hall, courtesy of WAM, Liverpool.

31 As quoted in Middlebrook, *Convoy*, p. 40.

32 Ibid., p. 190.

33 Laughton Mathews, *Blue Tapestry*, p. 119.

34 Ibid., p. 120.

35 Roberts, *The WRNS in Wartime*, p. 202.

36 Eulogy for Gilbert Roberts, George Phillips, kindly supplied by Susan Osman.

37 Elizabeth Osborne to author, May 2018.

38 Unpublished diaries of June Duncan, courtesy of Liverpool Museum, p. 8.

39 'Gilbert Roberts: Oral History', IWM, 2766.

40 Lamb, *Last Tales of a Dog-Watch*, p. 68.

41 Convoy HX.230.

42 Service Histories of RN Warships in World War 2: HMS *ORIBI* (G 66), NHN.

XIV

Nulli Secundus

1 Christian Lamb to author, 25th July 2018.

2 Lamb, *Last Tales of a Dog-Watch*, p. 69.

3 Lamb, *I Only Joined for the Hat*, p. 66.

4 Raeder to Hitler, 14th January 1943, cited in Sandhofer, *Dokumente zu militarischem Werdegang des Gr. Admls Doenitz*, p. 80.

5 'Message from Admiral Commanding U-boats,' 24th June 1941, TNA, HW 1/7.

6 Padfield, *Dönitz: The Last Führer*, p. 297.

7 Salewski, *Die deutsche Seekriegsleitung: 1935–1945*, p. 146.

8 Reynolds, *Rich Relations: The American Occupation of Britain, 1942–1945*, p. 86.

9 Collingham, *The Taste of War: World War II and the Battle for Food*, p. 243.

10 Smith, *Conflict over Convoys: Anglo-American Logistics Diplomacy in the Second World War*, p. 152.

11 Costello & Hughes, *Battle of the Atlantic*, p. 213.

12 Ibid., p. 304.

13 Ibid., p. 146.

14 Christian Lamb to author, 25th July 2018.

XV
The Battle of Birds and Wolves: Part I

1 Gannon, *Black May*, p. 131.

2 Doenitz, *Ten Years and Twenty Days*, p. 338.

3 Gretton, *Convoy Escort Commander*, p. 107.

4 Seth, *The Fiercest Battle*, p. 75.

5 Lund & Ludlam, *Nightmare Convoy: The Story of the Lost Wrens*, p. 76.

6 Monsarrat, *Life is a Four-Letter Word*, p. 104.

7 'Notes on the Gretton Family', unpublished family history, p. 17.

8 'Commodore's Report', TNA, ADM 237/113.

9 Ibid.

10 Gretton, *Convoy Escort Commander*, p. 147.

11 'Use of Special Intelligence in Battle of Atlantic, Convoy ONS.5, April–May 1943', TNA, ADM 223/88.

12 KTB–BdU, 27th April, p. 7, as referenced in Gannon, *Black May*, p. 140.

13 Gretton, *Convoy Escort Commander*, p. 140.

14 Middlebrook, *Convoy*, p. 316.

15 Ibid.

16 Captain Lake memorandum, as cited in Middlebrook, *Convoy*, p. 289.

17 Unpublished memoirs of Mary Hall, courtesy of WAM.

18 Elsie Pearsal to author, August 2018.

19 Gretton, *Convoy Escort Commander*, p. 143.

20 'Interview with Howard Oliver Goldsmith', *Daily Telegraph*, 8th February 1993.

21 Gannon, *Black May*, p. 155.

22 Gretton, *Convoy Escort Commander*, p. 147.

23 Padfield, *Dönitz: The Last Führer*, p. 303.

XVI
The Battle of Birds and Wolves: Part II

1 Lamb, *I Only Joined for the Hat*, pp. 79ff.
2 Ibid.
3 Gannon, *Black May*, p. 170.
4 'Special Intelligence Summary, April 29th–May 5th 1943, Convoy ONS.5, Analysis of U-boat Operations', TNA, ADM 223/16.
5 Lamb, *Last Tales of a Dog-Watch*, p. 71.
6 Gretton, *Convoy Escort Commander*, p. 141.
7 Nuremberg Trial Proceedings Vol. 13, Thursday, 9 May 1946, YLS.
8 Service Histories of RN Warships in World War 2: HMS *ORIBI* (G 66), NHN.
9 Gannon, *Black May*, p. 243.
10 Christian Lamb to author, 25th July 2018.
11 WAM documents.
12 Lamb, *Last Tales of a Dog-Watch*, p. 70.
13 *Daily Express*, 13th May 1943.
14 Seth, *The Fiercest Battle*, p. 17.
15 Commander-in-Chief Western Approaches to Lords Commissioners of the Admiralty, 20th June 1943, TNA, ADM 234/370 pp. 28–30.
16 Gretton, *Convoy Escort Commander*, p. 149.
17 Gretton, 'Notes on the Gretton Family', p. 83.
18 Offley, *Turning the Tide*, p. 354.
19 Gretton, 'Notes on the Gretton Family', p. 83.
20 Ibid., p. 18.
21 'Premier's Guildhall Speech: Freedom of the City,' AP, BM43824–4.
22 BdU–KTB, 23rd May 1943, as cited in Padfield, *Dönitz: The Last Führer*.
23 Padfield, *Dönitz: The Last Führer*, p. 320.
24 Boog, Rahn, Stumpf & Wegner (eds.), *Germany and the Second World War Volume 6: The Global War*.

XVII
Honours

1 Christian Lamb to author, 25th July 2018.

2 Hammond, *Food and Agriculture in Britain 1939–45: Aspects of Wartime Control*, p. 185.

3 Chalmers, *Max Horton and the Western Approaches*, pp. 199–200.

4 Offley, *Turning the Tide*, p. 373.

5 Hansard, 21 September 1943 vol. 392 cc69–170.

6 'Life and Letters of Gilbert Howland Roberts', unpublished diaries, (no page ref.).

7 Unpublished memoir of Elizabeth Osborne.

8 'Life and Letters of Gilbert Howland Roberts', unpublished diaries, p. 132.

9 Ibid.

10 Osborne, *Looking Astern After 50 Years*, p. 19.

11 Emma Stringfellow to author, May 2019.

12 Eulogy for Gilbert Roberts, George Phillips, kindly supplied by Susan Osman.

13 'It Was Once Hush-Hush', unattributed newspaper clipping from the papers of June Duncan.

14 'Mary Charlotte Horsfall: Oral History', IWM, 24920.

XVIII
The Gun in the Night

1 'Report from Captain Roberts on his visit to Germany', TNA, ADM 1/17561, Appendix I, pp. 1–2.

2 Ibid.

3 Ibid.

4 'Life and Letters of Gilbert Howland Roberts', unpublished diaries, p. 147.

5 'Getting Fritz to Talk', *Virginia Quarterly Review*, Spring 1978.

6 'Life and Letters of Gilbert Howard Roberts', unpublished diaries, p. 147.

7 'The Capture of 500 Enemy Wrens', *War Illustrated*.

8 'Report from Captain Roberts on his visit to Germany', TNA, ADM 1/17561, Appendix I, p. 1.

9 Schaeffer, *U-boat 977*, p. 163.

10 'Life and Letters of Gilbert Howland Roberts', unpublished diaries, pp. 148ff.

11 Ibid., p. 150.

12 'Interrogation of Senior German Officers at Flensburg', TNA, ADM
   1/18222.

13 'Visit to *U-3008* at Kiel, 25th May 1945,' TNA, ADM 1/17561.

14 Laughton Mathews, *Blue Tapestry*, p. 248.

15 'Life and Letters of Gilbert Howland Roberts', unpublished diaries,
   p. 152.

16 Ibid, p. 153.

XIX
The Sisterhood of the Linoleum

1 '*U-249*', UBA.

2 Private papers of Nancy Osborne.

3 Laughton Mathews, *Blue Tapestry*, p. 245.

4 Ibid., p. 247.

5 Roberts, *The WRNS in Wartime*, p. 171.

6 'Hitler's Testimony Before the Court for High Treason from
   Frankfurter Zeitung', Document 2512-PS, Cornell University Law
   Library, translated by Evelyn Glazier, P/O WRNS, 37371.

7 Thomas & Bailey, *WRNS in Camera*, p. 101.

8 'Olive', WW2 People's War Archive, BBC.

9 Nicholson, *What Did You Do in the War, Mummy?*, p. 133.

10 'A Service Which Astonished the World', *Western Morning News*, 25th
   October 1945.

11 Eulogy for Mary Charlotte Horsfall.

12 Roberts, *The WRNS in Wartime*, p. 223.

13 Ibid.

14 Paton, 'The Best of Women,' p. 39.

15 Last will and testament of Jean Laidlaw, 2007.

16 Eulogy for Wren Nan Wales, June 2005.

17 'Battle of the Atlantic', supplement to the *Daily Post*, 22nd March
   1993, p. 3.

18 'Glory days of model June', *Sidmouth Herald*, April 1990.

19 'Battle of the Atlantic', supplement to the *Daily Post*, 22nd March
   1993, p. 3.

20 Laughton Mathews, *Blue Tapestry*, p. 281.

Postscript

1 'Western Approaches Tactical Unit: Annual Report', 1944, TNA, ADM 1/17557.
2 Ibid., Appendix, pp. 2–3.
3 Ibid., Appendix, p. 3.
4 WAM archives.
5 Letter to Gilbert Roberts from A.V. Alexander, 8th June 1945, Roberts Family Papers.
6 As quoted in eulogy for Wren Nan Wales, June 2005.

Epilogue

1 http://www.warsailors.com/convoys/ucconvoys.html.
2 'The Life Story of Dynley Parkin', Parkin, pp. 4ff.
3 Statistics held at WAM.
4 'Russia's War Games With Fake Enemies Cause Real Alarm', *New York Times*, 13th September 2017.
5 https://twitter.com/veishnoriya_f_o.
6 'Russia's War Games With Fake Enemies Cause Real Alarm,' *New York Times*, 13th September 2017.
7 'Life and Letters of Gilbert Howland Roberts', unpublished diaries, p. 194.
8 Letter to Gilbert Roberts from Frank Carr, director of National Maritime Museum, 24th July 1948. Private Papers of Gilbert Roberts.
9 Susan Osman to author, October 2018.
10 'Life and Letters of Gilbert Howland Roberts', unpublished diaries, 'New Year 1976'.
11 Ibid., p. 144.
12 'He Left Sea To Create Modern Farm', *Western Morning News*, 18th June 1948, p. 2.
13 'Veteran Stories: Carol Elizabeth Duffus (née Hendry)', The Memory Project, https://bit.ly/2DgA5iq.
14 'Wren's Model Career', *Daily Post*, 22nd March 1993, p. 3.

Index

Picture Acknowledgements

Insets pages 1–16

AP/Shutterstock: 6 above. Courtesy Susan Armstrong: 12 above. Courtesy Tony Bridger: 14 below right. Bundesarchiv: 2 below (Bild 101II-MW-3491-06/photo Lothar-Günther Buchheim), 7 below (Bild 101II-MW-0951-24A/photo Mannewitz). © *Daily Herald* Archive/National Science and Media Museum/Science & Society Picture Library: 10, 11, 16. Courtesy Michael Gretton: 15 above left. Courtesy Janet and Nigel Hinings: 14 above right. IWM/Getty Images: 3 below. © Imperial War Museum London: 1 (HU52876), 2 above left (HU54058), 4 above (HU52877), 5 above (A27098), 6 below (A2828), 12 below (HU52887), 13 above (A18468), 13 below (A27824). Courtesy Simon Lamb: 7 above. Mirrorpix/Reach plc: 3 above (*Liverpool Daily Post* Saturday 14th July 1945). NARA: 2 centre right (80-G-21187). The National Archives Kew: 9 (ADM205/22). National Museums Liverpool: 15 below left (78686-WAG). Courtesy Michael Osborne: 15 above right. Courtesy Susan Osman: 5 below. Courtesy Pen & Sword Books Ltd/*Grey Wolves: The U-Boat War 1939–1945* by Philip Kaplan, 2013: 8. Courtesy Janet Reynolds: 14 below left. Courtesy Jez Robinson: 14 above left. Westminster City Archives: 4 below (CD1.3).

Every reasonable effort has been made to trace copyright holders, but if there are any errors or omissions, Little, Brown and Company will be pleased to insert the appropriate acknowledgement in any subsequent printings or editions.